Guide to

Designing and Implementing Wireless LANs

Mark Ciampa

COURSE TECHNOLOGY

THOMSON LEARNING

Australia • Canada • Mexico • Singapore • Spain • United Kingdom • United States

COURSE TECHNOLOGY

™

THOMSON LEARNING

Guide to Designing and Implementing Wireless LANs

is published by Course Technology.

Managing Editor:
Stephen Solomon

Product Manager:
Laura Hildebrand

Production Editor:
Jennifer Goguen

Development Editor:
Deb Kaufmann

Permissions Editor:
Abby Reip

Quality Assurance Manager:
John Bosco

Associate Product Manager:
Elizabeth Wessen

Editorial Assistant:
Janet Aras

Marketing Manager:
Toby Shelton

Text Designer:
GEX Publishing Services

Compositor:
GEX Publishing Services

Cover Design:
Efrat Reis

BRIEF

Contents

TABLE OF
Contents

Preface

The wireless revolution has begun! For years computer users have found themselves restricted to using a computer that was chained to the wall by a 3-meter patch cable connecting it to the network. Users were forced to do their computer work in rooms or offices that were often away from where they needed to be. Valuable time was wasted because they could only be connected to the network and Internet when they were sitting at a computer in a specific location.

But not anymore. Users have started to throw off these wires that chained their computers to the wall. Today they are beginning to experience the newfound freedom of being connected to the network from almost anywhere. Instead of being restricted by wires, new wireless technology has freed users to remain connected to the network no matter where they may roam.

Evidence of this revolution is everywhere around us. Magazines and newspapers regularly carry articles proclaiming "A World Without Wires" and "It's a Wireless Life." Schools across the country are installing wireless networks at a dizzying pace, allowing students to be connected from anywhere on campus. Computer manufacturers are building laptop computers with wireless antennae already built in. Airports, football stadiums, and coffee houses are all installing wireless networks for travelers, spectators, and customers to use. And estimates are that value of installed wireless networks by the year 2004 will exceed $35 *billion* dollars! Network computing will never be the same. The wireless revolution is here.

This book is designed to give you the necessary tools to help you become part of this tremendous wave of change in network computing as a manager of a wireless local area network (WLAN). It is designed to give you direct experience in planning, installing, using, configuring, managing, and troubleshooting WLANs. Each chapter in the book contains hands-on projects that cover many aspects of how wireless networks function and show how to install and manage a WLAN. The projects are designed to make what you learn come alive through actually performing the tasks. Besides the hands-on projects, each chapter gives you experience through realistic case projects that put you in the role of a consultant who works in different scenarios helping solve the problems of clients. And every chapter includes review questions to reinforce your knowledge while preparing you be a wireless network administrator.

Chapter 1, "It's a Wireless World," helps you see how WLANs fit into the big picture. This chapter explains how WLANs compare with other wireless technologies and provides real illustrations of how this technology is being used today.

In **Chapter 2**, "Wireless LAN Fundamentals," you learn the technology behind how a wireless network works and what hardware and software components make up a wireless network.

Chapter 3, "IEEE 802.11 Physical Layer Standards," explains the specifications for the IEEE Physical (PHY) layer.

Chapter 4 reveals the technical workings of the MAC and Network layer in "IEEE 802.11 Medium Access Control and Network Layer Standards."

Chapter 5, "Building and Securing a WLAN," helps you learn how to plan a wireless installation, what security options are available with wireless networks, and how to provide user support.

In **Chapter 6** you begin the actual process of installing a wireless local area network. "Installing the Cisco Aironet 340" explains in detail how to install the necessary hardware and software for the Cisco product, and how to set up both ad hoc and infrastructure networks.

Chapter 7, "Installing the 3Com AirConnect" covers the process for setting up 3Com's AirConnect wireless network system.

In **Chapter 8**, "Configuring the Cisco Aironet and 3Com AirConnect," you learn how to configure the access points, implement security features, conduct a site survey, and enable power management.

Chapter 9, "Managing the Cisco Aironet and 3Com AirConnect"explains how to monitor the network, upgrade the firmware, and modify radio parameters.

The last chapter, **Chapter 10**, "Network Settings and Troubleshooting the Cisco Aironet 340 and 3Com AirConnect," explains how the Ethernet settings can be modified to suit the particular needs of the users. In addition, warnings and troubleshooting tips are revealed. Finally, a series of helpful FAQs assist you in keeping the wireless network running at peak performance.

FEATURES

To ensure a successful learning experience, this book includes the following pedagogical features:

- **Chapter Objectives:** Each chapter in this book begins with a detailed list of the concepts to be mastered within that chapter. This list provides you with a quick reference to the contents of that chapter, as well as a useful study aid.

- **Illustrations, Photographs and Tables:** Numerous illustrations, photographs and tables aid you in understanding wireless LAN technology, design and setup.

- **End of Chapter Material:** The end of each chapter includes the following features to reinforce the material covered in the chapter:

- **Chapter Summaries:** Each chapter's text is followed by a summary of the concepts it has introduced. These summaries provide a helpful way to recap and revisit the ideas covered in each chapter.
- **Key Terms List:** A list of all new terms and their definitions.
- **Review Questions:** To test knowledge of the chapter, the review questions cover the most important concepts of the chapter.

 Hands-on Projects: Although it is important to understand the theory behind WLAN technology and design, nothing can improve upon real-world experience. To this end, along with theoretical explanations, each chapter provides numerous hands-on projects aimed at providing you with real-world research and implementation experience.

 Case Projects: Located at the end of each chapter is a multi-part case project. In this extensive case example, as a consultant at the fictitious Northridge Consulting Group, you implement the skills and knowledge gained in the chapter through real-world WLAN research, implementation and troubleshooting.

 Optional Team Case Project: Each chapter concludes with an optional team case project that enables you to work in a small group of students to solve a real-world problem or to extensively research a topic. These projects give you experience working as a team member, which is a common format used by many businesses and corporations.

TEXT AND GRAPHIC CONVENTIONS

Wherever appropriate, additional information and exercises have been added to this book to help you better understand what is being discussed in the chapter. Icons throughout the text alert you to additional materials. The icons used in this textbook are as follows:

 Tips are included from the author's experience that provide extra information about how to set up Cisco Aironet 340 and the 3Com AirConnect equipment.

 The Note icon is used to present additional helpful material related to the subject being described.

 Cautions are included to help you anticipate potential mistakes or problems so you can prevent them from happening.

Each Hands-on Project in this book is preceded by the Hands-On icon and a description of the exercise that follows.

 Case project icons mark the case project. These are more involved, scenario-based assignments. In this extensive case example, you are asked to implement independently what you have learned.

 Optional case projects for teams icons indicate special projects that students can tackle as a group and that often require extra research and group decision making, which simulates the team environment stressed in many organizations.

INSTRUCTOR'S MATERIALS

The following supplemental materials are available when this book is used in a classroom setting. All of the supplements available with this book are provided to the instructor on a single CD-ROM.

Electronic Instructor's Manual. The Instructor's Manual that accompanies this textbook includes:

- Additional instructional material to assist in class preparation, including suggestions for lecture topics, suggested lab activities, tips on setting up a lab for the hands-on assignments, and alternative lab setup ideas in situations where lab resources are limited.
- Solutions to all end-of-chapter materials, including the Review Questions, Hands-on Projects, Case and Optional Team Case assignments.

ExamView Pro 3.0. This textbook is accompanied by ExamView®, a powerful testing software package that allows instructors to create and administer printed, computer (LAN-based), and Internet exams. ExamView includes hundreds of questions that correspond to the topics covered in this text, enabling students to generate detailed study guides that include page references for further review. The computer-based and Internet testing components allow students to take exams at their computers, and also save the instructor time by grading each exam automatically.

PowerPoint presentations. This book comes with Microsoft PowerPoint slides for each chapter. These are included as a teaching aid for classroom presentation, to make available to students on the network for chapter review, or to be printed for classroom distribution. Instructors, please feel at liberty to add your own slides for additional topics you introduce to the class.

READ THIS BEFORE YOU BEGIN

To the Student

This book helps you understand how to install, use, manage, configure, and troubleshoot a WLAN. Every chapter is designed to present you with easy-to-understand information about wireless networks to help you plan and implement this system in different environments. Each chapter of the book ends with review questions, hands-on projects, case assignments, and team case assignments that are written to be as realistic as the work you will soon be performing on the job. Your instructor can provide you with answers to the review questions and additional information about the hands-on projects.

Setting up the WLAN. To complete the projects and assignments in the book, the students will need access to a Cisco Aironet 340 wireless system or a 3Com AirConnect or both. To maximize the learning experience, it is recommended that you have one or more access points that can be dedicated for classroom use. In addition, each student should have a computer with a wireless NIC adapter installed along with the appropriate Cisco and/or 3Com software. Although each computer server need not be an expensive model, it should have adequate RAM, hard drive, and processor capabilities to ensure that the systems will function at an optimum level on the network. Although it is not required, it is desirable for each access point to be connected to a wired Ethernet network in order that the full advantages of a wireless network can be experienced.

Internet assignments. Some projects require Internet access for information searches. These projects will help train the student in using this resource as a prospective network administrator.

System requirements. The recommended software and hardware configurations are as follows:

Wireless Clients

- Portable laptop computer with Type II or Type III PC Card slot
- Windows 95, Windows 98, Windows ME, Windows NT or Windows 2000 operating system
- Netscape Navigator 5.0+ or Internet Explorer 4.0+ browser installed
- Minimum Pentium 133 MHz processor
- Minimum 32 MB of RAM
- VGA monitor
- Mouse or pointing device
- Wireless NIC adapter
- Hard disk drive
- At least one high density 3.5-inch floppy disk drive
- Internet access (recommended but not required for selected research assignments)

ACKNOWLEDGMENTS

An author alone does not create a book; it takes an entire team to produce the finished product. And the team that worked on this book was one of the very best. Managing Editor Stephen Solomon, with his clear vision of networking trends, did a fantastic job of turning a vague notion into a workable concept for a textbook. Laura Hildebrand as Product Manager was excellent at keeping the project on track and keeping tabs on all of the loose ends. Development Editor Deb Kaufmann was marvelous at making suggestions and correcting mistakes. Roger Simerly at Volunteer State was again exceptional in helping me solve WLAN problems. To these and all of the Course Technology staff behind the scenes, my sincere thanks.

And finally, a big hug goes to my family—my wife Susan, and my sons Brian and Greg. Their constant support, patience, and love helped see me through another project.

PHOTO CREDITS

DEDICATION

To my wife Susan and my sons Brian and Greg

IT'S A WIRELESS WORLD

> **After reading this chapter and completing the exercises, you will be able to:**
>
> ♦ Explain how wireless technologies are used today in the home, school, car, office, and field
> ♦ Describe the applications for wireless local area networks
> ♦ List and explain the advantages of a wireless local area network
> ♦ List and explain the disadvantages of a wireless local area network

Fifty years ago, scientists tried to peer into the future and predict what our world would be like in the year 2000. Flying cars, disposable aluminum clothing, household robots, and underwater cities were just a few of their predictions. Although none of these became reality, one prediction did come true: Scientists predicted that someday we would be able to send and receive messages from anywhere on earth through a vast wireless communications network. By a device that was hooked onto our belt or attached to our wristwatch, we could always be in touch with one another.

What these scientists *didn't* realize is just how common wireless communications would become in our everyday lives even before the new millennium. When was the last time that you walked over to the television set to change channels instead of using the remote control? Or opened the garage door by hand instead of pressing the button on the garage door opener? Or ran inside to answer the phone instead of carrying the cordless phone with you in the yard? Household wireless communication has become commonplace in today's world.

Wireless communication is likewise becoming the standard in the business world. Remote wireless Internet connections and wireless computer networks are appearing on the scene and will dramatically impact the way business does business in the future. It has truly become a wireless world.

A Day in the Life of a Wireless User

The extent to which wireless devices are used today can be easy to overlook. A day in the life of a typical user, Anthony Winters, may reveal something of today's vast wireless landscape.

Home

Anthony starts to get ready for a typical day. He will use several household wireless devices—remote CD player control, cordless telephone, and garage door control—just to help him get out the door. However, before he leaves, Anthony must first print a copy of the paper that he finished writing last night. Because he has more than one computer in his house, Anthony set up a wireless computer network. This network is based on the **Shared Wireless Access Protocol (SWAP)**. This protocol defines a set of specifications for wireless data and voice communications around the home. Devices can be as far as 150 feet (45 meters) apart, can send and receive data up to 5 million bits per second (Mbps), and can include not only computer equipment but also cordless telephones and home entertainment equipment.

SWAP was established by the **HomeRF Working Group**, which is made up of over 40 different companies from the personal computer, consumer electronics, communications, and software industries.

Anthony sits down at his desktop computer upstairs and retrieves his document using a word processor. He then clicks the print icon. A device called a **wireless home networking adapter** is connected to his computer. This adapter upstairs sends the data over radio waves to the computer downstairs, which also has a home networking adapter as well as the laser printer connected to it. By the time he gets downstairs, the last page is coming out of the printer. This wireless network is ideal for Anthony. He can have all of his home computing and electronic devices connected without the expense of installing cabling, and can share printing, files, and even Internet connections among them. Figure 1-1 illustrates Anthony's home wireless network.

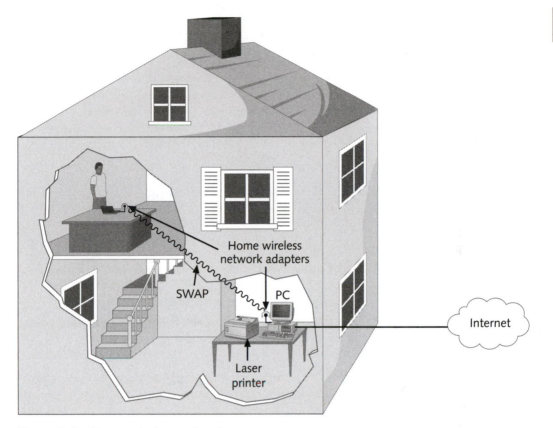

Figure 1-1 Home wireless network

College

Anthony stops at the library of the local community college before he heads to work. As a part-time instructor, he teaches a class on electronic commerce (e-commerce) one evening a week. Anthony has promised Tracy Li that he would help her with her new digital camera. Tracy's camera conforms to the **Bluetooth** wireless standard. Bluetooth devices communicate using small radio transceivers, called **radio modules**, built onto microprocessor chips. Each Bluetooth device also uses a **link manager**, which is special software that helps identify other Bluetooth devices, creates the links with them, and sends and receives data. A Bluetooth device can transmit data at up to 1 Mbps over a distance of 33 feet (10 meters). Bluetooth can send data through physical barriers such as walls and can send to one or many different devices all at the same time, and the devices don't even have to be aimed at each other.

Over 1,500 different computer, telephone and peripheral vendors have agreed to create products based on the Bluetooth standard.

Bluetooth is named after the 10th century Danish king Harold Bluetooth, who was responsible for unifying Scandinavia.

Anthony takes a picture of Tracy with her camera. He then takes the camera into the Student Production Center that contains a Bluetooth-enabled color laser printer. As soon as he walks into the room, the camera automatically establishes a connection with the printer. This connection creates a **personal area network (PAN)**. A PAN is two or more Bluetooth devices that are sending and receiving data with each other. Anthony presses the Print button on the camera and it begins transmitting the picture from the camera to the printer. A glossy color picture of Tracy soon appears as Anthony pays the printing fee. Figure 1-2 illustrates the wireless college network.

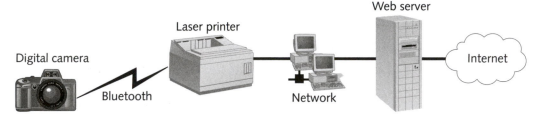

Figure 1-2   College wireless network

Car

After helping Tracy, Anthony gets into his car to drive to his office across town. However, road construction causes the traffic to come to a standstill. While stopped, Anthony pulls out his cellular telephone in order to read his e-mail. He can do this because his cell phone uses the **Wireless Application Protocol (WAP)**. WAP provides a standard way to transmit, format, and display Internet data for devices such as cell phones. With traditional computers, software known as a **Web browser** runs on a local PC. The Web browser software makes a request from the World Wide Web file server for a Web page. That page is transmitted back to the Web browser in **Hypertext Markup Language (HTML)**, which is the standard language for displaying content on the Internet. This model is illustrated in Figure 1-3.

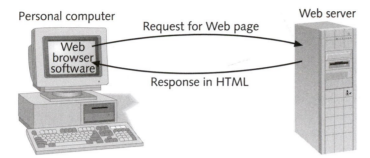

Figure 1-3   Browsing the World Wide Web

 When a Web server sends a Web page back to a PC, it is sending only HTML code; the Web browser is responsible for interpreting that code and displaying the results on the screen.

WAP follows this standard Internet model with a few variations. A WAP cell phone runs a tiny browser program (called a **micro browser**) that uses **Wireless Markup Language (WML)** instead of HTML. WML is designed to display text-based Web content on the small screen of a cell phone, as seen in Figure 1-4. However, since the Internet standard is HTML, a **WAP gateway** (sometimes called a **WAP proxy**) must translate between WML and HTML. This WAP model is illustrated in Figure 1-5.

Figure 1-4   WAP cell phone

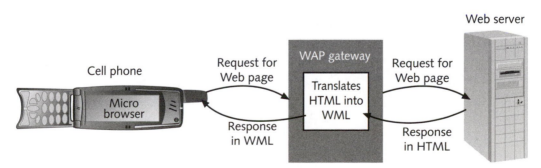

Figure 1-5   WAP communications

The WAP gateway takes the Web page sent from the Web server in HTML code and changes it to WML language before forwarding it to the cell phone.

Anthony uses his cell phone to connect to his e-mail server and read his mail. The cell phone connects to the nearest cellular tower, which connects to the local telephone company, which then calls his local Internet provider and completes the connection to his e-mail server. The e-mail messages are sent back to Anthony in HTML format to the WAP gateway, which extracts only the necessary text data, converts it to WML, and sends it to his cell phone display. After Anthony reads his last message, traffic starts to move again, so Anthony shuts off his cell phone for the drive to the office. Figure 1-6 illustrates the wireless WAP network.

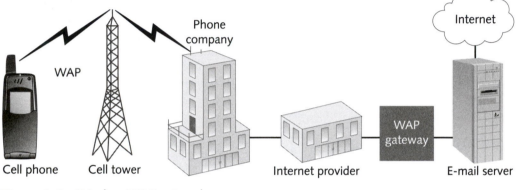

Figure 1-6   Wireless WAP network

Office

When Anthony arrives at the office, he heads for his cubicle. He does not have a desktop computer there. Instead, his company provides its employees with portable laptop computers that they use while at home, in the office, or on the road. None of the laptop computers in the office are connected to the local area network by cables. Instead, the company has set up a **wireless local area network (WLAN)**. A WLAN is identical to a standard LAN except that the computers are not connected to the LAN by wires. The WLAN is based on the **Institute of Electrical and Electronic Engineers (IEEE) 802.11b** standard. This standard allows WLAN computers to transmit at up to 11 Mbps over a distance of about 375 feet (114 meters).

Each computer on the WLAN has a **wireless network interface card** installed. This card performs the same basic functions as and looks similar to a traditional network interface card (NIC) except that it does not have a cable that connects it to a jack in the wall. Instead, the wireless NIC has an antenna either built in (Figure 1-7) or as a small telescoping external device.

Figure 1-7   Wireless NIC

The wireless NIC sends its signals through radio waves to an **access point**. The access point, as seen in Figure 1-8, receives the signals and transmits them back to the wireless NIC. The access point is also connected by a standard cable to the local area network. Through this connection, the access point (and the wireless devices that communicate with it) is able to communicate with all of the devices connected to the network, such as file servers, printers, and even other access points (and the wireless devices connected to them). The access point is fixed in one place (although it can be moved when necessary), whereas the computing devices with wireless NICs have the freedom to move around.

Anthony opens up his laptop on his desk and turns it on. The laptop starts up and establishes a connection with the access point located behind a green plant around the corner. Anthony can perform any network activity just as if he were connected to the network with a cable. For his next meeting, he carries his laptop with him down the hall to the conference room. Once there he opens it up and it's still connected to the network, along with the laptops of the five other people in the room. Figure 1-9 illustrates the WLAN office.

Figure 1-8   Wireless LAN access point

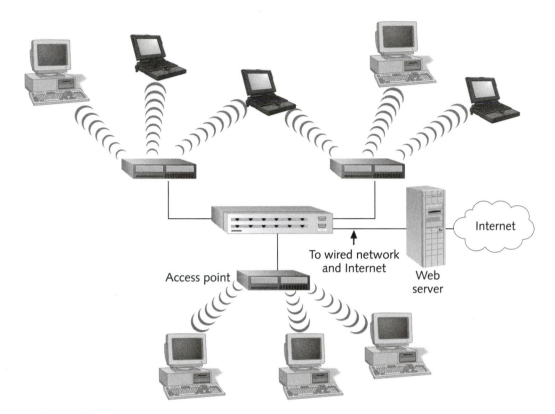

Figure 1-9   Wireless LAN layout

Field

Anthony drives to a customer's office for a meeting. While there he meets the new office manager, Tashica Dobbins. Anthony wants to record Tashica's contact information (telephone number, e-mail address, etc.), so he takes out his **Personal Digital Assistant (PDA)**. The PDA is a hand-held device that he uses for taking notes and making records. Anthony needs to transmit this information back to the server on the company's computer network that contains the customer database. He connects his digital cellular telephone to the PDA. The cell phone uses **Personal Communications Service (PCS)**. PCS sends a digital transmission signal instead of an analog signal. PCS is also a **circuit-switched** technology. Circuit-switched means that a dedicated connection circuit is established between the sending and receiving devices, and this circuit remains open until the entire transmission is terminated. In Figure 1-10, a dedicated Circuit A is created between the two PCs while another dedicated circuit exists between two telephones. Only data between the two PCs is transmitted on Circuit A, whereas only the voice transmission travels across Circuit B.

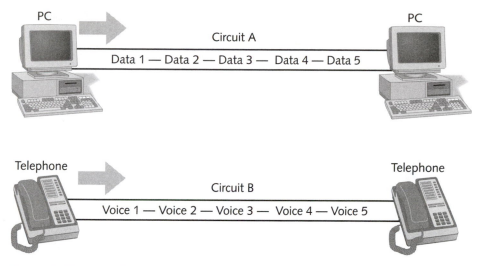

Figure 1-10   Circuit-switched network

 "Regular" (noncellular) telephones send an analog signal and use circuit-switched technology.

PCS is replacing **Cellular Digital Packet Data (CDPD)**, which used an analog packet–switched technology. **Packet switching** technology breaks the message into small data packets that then seek out the most efficient route to the destination as circuits become available. Each packet may go a different route but is reassembled at the final destination point. This is illustrated in Figure 1-11.

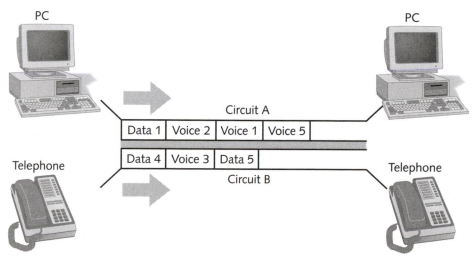

Figure 1-11   Packet-switched network

Anthony connects his digital cellular telephone to the PDA. He then sends data back to a server on the company's computer network, using the cell phone like a wireless modem. The data can then be ported over to the company's Web server so that other employees can access the data over the Internet. Figure 1-12 illustrates the wireless cellular modem technology.

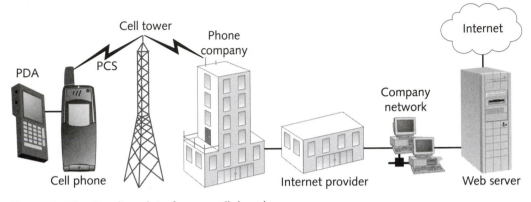

Figure 1-12   Sending data from a cellular phone

The Wireless Landscape

Anthony's typical day is built around the total wireless technology landscape, as seen in Figure 1-13. Many of these functions could not have been easily completed—much less attempted—without wireless technology. Wireless communication is no longer a special means of transmitting signals reserved for high-end users. Instead, it has become a standard means of communication for people in all walks of life. And the prospects for the future reveal nothing short of exponential growth in this area.

Although the field of wireless communications covers many areas (such as SWAP, Bluetooth, WAP, and PCS) and several of them overlap, this book focuses on the fastest-growing segment of the wireless landscape: wireless local area networks (WLANs). It is estimated that sales of WLANs will grow from $300 million in 1998 to over $1.6 billion in 2005, and that there will be over 34 million wireless devices by the year 2002.

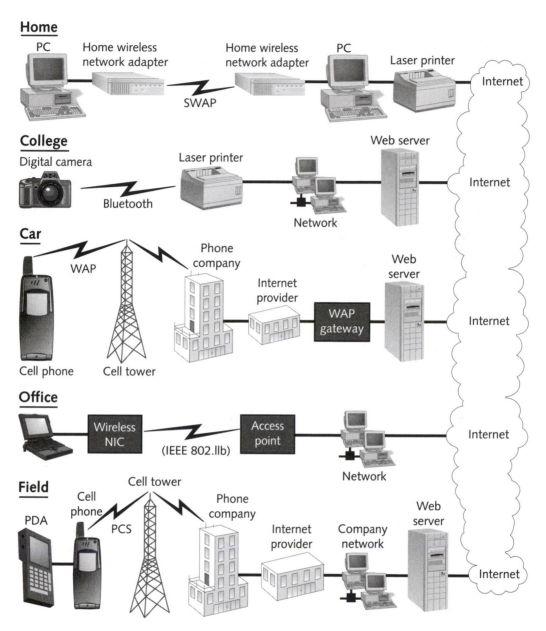

Figure 1-13   Wireless landscape

WLAN APPLICATIONS

Wireless local area networking can be found in almost every industry that has employees who need the mobility and freedom to conduct business without being chained to their desk. This section describes several of the leading industries.

Education

WLAN technology is an ideal application for colleges and schools. Teachers can create classroom presentations on the laptop computer in their office and then carry that computer with them right into the classroom. Once there they do not have to take time using cables to connect to the campus LAN; rather, their laptop automatically makes the wireless connection as soon as they walk into the room. Teachers can also send class material directly to students sitting in the classroom who have brought their own wireless laptops with them to class.

The wireless connection also offers students a degree of freedom that they have not experienced before. Students can access the school network "wirelessly" from almost any location on campus. As they move to different classrooms in different buildings, they always remain connected to the network. Many schools that require students to own a laptop computer now require that those same computers have wireless network connections.

Warehouse Management

Managing a warehouse stocked with inventory can be a nightmare. New products arrive continuously and must be inventoried and stored. When products are shipped out of the warehouse, personnel must first locate and then transfer them to the right loading dock so workers can place the goods on the correct truck. A mistake in any one of these steps can result in a warehouse stocked with products that employees cannot locate, in irate customers receiving the wrong item, or in a store running out of goods to sell.

Implementing a WLAN solution can turn this nightmare into a dream. All forklift trucks in the warehouse can be outfitted with a wireless computer device. Employees can also be given portable wireless devices. All of these devices can be connected to the wireless LAN. Warehouse management system (WMS) software can manage all of the activities from receiving through shipping. And since this network is tied into the front office computer system, managers can have statistics that are current at any given moment.

Pallet loads arriving from other locations come with bar-coded pallet labels. The bar coding includes product identification numbers, product code dates or expiration dates, originating plants and lines of manufacture, and sequentially assigned serial numbers. As pallets arrive, a forklift truck operator scans the bar code label with a portable wireless device. This device sends the data to the WLAN, where the warehouse software immediately designates a storage location for the pallet and relays the information back to the computer on the forklift truck. A bar code is immediately printed and affixed to the pallet. The forklift operator then transports the pallet to a storage location in the warehouse, as seen in Figure 1-14. A bar code label suspended from the ceiling for floor locations or attached to a rack face identifies every storage location. The forklift operator scans the bar code to confirm that the pallets are being put away in the correct location before depositing the load.

Figure 1-14 Forklift using a WLAN

 One warehouse facility that didn't use a WLAN dedicated two full-time employees just to walk around the 300,000-square-foot warehouse to find open storage locations for incoming pallet loads.

In the front office, clerks receive and enter orders into the computer that connects to the WLAN in the warehouse. The WMS software manages order picking, balances workloads, and selects pick sequences for lift truck operators. The dock control module then releases orders for picking. A forklift operator locates the correct storage location, scans the bar code of the pallet, and then ferries it to the shipping dock to be loaded onto a truck.

One warehouse that recently installed WLANs along with WMS software and bar codes was able to ship an additional 1.8 million cases of their product in 2,200 fewer worker hours while decreasing the amount of stock in inventory by 121,000 cases—all during the first year of implementation. In addition, inventory accuracy now exceeds 98%, every item shipped is 100% lot traceable, and workers can load the product in minutes.

Investment Banking

In investment banking, communicating quickly with clients and fellow traders and remotely monitoring changes in the stock market are critical to success. Several investment banking firms have installed WLANs so that their employees can securely monitor the stock market wirelessly and communicate with others from anywhere in the building.

Health Care

WLANs in hospitals allow the health care industry to improve in two primary areas: maintaining patient records and documenting medication administration. Typically, nurses must write a note on paper regarding a patient's condition or treatment and then take it back to the nurses' station for entry into the computer. However, having multiple patients to care for and sometimes only a single computer at the nurse's station can make it difficult for nurses to perform the clinical documentation on the computer in a timely fashion. As a result, a nurse who administered treatment in the morning may be forced to wait until the end of the shift to document it in the system.

Administering medication is another problem area. Typically, medication printouts are posted at the medication area. As nurses administer medication, they cross off the treatment from the list and initial their changes to the list. However, since nurses cannot update the paper record immediately, a patient could get an extra dose of medication before an order for a new or changed medication was processed. This problem also forces duplicate documentation. Nurses first check the medication printout to determine the medication to be given. Then, they document on paper that the medication was actually given, and later enter the data on the computers.

However, wireless point-of-care computer systems connected to WLANs allow hospital staff to access and update patient records immediately. Many hospitals are using laptop computers equipped with the wireless NICs on mobile carts that provide space for a laptop, mouse, and medication cups. Nurses can now document a patient's treatment immediately on the computer as they move from room to room, without worrying about connecting and disconnecting cables. Also, nurses can document medication administration at bedside. The system immediately verifies that medication is being administered to the correct patient, in the correct dosage, which eliminates potential errors and documentation inefficiencies. The documentation process now takes place at the bedside where care is delivered, which improves accuracy. In addition, all hospital personnel now have real-time access to the latest medication and patient status information. One hospital recently reported that after it implemented the point-of-care computers with WLANs, noncompliance with documentation requirements went from over 13% noncompliance to less than 1% noncompliance.

WLANs likewise hold the potential for more radical changes in the health care industry. Wireless network devices can dramatically improve patient care and surgery. Scientists have recently developed a high-tech capsule the size of a pill that contains a miniature camera and transmitter that a patient can swallow to give doctors a wireless visual tour of the patient's digestive tract, as seen in Figure 1-15.

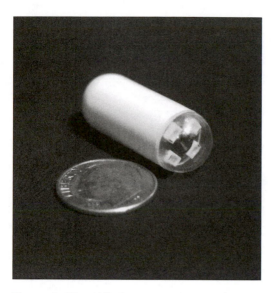

Figure 1-15   Wireless camera capsule

Entertainment

Managing spectators attending a sporting event or concert can be a daunting task. Each attendee has a ticket, and there are special passes for the press and team officials. However, tickets can be lost, stolen, or even counterfeited. Attempting to identify a stolen or counterfeit ticket as tens of thousands of spectators swarm to the event minutes before it is to begin is almost an impossible task. Several large arenas and stadiums are now turning to WLAN systems to facilitate this process.

Event tickets are printed with a unique bar code that ticket takers then scan at the venue's point of entry using hand-held or integrated turnstile hardware, which is connected to a WLAN. The network instantaneously validates the ticket via the wireless LAN and then signals back to the turnstile at the gate to allow the entry of the patron into the arena. Not only does this prevent the use of counterfeit tickets, but it also can be used to identify stolen tickets.

The wireless point-of-entry turnstiles can also give a real-time look at traffic flow. It helps the venue more effectively manage its manpower and deploy personnel where they are needed. Data about who enters which gate can even be used by advertisers to tailor their marketing efforts.

Manufacturing

Almost all manufacturing operations have one thing in common: They cover a large amount of space. Most manufacturing operations are spread out over several different buildings and offices that receive, process, and ship products. Wiring between the buildings can be very costly and typically involves a monthly charge for the connectivity. Within each building there likewise can be a vast amount of space. Wiring within these large buildings becomes very expensive. And if the computers are in fixed locations, performing such jobs as taking inventory involves making notes and then later entering the data by hand into a computer.

WLANs can help provide the solution to these problems. Users on the manufacturing floor, shipping dock, or office can freely move about while they are connected to the network. In addition, new wrist-mounted fingertip scanners such as those shown in Figure 1-16 can dramatically increase the speed and accuracy of the data being read. And wireless transmissions between buildings can help tie everyone together without expensive recurring communications charges.

Figure 1-16   Fingertip scanner

WLAN Advantages and Disadvantages

As with any new technology, there are advantages and disadvantages to consider. WLANs are no exception. This section discusses several of those advantages and disadvantages.

Advantages

There are many advantages to a wireless local area network, including mobility, easier and less expensive installation, easier network modification, increased network reliability, and speedier disaster recovery.

Mobility

The freedom to move about without being tethered to the network by wires is certainly the primary advantage of a WLAN. A WLAN enables a user to use a device like a laptop computer that is always in contact with the network as the user moves around in the building.

Many occupations require workers, such as police officers and inventory clerks, to be mobile. WLANs are vital to them.

An increasingly mobile workforce is one characteristic of the business world of today. Many employees spend much of their time away from the office. Because of this, companies are equipping their workers with notebook computers and other portable devices. However, these employees still need immediate access to the company network. WLANs fit well in this work environment, giving mobile workers the freedom they need but still allowing them to access the network resources that they need. With a wireless network, workers can access information from almost anywhere.

Another characteristic of the business world of today is "flatter" organizations—that is, many organizations tend to be less hierarchical (a vertical structure) and incorporate more work in teams or groups that cross traditional organizational boundaries (a more horizontal, flatter structure). Much of today's work occurs in team meetings away from individual workers' desks, yet the need for immediate access to network resources still exists. WLANs are again the solution to the problem. They enable team-based workers to access the network resources that they need while collaborating in a team environment.

 Several airports around the nation are installing wireless networks as a free service to business travelers. Those travelers with wireless NICs installed in their laptops can connect to access points located around the terminal and access the Internet while waiting for their flights.

Easier and Less Expensive Installation

Installing network cabling in older buildings can be a difficult and costly task. These buildings were built with no thought of running computer wiring between the rooms. Thick masonry walls and plaster ceilings are difficult to drill holes through and snake cabling around. Sometimes an older building may have asbestos that would first have to be completely removed before any new cabling could be installed. And often there are restrictions on modifying older facilities that have a historical value.

In these instances, a wireless LAN is the ideal solution. Historical buildings are preserved, dangerous asbestos is left undisturbed, and difficult drilling can be avoided by using a wireless system. And of course, eliminating the need for installing cabling results in a significant cost savings.

Also, the time required to install network cabling is generally significant. Installers must pull wires through the ceiling and then drop cables down walls to network outlets. This can usually take days or even weeks to complete. During that time, employees must somehow continue their work in the midst of the construction zone, which is often difficult to do. Using a wireless LAN eliminates any such disruption because there are no cables to install.

Easier Network Modification

Wireless networks also make it easier for any office—in either an old or new building—to be modified with new cubicles or furniture. No longer does the design for a remodeled office first have to consider the location of the computer jack in the wall before relocating furniture. Instead, the focus can be on creating the most effective work environment for the employees.

Increased Network Reliability

Network cable failures are perhaps the most common source of network problems. Moisture from a leak during a thunderstorm or a coffee spill can erode metallic conductors. A user who moves a wired computer may break the network connection. A cable splice that is done incorrectly can cause problems that result in baffling errors that are very difficult to identify. A wireless LAN eliminates these types of cable failures and increases the overall reliability of the network.

Speedier Disaster Recovery

Accidents happen every day: Fires, tornados, and floods can occur with little if any warning. Any business that is not prepared to recover from these or other disasters may find itself quickly out of business. A disaster recovery plan is a vital document that every business must have in place if it is to get back on its feet quickly after a calamity.

Because the computer network is such a vital part of the daily operation of a business, the ability to have the network back up and working after a disaster is critical. Many businesses are turning to WLANs as a major piece of their disaster recovery plan. Laptop computers with wireless NICs and access points are kept in reserve along with backup network servers. In the event of a disaster, another office building is quickly located. The business need not consider whether the network wiring of the building is adequate, for it will not use such wiring. Instead, the network servers are installed in the building along with the access points, and the laptop computers are distributed to the resettled employees. The network can be immediately up and running so that business may proceed as normally as possible.

Disadvantages

Along with the many advantages to a wireless local area network, there are likewise disadvantages and concerns such as radio signal interference, security, interoperability, and health risks.

Radio Signal Interference

Because most WLANs operate using radio signals, there is the potential for signal interference. Signals from other devices can disrupt what a WLAN is trying to transmit, or the WLAN may itself be the source of interference for other devices, as seen in Figure 1-17.

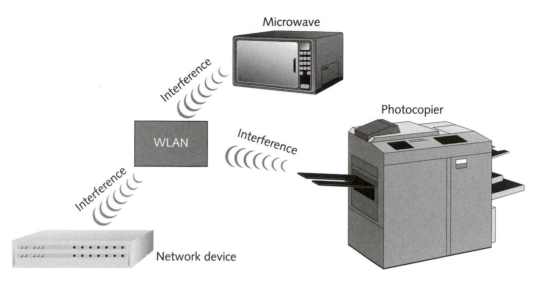

Figure 1-17   Radio signal interference

Several different types of devices transmit a radio signal that may interfere with a WLAN. These devices include microwave ovens, elevator motors, photocopying machines, certain types of outdoor lighting systems, theft protection devices, and cordless telephones. These may cause errors to occur in the transmission between a wireless device and an access point.

Interference, however, is also a problem for wired computer networks. Even when cables are used to connect network devices, interference from fluorescent light fixtures and electric motors can sometimes disrupt the sending and receiving of data. The solution for wireless devices is the same as that for standard cabled network devices: Locate and eliminate the source of the interference. For example, you can move a photocopying machine or microwave oven across the room or to another room. In addition, wireless LANs, just like standard LANs, can identify that errors occurred in the transmission and retransmit the data as necessary.

 Outside interference from AM or FM radio stations, TV broadcast stations, or other large-scale transmitters cannot occur since these stations and WLANs operate at different radio frequencies.

The other source of disruptive signals, the WLAN itself, is a far less frequent problem. Because the WLAN operates at a set frequency and because the strength of the signal itself is very low, the number of devices with which the WLAN interferes is very small. A device would have to be located extremely close to a WLAN for a disruption to take place.

 A WLAN will not necessarily return interference to the same devices. That is, although a microwave oven may interfere with a WLAN, a WLAN will not usually interfere with the operation of a microwave.

Security

Because a wireless LAN transmits radio signals over a broad area, security is a major concern. It is possible for an intruder to be lurking in his or her car in the parking lot with a laptop and wireless NIC in order to intercept the signals from the wireless network. Because much of a business' network traffic may contain sensitive information, security is a real concern to many users and businesses.

However, wireless LANs can provide a level of security that meets—and in some cases even exceeds—that of standard LANs. To prevent unauthorized eavesdropping on a WLAN, a business can take several different steps. First, the business can program a special coded number into each access point and every authorized wireless device. For anyone to gain entrance to the access point, the wireless device must first transmit the special number; if it cannot, then the system denies access to that device. In addition, a list of approved wireless devices can also be programmed into the access point. The system then allows access to only those on the list. As a further protection, a business can encode data transmitted between the access point and the wireless device in such a way that only the recipient can decode the message using a special electronic "key." If an unauthorized user were to intercept the radio signals being transmitted, he or she still could not read the messages being sent, as seen in Figure 1-18.

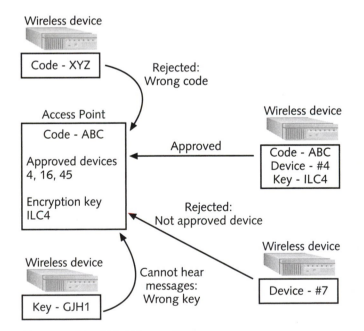

Figure 1-18   WLAN security

 All of the WLAN security provisions are in addition to the standard network levels of security that require authentication (such as passwords) in order for a user to access the network.

Interoperability

When any new technology is introduced, the question is always raised as to whether a product purchased from one vendor will work with a product purchased from another vendor. This is known as **interoperability**. In the early days of standard LANs (1980s), this issue was of great concern.

However, it appears that interoperability will not be a problem with WLAN. First, all of the major WLAN vendors have agreed to follow the specifications as set forth in the IEEE 802.11b standard. Second, the **Wireless Ethernet Compatibility Alliance (WECA)** in early 2000 started certifying WLAN vendors whose products met that standard. The WECA seal (called the **Wi-Fi certification**) guarantees that WLAN products from different vendors will work together out of the box. Those products include wireless NICs and access points.

Health Risks

Wireless network devices have continued to come under close scrutiny because of the possible health risks that they pose for users. Data regarding cellular telephone users continues to be analyzed to determine whether these devices pose significant health risks, such as cancer caused by the electromagnetic radiation that cell phones emit.

To date, no conclusive evidence suggests a link between wireless devices and health risks. In any event, WLANs pose even less of a threat than cellular telephones would. Wireless LANs operate at much lower power levels than cellular telephones. In addition, WLANs transmit for a much shorter period of time.

Although there is no evidence of any health risks associated with using any wireless device, it is always wise to be aware of the concern and monitor any studies that take place.

CHAPTER SUMMARY

❑ Household wireless communications have become commonplace in today's world, and wireless communication is becoming the standard in the business world as well. Remote wireless Internet connections and wireless computer networks are appearing on the scene and will dramatically impact the way business does business in the future.

❑ Today, wireless networks and devices can be found nearly everywhere people live and work. Home users can implement SWAP to connect different devices, and Bluetooth can connect devices over a short distance. WAP is used for cell phones to display text-based Internet information, whereas the PCS protocol can send digital circuit-switched signals. WLANs are becoming essential to business networks.

❑ WLAN applications are found in a wide variety of industries, including education, warehouse management, investment banking, health care, entertainment, and manufacturing.

❑ Mobility, or the freedom to move without being connected to the network by a cable, is the primary advantage of a WLAN. Other advantages include quicker and less expensive installation, increased network reliability, and support for disaster recovery.

❑ There are some disadvantages to a WLAN. Radio signal interference, security concerns, possible problems with interoperability of devices from different vendors, and health risks are sometimes considered disadvantages.

KEY TERMS

access point — A device connected to the local area network that receives signals and transmits signals back to wireless NICs.

Bluetooth — A wireless standard for devices to transmit data at up to 1 Mbps over a distance of 33 feet (10 meters).

Cellular Digital Packet Data (CDPD) — An analog packet-switched transmission signal used by cell phones.

circuit-switched — A technology that establishes a dedicated connection circuit between a sending and receiving device; that circuit remains open until the entire transmission is terminated.

HomeRF Working Group — A group of over 40 different companies from the personal computer, consumer electronics, communications, and software industries that established the SWAP standard.

Hypertext Markup Language (HTML) — The standard language for displaying content on the Internet.

Institute of Electrical and Electronic Engineers (IEEE) 802.11b — The networking standard for wireless local area networks.

interoperability — The ability of a product manufactured by one vendor to work with a product made by another vendor.

link manager — Special software in Bluetooth devices that helps identify other Bluetooth devices, creates the links between them, and sends and receives data.

micro browser — A tiny browser program that runs on a WAP cell phone.

packet switching — A communications technology that breaks a message into small data packets and then seeks out the most efficient route to the destination as circuits become available.

personal area network (PAN) — Two or more Bluetooth devices that send and receive data to and from each other.

Personal Communications Service (PCS) — A digital circuit-switched transmission signal used by cell phones.

Personal Digital Assistant (PDA) — A hand-held device used for taking notes and making records.

radio module — A small radio transceiver built onto a microprocessor chip embedded into Bluetooth devices that enable them communicate.

Shared Wireless Access Protocol (SWAP) — A set of specifications for wireless data and voice communications around the home that can include computer equipment, cordless telephones, and home entertainment equipment.

WAP gateway — A device that translates HTML to WML so that it can be displayed on a WAP cell phone; also called a WAP Proxy.

WAP proxy — A device that translates HTML to WML so that it can be displayed on a WAP cell phone; also called a WAP Gateway.

Web browser — Software that runs on a local PC and makes a request from the World Wide Web file server for a Web page.

Wi–Fi certification — The seal granted by the WECA that guarantees that a wireless LAN product will work with products from other vendors.

Wireless Application Protocol (WAP) — A standard for transmitting, formatting, and displaying Internet data for devices such as cell phones.

Wireless Ethernet Compatibility Alliance (WECA) — A standards group that certifies wireless LAN vendors whose products meet the IEEE 802.11b standard.

wireless home networking adapter — A device that connects to a home computer to transmit and receive data over radio waves.

wireless local area network (WLAN) — A local area network that is not connected by wires but instead uses wireless technology.

Wireless Markup Language (WML) — The language for displaying Internet content on WAP cell phones.

wireless network interface card — A card installed in a computer that performs the same functions as a standard network interface card, except that it does not have a cable that connects it to the network.

REVIEW QUESTIONS

1. The Shared Wireless Access Protocol (SWAP) is used in the _____.

   a. home

   b. office

   c. car

   d. cell phone

2. Bluetooth devices communicate using a small radio transceiver called a _____, which is built onto microprocessor chips.

   a. receiver

   b. transponder

   c. radio module

   d. link manager

3. _____ provides a standard way to transmit, format, and display Internet data for devices like cell phones.

   a. WLAN

   b. WAP

   c. HTML

   d. WML

4. The WLAN standard is the Institute of Electrical and Electronic Engineers (IEEE) _____.

   a. 802.11b

   b. WAP

   c. 501

   d. HTTP

5. PCS is a(n) _____ technology.

   a. packet-switched

   b. circuit-switched

   c. analog

   d. serial

6. SWAP devices can be as far as 150 feet apart, and can send and receive data up to 5 Mbps. True or false?

7. A Bluetooth device can transmit data at up to 1 Mbps over a distance of 33 feet. True or false?

8. A wireless network interface card performs the same functions as and looks identical to a traditional network interface card (NIC) card. True or false?

9. Applications for WLANs include education, warehouse management, investment banking, health care, entertainment, and manufacturing. True or false?

10. Eliminating installation costs is a disadvantage of a WLAN. True or false?

11. SWAP can connect not only computer equipment but also _____ and home entertainment equipment.

12. SWAP was established by the _____, which is made up of over 40 different companies from the personal computer, consumer electronics, communications, and software industries.

13. The wireless NIC sends its signals through invisible radio waves to a(n) _____.

14. PCS sends a digital transmission signal instead of a(n) _____ signal.

15. _____ failures are the most common source of network problems.

16. A network of two or more Bluetooth devices is called a(n) _____.

17. Explain how a WAP cell phone sends and receives Internet data.

18. Explain the difference between packet-switching and circuit-switching technologies.

19. Tell how WLANs can eliminate installation time.

20. Explain how a WLAN can aid in a disaster recovery.

HANDS-ON PROJECTS

1. Write a one-page paper outlining the differences and similarities between SWAP and Bluetooth. Use the Internet as well as material from SWAP and Bluetooth vendors. Include their advantages and disadvantages. When would you use SWAP instead of Bluetooth, and vice versa?

2. Research the differences between HTML and WML. How are they similar? How are they different? Be sure to include information about WML "decks" and "cards." What type of WAP browsers are available to display WML?

3. Use the Internet or your local telephone provider to find out more information on PCS and CDPD. What are the technical differences between PCS and CDPD? What is the difference in cost in your area? Which do you recommend for a new cell phone purchaser?

4. Locate a school, hospital, manufacturing plant, warehouse, or other business that is switching to a WLAN. Interview appropriate people to determine why they are making the change. Ask what benefits and drawbacks they considered. Write a one-page paper on your findings.

5. Write a one-page paper that addresses WLAN security concerns. Use the Internet and information from vendors as additional resources.

6. Using the Internet, find the latest information about health concerns using wireless technologies. What studies are currently under way? What issues are concerns? What is your conclusion? Write a one-page paper about your findings.

7. How could wireless technology change what you do every day? How has it changed your activities already? Write a one-page paper outlining how the world of wireless technology could impact your life.

CASE PROJECT

Northridge Consulting Group

You are employed by Northridge Consulting Group (NCG), a company of 20 consultants that assists organizations and businesses with issues involving network planning, design, implementation, and problem solving. You have recently been hired by NCG to work with one of the company's new clients, Pickup Packages, on its networking needs.

Pickup Packages is a local package pickup and delivery service that offers two-hour delivery of packages and letters in your city. The company also picks up out-of-town deliveries and takes them to the company's main office, where they are transferred to a national package delivery system.

1. Pickup Packages has recently moved into an older building that will be used for offices as well as space for company vehicles, bicycles, and a central location for pickup by the national package delivery system. The service needs a network of computers both in the office as well as in the warehouse. NCG believes that a WLAN may be a good application for this project. Create a presentation to deliver to Pickup Packages' management team about WLANs. Be sure to cover the following points:

    ❐ Mobility

    ❐ Easier and less expensive installation

    ❐ Easier network modifications

    ❐ Increased network reliability

    ❐ Speedier disaster recovery

    ❐ Radio signal interference

    ❐ Security

    ❐ Interoperability

2. After your presentation, Pickup Packages is interested in WLANs, but the president has a concern regarding health risks. Create another presentation that shows the issues of health risks with WLANs. Compare and contrast them with the health issues for wired LANs, cellular telephones, and microwave transmissions.

3. Pickup Packages is also interested in providing its drivers or bicyclists with another means of communication besides pagers and analog cellular telephones. The management team wants the carriers to receive their pickup and delivery messages from the company's Web server. The managers have asked your opinion regarding using WAP with cellular telephones or wireless PDAs. Prepare to present your recommendations to Pickup Packages' management team.

OPTIONAL TEAM CASE PROJECT

A local newspaper, *The News-Examiner*, is writing an article about Bluetooth technology and has asked Northridge Consulting Group (NCG) for information. Form a team of two or three consultants and research Bluetooth technology. Specifically, investigate the future of Bluetooth. Provide information regarding its problems and the concerns of some vendors. Also provide estimates regarding how you envision Bluetooth will be used in home applications.

2

WIRELESS LAN FUNDAMENTALS

After reading this chapter and completing the exercises, you will be able to:

♦ Tell how a light-based WLAN sends and receives data

♦ List and explain the advantages and disadvantages of light-based WLANs

♦ Explain how radio waves can be used to transmit data signals

♦ Discuss the similarities and differences between frequency hopping spread spectrum (FHSS) and direct sequence spread spectrum (DSSS)

♦ Describe the hardware and software components of a WLAN

Most users of computers, cars, telephones, audio systems, and other complex modern devices approach them with a "black box" philosophy. This simply means that users view the device as a mysterious black box that magically does something to produce the desired service or effect. All the user cares about is how to manipulate the "box" to achieve the desired benefit, as seen in Figure 2-1. How the device actually works is considered irrelevant.

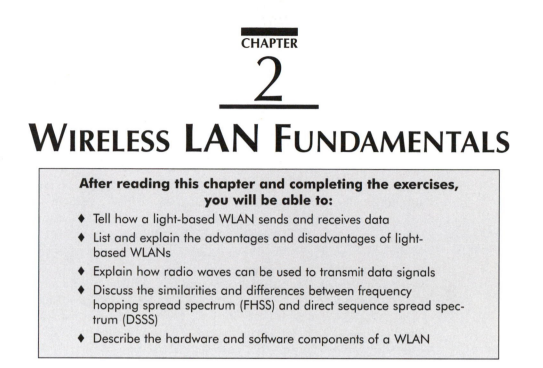

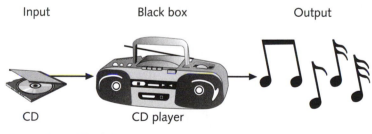

Input   Black box   Output

CD   CD player

Figure 2-1 Black box concept

For users, this philosophy usually is satisfactory. However, for those more closely involved with the technology, an in-depth understanding of how the technology actually functions is important. This understanding can help in troubleshooting and fixing problems when something goes wrong, and can be critical when it comes time to expand, upgrade, or even replace the technology.

Knowledge of how a WLAN functions is essential for anyone with WLAN responsibilities greater than those of the basic user. This chapter looks at the scientific principles that underlie WLANs and how they operate.

Light-Based WLANs

One of the two ways in which a wireless LAN can send and receive information is by using light. Transmitting information by light has been used for many years in several types of applications. For example, before radios were commonplace, ocean ships flashed Morse code signals across the water to one another using light. Transmitting network data using light follows the same basic principle.

Alexander Graham Bell in 1880 demonstrated an invention called the photophone, which used the concept of light waves to transmit voice information. The device was used to transmit sound, but the technology was not available to produce a strong enough image that could work during the day or be unaffected by weather. It wasn't until the 1960s that the concepts learned from the photophone would help establish the operating principles of laser communication over fiber-optic cables.

Coding Signals

Transmitting a network signal using light is a straightforward task. This is because of the way that computers store and transmit data internally. Every number, letter of the alphabet, and symbol (such as a dollar sign) that can be entered into a computer is assigned an arbitrary number based on a specific coding scheme. One of these arbitrary coding schemes uses the numbers from 0 to 255 and is called the **American Standard Code for Information Interchange (ASCII)**. The uppercase letter *A*, for example, has been assigned the number 65 in ASCII. Instead of storing the character *A*, a computer will instead store its ASCII equivalent number (65).

Yet computers store and internally transmit these ASCII numbers in a format different than people use. Computers are based on **binary code**. This code, also known as **base 2**, can represent any number by using just two digits, 0 and 1. Computers represent everything as a series of ones and zeros using binary code. The number 65, for example, can be represented in binary code as 01000001. Thus, to store the letter *A*, the computer first converts it to its ASCII equivalent (65) and then stores the number as binary code (01000001), as seen in Figure 2-2.

2

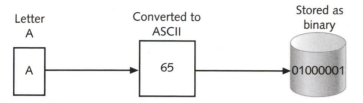

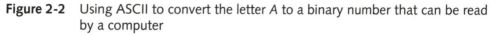

Figure 2-2   Using ASCII to convert the letter *A* to a binary number that can be read by a computer

 One of the limitations of ASCII is that there are not enough codes for all the symbols used by world languages. Another coding scheme called Unicode can represent 65,535 different characters.

Because computers use coding schemes and binary code, it is easy to transmit information across a WLAN by using light. Just as binary code uses only two digits (0 and 1), light has only two properties (off and on). To send a 1 in binary code would result in a light flashing on; to send a 0, the light would remain off. Thus the letter *A* could be transmitted by light as seen in Figure 2-3 as "off-on-off-off-off-off-off-on." A WLAN that transmits data in this way is called a **light-based WLAN**.

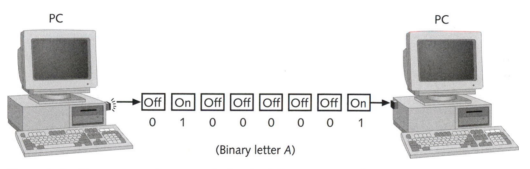

Figure 2-3   Transmitting binary code for the letter *A* using light

Infrared Light

If visible light flashes were used to transmit data over a network, the transmission could be very unreliable. Other bright lights could be mistaken for the network transmission signal and confuse the receiving device. And an even brighter light—such as sunlight coming through a window—could "wash out" the light flashes. Instead of using visible light, another type of light is needed to transmit network signals.

There are several different types of light on earth. All the different types of light that travel from the sun to the earth make up the **light spectrum**, as seen in Figure 2-4. The light that is actually seen by humans (called visible light) is just a small part of that entire spectrum. All other types of light are invisible to the human eye. These include X-ray light, ultraviolet light, and **infrared light**. Infrared light is next to visible light on the light spectrum, and thus has many of the same characteristics as visible light: It travels in straight lines and cannot penetrate through opaque (solid) objects such as walls or ceilings. All light-based WLANs today use infrared light to send and receive signals.

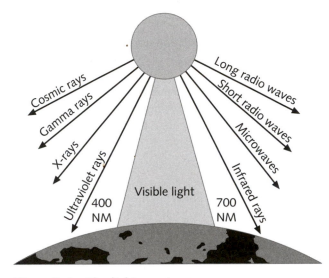

Figure 2-4   The light spectrum

In the early 19th century, William Herschel took a prism and saw seven colors (violet, indigo, blue, green, yellow, orange, and red) split out of the white light. He then placed a thermometer to the right of the red area and noticed that the thermometer showed increased heat. He called this infrared, and it was the first detection of a form of light invisible to the human eye.

Some animals are able to see forms of light that are not visible to humans, including ultraviolet and infrared.

Light-based infrared WLAN systems require that each device on the network have two components: an **emitter** that transmits a signal and a **detector** that receives the signal (these two components are sometimes combined into one device). An emitter is usually a laser diode or a light-emitting diode (LED). To transmit a *1*, the emitter increases the intensity of the current and sends a "pulse" using infrared light. The detector senses the higher-intensity signal and produces a proportional electrical current. Thus an infrared WLAN sends data by the intensity of the light wave instead of "on-off" signals of light: A higher impulse is a 1, whereas a lower impulse is a 0, as seen in Figure 2-5.

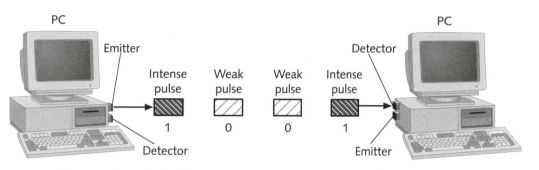

Figure 2-5   An infrared WLAN uses weak and intense pulses of light

Directed and Diffused Transmissions

Infrared transmission in WLANs can be either directed or diffused. A **directed** WLAN requires that the emitter and detector be aimed directly at one another (called **line-of-sight transmission**), as seen in Figure 2-6. The emitter sends a narrowly focused beam of infrared light. The detector has a small receiving or viewing area.

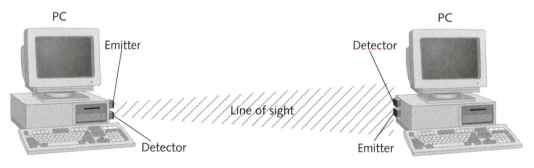

Figure 2-6   Line-of-sight transmission

Directed WLANs use a line-of-sight principle. It is thus impractical for mobile users to use a directed WLAN, since the alignment between the emitter and the detector would have to be continuously adjusted. In addition, other objects, such as people walking through the signal or someone placing a plant on a desk, could disrupt the transmission signal. Because of this, directed WLANs are not suitable in an environment where the users need to be mobile. Instead, they are best designed for a setting where the network devices are fixed in a stationary position without the possibility of something interfering with the line of sight.

A **diffused** WLAN does not require line of sight. Instead, it relies on reflected light. The emitters on a diffused WLAN have a wide-focused beam instead of a narrow beam. Emitters are usually pointed at the ceiling and use it as the reflection point. When the emitter transmits an infrared signal, it bounces off the ceiling and fills the room with the signal, much as the light from a flashlight will reflect off the walls and ceilings of a room. Detectors are likewise pointed at the same reflection point and can detect the reflected or "bounced" signal, as seen in Figure 2-7.

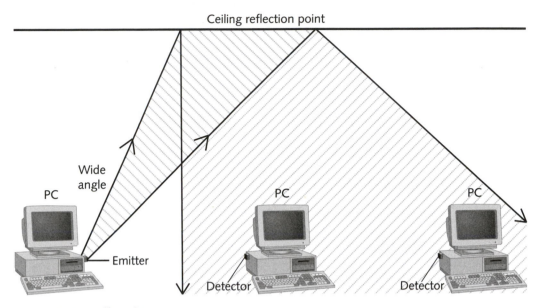

Figure 2-7   Diffused transmission

 The emitters used in diffused infrared WLANs radiate less infrared energy than a standard light bulb and do not pose any health or safety hazards.

Advantages and Disadvantages of Light-Based WLANs

Light-based WLANs have several advantages. Infrared light does not interfere with other communications signals and is not affected by other signals. And, because infrared signals do not penetrate walls, the signals are kept inside the room. This makes it almost impossible for someone elsewhere to "eavesdrop" on the transmitted signal. And the overall power consumption is low for emitters.

However, there are serious limitations to light–based WLANs. The first limitation involves the range of coverage. Because directed WLANs require a line of sight, they cannot be placed in an environment where the users are mobile or there is the possibility that anything could be placed in the way of the infrared beam. Due to the angle of deflection, network devices in diffused WLANs can cover a range of only about 50 feet (16 meters). And because diffused WLANs require a reflection point, they can only be used indoors.

 The ceiling height of a room will also affect the range of a diffused WLAN. A ceiling height of 10 feet (3 meters) will limit the range to about 40 feet (13 meters).

The second limitation of a light-based WLAN involves speed. Diffused infrared WLANs can send data at a rate of only up to 4 Mbps. This is because the wide angle of the beam loses energy as it reflects. This loss of energy forces the data rate to be lower (the loss of energy is also the same reason that a diffused WLAN signal cannot be transmitted over long distances).

Because of the limited range of coverage and the slow data speed, there are very few light-based infrared WLANs. Most infrared data transmissions are between laptop computers and printers based on the **Infrared Data Association (IrDA)** specification, which is a 115 Kbps directed transmission. This transmission speed has proven to be satisfactory for smaller quantities of data, like print jobs, that are quickly transmitted between two devices within line of sight. Almost all WLANs are based on another method of transmitting data signals—radio waves.

RADIO-BASED WLANS

The second means by which a WLAN can send and receive information is by using radio waves. This has proven to be the most effective means for transmitting data for a local area network.

Radio Waves

Suppose you were to hand a 10-foot length of rope to a friend and ask your friend to hold one end of it tightly while you hold the other end. As you shake your end up and down, the rope will create what look like waves that move up and down, as seen in Figure 2-8.

Shake slowly

Figure 2-8   Rope waves

This movement of a rope is an excellent illustration of waves. Light from a bulb or heat from the sun reaches the earth by moving through space as **electromagnetic waves**. These waves require no special medium for traveling from the bulb or sun to us (early 17th-century scientists theorized that there was a medium in space called the **ether** through which light and heat traveled; however, this was later proven to be incorrect). These waves travel freely through space at the speed of light, which is 186,000 miles (62,000 meters) per second.

The network type Ethernet was named for the ether posited in these early theories.

However, light and heat waves have obvious limitations as transmission media. Light waves cannot penetrate through opaque material such as wood or concrete. In addition, surrounding objects absorb heat waves. Thus the distance that light and heat waves can travel is limited because of obstacles that they encounter.

Yet light and heat are not the only things that travel as waves. Another type of wave that travels in this same fashion is called a **radiotelephony wave** or **radio wave**. When an electric current passes through a wire, it creates a magnetic field in the space around the wire. As this magnetic field radiates or moves out, it creates an electromagnetic radio wave. Unlike a signal that is confined to and travels down a wire to its destination, a radio wave spreads out over space, as seen in Figure 2-9.

Figure 2-9   Radio waves

 The word *radio* comes from the term *radiated energy*.

Radio waves do not have the same limitations as light and heat waves. Radio waves can travel great distances and can also penetrate through nonmetallic objects. However, unlike visible light waves and heat waves that you can see and feel, radio waves are invisible.

Radio Frequencies

Considering the rope again, if you move your hand up and down slowly while holding the rope, you will create large waves that reach the hand of your friend holding the other end of the rope. However, if you shake your hand up and down rapidly, the waves are shorter. Depending upon how fast you shake your hand, the waves may be several inches or several feet long, as shown in Figure 2-10.

2

Shake slowly

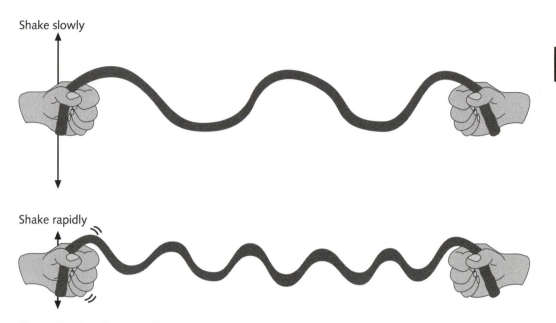

Shake rapidly

Figure 2-10 Short and long rope waves

The same is true with radio waves. The rate at which the device that generates the waves moves or cycles up and down will create different radio waves. The different rates establish a radio wave's **frequency**; how *frequently* something moves to generate the wave creates different *frequencies*.

Frequencies are measured in the number of cycles per second. Today the term **hertz (Hz)** is used instead of "cycle." A radio wave measured as 710,000 Hz means that its frequency was created by a device that moved 710,000 cycles per second. Because of the high number of cycles required, metric prefixes are generally used when referring to frequencies. A **kilohertz (KHz)** is one thousand hertz, a **megahertz (MHz)** is one million hertz, and a **gigahertz (GHz)** is one billion hertz. The wave measured as 710,000 Hz would more properly be listed as 710 KHz.

What frequencies are used when broadcasting over radio waves? If many devices were sending out radio waves on the same frequency, then the receiving station would become confused with the multiple signals it receives. Frequencies, then, must be regulated. In the United States, the **Federal Communications Commission (FCC)** is responsible for establishing how frequencies should be used. Figure 2-11 illustrates part of the radio frequency spectrum.

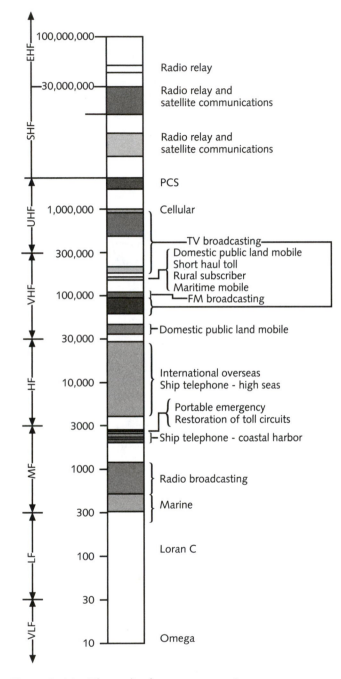

Figure 2-11 The radio frequency spectrum

2

 The International Telecommunication Union (ITU) is made up of representatives of 180 nations. The ITU is responsible for making recommendations regarding telecommunications issues that can have an impact worldwide. The United States is a member of the ITU.

Radio waves can be transmitted and received using an antenna. An **antenna** is a copper wire or similar device that has one end up in the air and the other end connected to the ground. Some antennae do not have protruding wires but are enclosed. When transmitting, the radio waves are directed to strike this wire. This sets up an electrical pressure, or **voltage**, along the wire. This pressure causes a small electrical current to flow up and down the wire. The voltage causes a back and forth movement of the electricity in the antenna at the same frequency as the radio waves. Broadcasting is accomplished simply by forcing the electricity in the antenna to move at the same frequency as the radio waves.

To pick up transmitted radio signals, a receiver also uses an antenna. The electricity in the receiving antenna moves back and forth in response to the radio signals reaching it. The motion causes a voltage that leads from the antenna into the receiver, as seen in Figure 2-12.

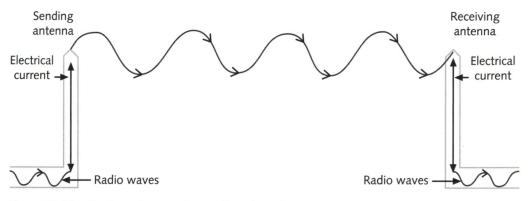

Figure 2-12   Radio antennae transmit and receive

 The length of an antenna should be close to one-quarter of the wavelength. If the antenna is smaller than one-20th of the wavelength, then very little power actually travels out into space.

Transmissions

Suppose you want to send a message to your friend at the other end of the rope. How could you do it? It might be possible to do it through a series of predefined shakes of the rope, like sending a Morse code signal. A long shake could mean a "dash," whereas a short shake could stand for a "dot," as seen in Figure 2-13.

Figure 2-13   Rope Morse code

However, shaking a rope for Morse code would be difficult to do. Another way would be to write the message on a piece of paper and then attach that paper to a large ring. Sliding the ring onto the rope would allow you to "scoot" the message over to your friend by shaking the rope, as seen in Figure 2-14.

Figure 2-14   Scooting over a message

Narrowband Transmissions

The same principle of "scooting" a message over to your friend by shaking the rope can also be used with radio waves. A single radio frequency by itself carries no useful information. The signal is simply known as the **carrier signal**. However, a process known as **modulation** can modulate or change the carrier signal so it can also carry information, much like the ring with paper attached. Modulation attaches useful information to the carrier signal. Two types of modulation, **amplitude modulation (AM)** and **frequency modulation (FM)**, are commonly used for transmitting conventional radio station signals, as shown in Figure 2-15.

These conventional radio signals are referred to as **narrowband** transmissions. This means that they transmit all of their power in a very narrow portion of the radio frequency spectrum, as shown in Figure 2-16. Thus narrowband transmissions are very vulnerable to outside interference from another signal. Much like an accident on a narrow one-lane road can stop all traffic from moving because there's no way to get around it, a single interfering signal at or near the transmission's frequency can easily render the radio inoperable.

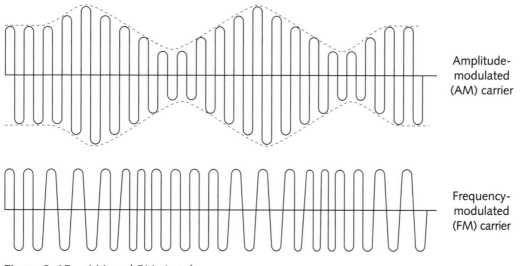

Amplitude-
modulated
(AM) carrier

Frequency-
modulated
(FM) carrier

Figure 2-15   AM and FM signals

 FM stations broadcast between 88 MHz and 108 MHz, whereas AM stations
transmit between 535 KHz and 1,700 KHz.

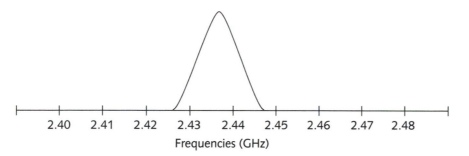

Frequencies (GHz)

Figure 2-16   Narrowband transmission

Spread Spectrum Transmissions

An alternative to narrowband transmission is spread spectrum transmission. **Spread spectrum**
is a technique that spreads a narrow signal over a broader portion of the radio frequency band,
as shown in Figure 2-17. Spread spectrum is more resistant to outside interference. This is
because any interference would affect only a small portion of the signal instead of the entire
signal. Although an accident on an eight-lane freeway is inconvenient, there still are seven other
lanes by which traffic can move around the accident and keep going. Spread spectrum likewise
results in less interference and fewer errors. Another advantage is that spread spectrum transmissions are more difficult to detect and intercept.

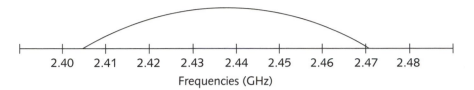

Frequencies (GHz)

Figure 2-17   Spread spectrum transmission

Spread spectrum uses two different methods to spread the signal over a wider area. The first method is **frequency hopping spread spectrum (FHSS)**. Instead of sending a signal on just one frequency, frequency hopping uses a range of frequencies and changes frequencies during the transmission. FHSS transmits a short burst at one frequency, then another short burst at another frequency, and so on, until the entire signal has been sent.

Hedy Lamarr, a well-known film actress during the 1940s, and George Antheil, who had experience synchronizing the sounds of music scores with motion pictures, originally conceived the idea of frequency hopping spread spectrum during the early part of World War II. Their goal was to keep the Germans from jamming the radios that guided U.S. torpedoes against German warships. Lamarr and Antheil received a U.S. patent for their idea in 1942.

The example FHSS transmission shown in Figure 2-18 starts by sending a burst of data at the 2.44 GHz frequency for 1 millisecond. Then the transmission switches to the 2.41 GHz frequency and transmits for the second millisecond. At the third millisecond, the transmission takes place at the 2.42 GHz frequency. This continual switching of frequencies takes place until the transmission is complete.

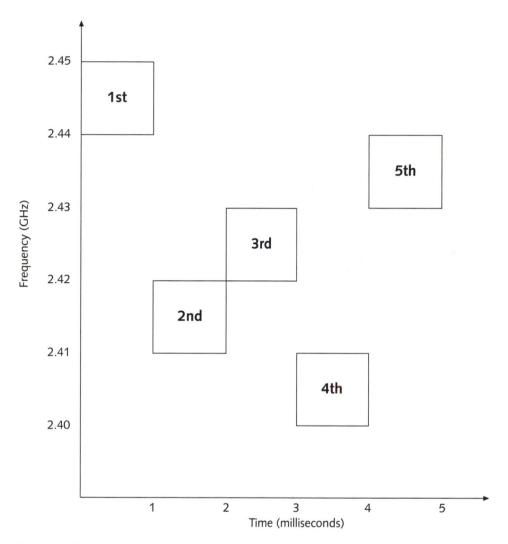

Figure 2-18 FHSS transmission

Naturally, the receiving station must know which frequencies will be used in which sequence. This is known as the **hopping code**. In Figure 2-18, the hopping code would be as follows: 2.44–2.41–2.42–2.40–2.43. During a transmission that requires frequency hopping, if interference is encountered on a frequency, that part of the signal affected by the interference will be retransmitted on the next frequency as established in the hopping code. In Figure 2-19, the second transmission received interference, so it was retransmitted on the frequency that would normally carry the third transmission. All other transmissions are then sent on the next frequency of the hopping code.

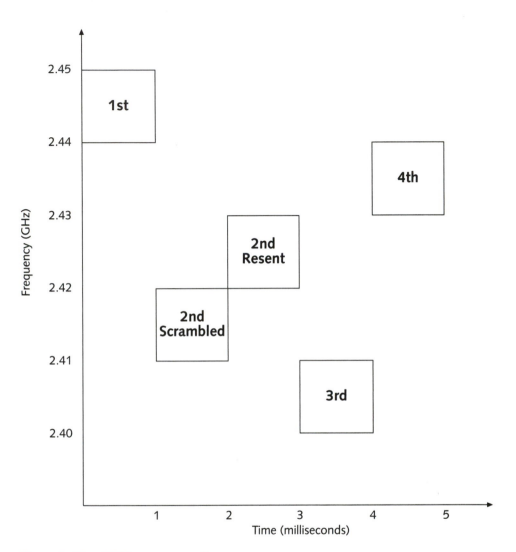

Figure 2-19   FHSS error correction

Frequency hopping can also reduce the impact of interference from other radio signals. An interfering signal will affect the FHSS signal only when both are transmitting at the same frequency at the same time. Because FHSS transmits short bursts over a wide range of frequencies, the extent of any interference will be very small and can easily be corrected by error checking. In addition, FHSS signals create minimal interference for other signals. To an unintended receiver, FHSS transmissions appear to be of a very short duration and again can be easily corrected by error checking.

It is possible for multiple FHSS devices to send radio signals using the same set of frequencies as long as they do not use the same frequencies at the same time. While one device is transmitting at one frequency, another device is using a different frequency, as shown in Figure 2-20. A set of hopping codes that never use the same frequencies at the same time is called **orthogonal FHSS**.

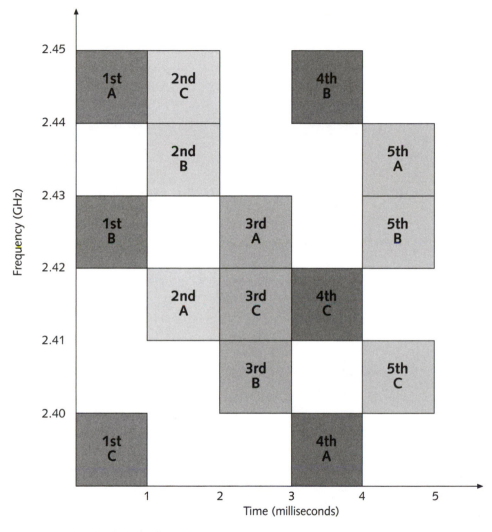

Figure 2-20   Orthogonal FHSS

The other type of spread spectrum technology is **direct sequence spread spectrum (DSSS)**. DSSS uses an expanded redundant code to transmit each data bit. In Figure 2-21, the top line represents three original data bits (ODBs) to be transmitted—in this case, 1, 0, and 1. However, instead of transmitting these three ODBs, DSSS substitutes a different sequence of bits, as seen in the middle line of Figure 2-21. This bit pattern is called the **Barker code** or the **chipping code** (because a single radio bit is commonly referred to as a "chip").

In Figure 2-21, the chipping code is 1001. That means instead of sending a 1 ODB, DSSS substitutes the chipping code of 1 (1001), and instead of sending a 0 ODB, DSSS substitutes the chipping code of 0 (0110).

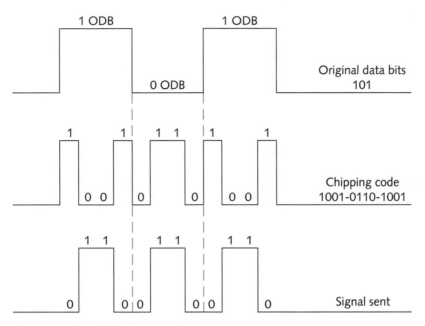

Figure 2-21   DSSS transmission

 If the chipping code of 1 is 1001, then the inverse of that code (0110) is the chipping code for 0.

 Most chipping codes are actually 11 bits long.

The last step is to "combine" the original data bit with the chipping code, as seen in the bottom line of Figure 2-21, to create the signal that is actually sent. If a 1 ODB is to be transmitted, then 1 is added to each bit of the chipping code:

ODB is 1

Chipping code for 1:	1	0	0	1
Value to add to chipping code:	1	1	1	1
Signal sent	0	1	1	0

If a 0 data bit is to be transmitted, then 0 is added to each bit of the chipping code:

	ODB is 0			
Chipping code for 0:	0	1	1	0
Value to add to chipping code:	0	0	0	0
Signal sent	0	1	1	0

Note Although it may appear that 0-1-1-0 would be sent for all 0 and 1 ODBs, that is not the case. When the ODBs are consecutive 1 bits, an extra 0 is placed between them in the chipping code so that it becomes [1001]-[0]-[1001], which would result in a transmitted code of [0-1-1-0]-[1]-[0-1-1-0].

Why send several bits when you could just send the single original bit? There are many reasons. First, if there is interference in the transmission when sending only one ODB, the signal would have to be resent, which takes time. However, if there is interference when sending the chipping code, statistical techniques embedded in the receiving device can recover the original data without having to retransmit the signal. Second, if an unintended device picks up the DSSS signal, the signal will appear as low-powered "noise" and will be rejected.

The greatest advantage of sending several bits with DSSS instead of just one is security. If an eavesdropper picks up the signal of the original data bit, reading the message is a simple task. A chipping code makes reading the message more difficult. And the longer the chipping code, the more difficult decoding becomes. If the chipping code were 4 bits long, then the eavesdropper would need to try up to 16 (2^4) combinations before breaking it. If the chipping code were 11 bits, then he or she would have to try 2,048 combinations. A chipping code of 16 bits would require 65,535 combinations and make the message far more secure.

There are two significant differences between using DSSS and FHSS in a WLAN. First, FHSS WLANs are less prone to interference from outside signals than DSSS. This is because FHSS transmits short bursts over a wide range of frequencies and the extent of any interference is very small. The second difference is in overall network capacity (known as **bandwidth**). DSSS WLANs have the potential for greater transmission speeds than FHSS. FHSS transmits a short burst on one frequency that is typically only 1 MHz. On the other hand, DSSS transmits on a frequency that is 22 MHz wide. This is illustrated in Figure 2-22. As you can see, the amount of data that a DSSS channel can send and receive is much greater than that of FHSS. DSSS has a bandwidth of up to 11 Mbps, whereas FHSS can only transmit at 3 Mbps.

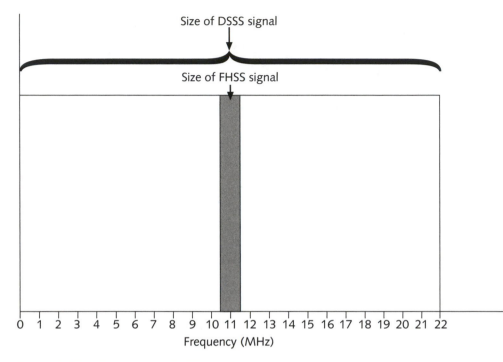

Figure 2-22   DSSS versus FHSS bandwidth

A comparison of the features of light-based infrared, FHSS, and DSSS wireless networks is summarized in Table 2-1. This table reveals that although each type of network has advantages, two of the most critical factors in a LAN—bandwidth and range of coverage— make the DSSS the most attractive WLAN technology. This conclusion is reinforced by the WLAN industry itself. Almost all WLAN vendors have selected to use the DSSS technology as the basis for their networks.

Table 2-1   WLAN Comparison

Feature	Light-Based WLAN	FHSS	DSSS
Causes interference	No	Yes	Yes
Can be interfered with	No	Yes	Yes
Power consumption	Low	Moderate	Moderate
Range of coverage	Limited to line of sight	Broad	Broad
Bandwidth (Mbps)	2	2	11

Components

The hardware and software components that make up a radio-based WLAN are very basic and in many ways similar to those used in a standard LAN. They include:

- Wireless network interface card
- Access point
- Remote wireless bridge

Wireless Network Interface Card

One of the most important pieces of hardware in a computer network is the **network interface card (NIC)**. A NIC is installed or built into each computer that is connected to the network and plays a critical role in sending and receiving data between the computer and the network. The functions that both a wireless NIC and standard NIC perform in a computer sending network data are the same:

1. Change the data from parallel to serial transmission.
2. Divide the data into **packets** (smaller blocks of data) and attach the sending and receiving computers' addresses.
3. Determine when to send the packet based on the network topology being used.
4. Transmit the packet.

Like a standard NIC, a wireless NIC is installed inside the computer and connects to the computer's expansion slots. Wireless NICs can be installed in an Industry Standard Architecture (ISA) expansion slot, a Peripheral Component Interface (PCI) expansion slot, or the PC Card slot typically found on a laptop computer. There are also external devices that function like a wireless NIC that connect to the computer's serial port or the Universal Serial Bus (USB) connection.

 The ISA expansion slot connects to the ISA bus that transmits 16 bits at 10 MHz or a total of 5 million bytes per second. A PCI bus in a computer can transmit 32 bits at 33 MHz (132 million bytes per second) or at 100 MHz.

 Because of the electrical principle known as capacitance, the number of available PCI connections on a computer is limited to three.

A wireless NIC is the same as a standard NIC, with one major exception: Whereas a standard NIC has a connection for cables (such as RJ-45) to connect it, a wireless NIC has an antenna for transmitting radio waves. The antenna can either be built into the wireless NIC, as shown in Figure 2-23, or be external, as shown in Figure 2-24. Some wireless NIC cards even have retractable antennae that can slide into the card when not in use, or a removable antenna.

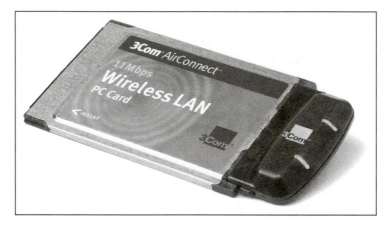

Figure 2-23   Wireless NIC PC card

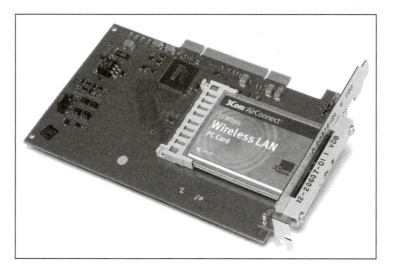

Figure 2-24   Wireless NIC PCI card

The driver software that interfaces between the wireless NIC and the computer on which it is installed is of the same type as for a standard NIC. Software drivers that follow the Microsoft Network Driver Interface Specification (NDIS) for Microsoft networks or the Novell Open Datalink Interface (ODI) for Novell networks are typically used. The network operating system of the WLAN is unaware that a wireless NIC is being used instead of a standard NIC.

Access Point

An **access point (AP)**, shown in Figure 2-25, is a device that consists of three components. First, it contains an antenna and a radio transmitter/receiver used to send and receive signals. Second, it has a wired network interface, such as an RJ-45, that allows it to connect to a standard wired network. Finally, an access point has special bridging software installed.

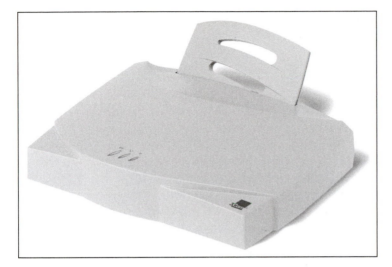

Figure 2-25 Access point

It is possible to use a standard PC as the access point. Installing a wireless NIC (which functions as the transmitter/receiver), a standard NIC (which serves as the wired network interface), and special AP control software will allow a PC to serve this function.

An access point has two basic functions. First, the access point acts as the base station for the wireless network. All of the devices that have a wireless NIC can transmit to the AP, which will in turn redirect the signal to the other devices. The range of an access point acting as the base station is approximately 375 feet (114 meters); however, certain types of obstacles may affect the radio waves and the distance that they can travel. The number of users that a single access point can support varies but is generally 60–200 users.

The second function of an AP is to act as a bridge between the wireless and wired networks. The AP can be connected to the standard network by a cable, allowing the wireless devices to access the wired network through the AP, as shown in Figure 2-26.

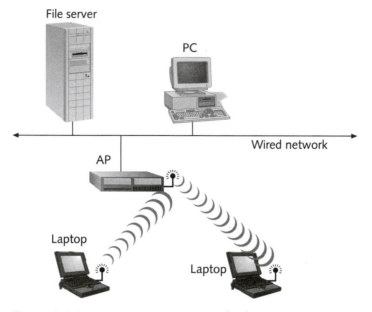

Figure 2-26   Access point (AP) as a bridge

Remote Wireless Bridge

The third component of a radio-based WLAN is a **remote wireless bridge**. A remote wireless bridge is used to connect network devices using radio-based technology. Whereas an AP connects network clients (such as PCs and laptops) to the network, a remote wireless bridge connects network segments, as shown in Figure 2-27. A remote wireless bridge can connect small-to medium-size LAN segments using radio waves. These LAN segments can either be wireless or wired. Remote wireless bridges are typically used for outdoor rather than indoor connections. These connections are usually between devices in different buildings and can be as far as 25 miles apart. They are often used as an alternative to installing cable or leasing telephone lines.

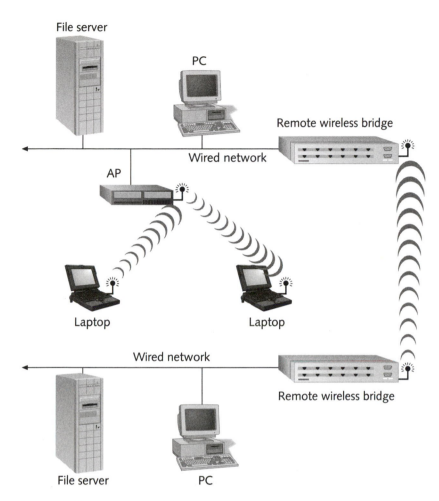

Figure 2-27   Remote wireless bridges

Modes

There are two modes in which data can be sent and received in a radio-based WLAN: peer-to-peer and infrastructure.

Peer-to-Peer Mode

The **peer-to-peer mode** of sending and receiving radio-based data is also called the **ad hoc** or **Independent Basic Service Set (IBSS)** mode. Peer-to-peer mode functions as its name implies—that is, the wireless stations communicate directly among themselves without using an access point, as shown in Figure 2-28. This mode is useful for quickly and easily setting up a wireless network anywhere that a wired network infrastructure does not exist or is not required, such as in a hotel room, convention center, or airport. The drawback is that the wireless stations can communicate only among themselves; there is no access to a wired network.

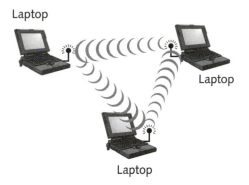

Laptop

Laptop

Laptop

Figure 2-28   Peer-to-peer mode

Infrastructure Mode

The second mode for radio-based wireless data transmission is the **infrastructure mode**, also known as the **Basic Service Set (BSS)**. Infrastructure mode, or BSS, consists of wireless stations and one access point. This configuration allows up to 100 wireless users over an area of 300 feet (100 meters) to send and receive data.

If you need to add more users or increase the range, you can create an **Extended Service Set (ESS)**. An ESS is simply two or more BSS wireless networks. That is, multiple access points are set up to accommodate additional users over a wider area, as shown in Figure 2-29.

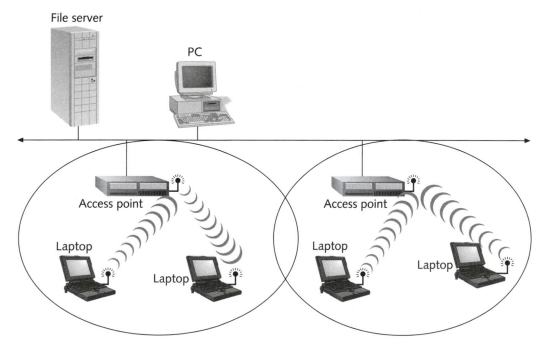

Figure 2-29   Extended service set (ESS)

2

As Figure 2-29 illustrates, when multiple access points are used, they create areas of coverage, much like cells in a cellular telephone system. These cells overlap to facilitate movement known as **roaming**. When a mobile wireless user (perhaps carrying a wireless notebook computer) enters into the range of more than one AP, the user's wireless device will choose an AP to connect with based on signal strength (some APs also look at packet error rates). Once the AP accepts that device, the client device "tunes" to the radio channel at which the AP is set.

The mobile device surveys all the radio frequencies at regular intervals to determine whether a different access point can provide better service. If the device finds one (perhaps because the user has moved), then it connects the new AP (a process called a **handoff**), tuning to the radio frequency of the new AP. The handoff is seamless to the user because the wireless device never has an interruption of service.

CHAPTER SUMMARY

- All light-based WLANs today use infrared light to send and receive signals. An infrared WLAN sends data using the intensity of the light wave instead of "on-off" signals of light: A higher-intensity impulse is a 1, whereas a lower-intensity impulse is a 0. Infrared transmission in WLANs can be either directed or diffused. A directed WLAN transmission requires that the emitter and detector be aimed directly at one another. A diffused WLAN transmission does not require the sender and receiver to be within line of sight. Instead, it relies on reflected light.

- Light-based WLANs have several advantages: Infrared light does not interfere with other communications signals and is not itself affected by other signals; it is almost impossible for someone elsewhere to "eavesdrop" on the transmitted signal; and overall power consumption is low for emitters. However, there are serious limitations to light-based WLANs: The range of coverage is only about 50 feet; they can be used only indoors; and the data transmission rate is low.

- Radio waves do not have the limitations of light and heat waves, and thus make an excellent medium for data transmission. Radio waves can travel great distances and can also penetrate nonmetallic objects. Unlike visible light waves and heat waves, radio waves are invisible. Narrow-band transmissions, such as conventional AM and FM radio signals, transmit all of their power in a very narrow portion of the radio frequency spectrum. Spread spectrum is a technique that spreads a narrow signal over a broader portion of the radio frequency band.

- There are two methods of spreading the signal in spread spectrum WLANs: frequency hopping spread spectrum (FHSS) and direct sequence spread spectrum (DSSS). FHSS WLANs are less prone to interference from outside signals than DSSS, but DSSS WLANs have the potential for greater transmission speeds. DSSS has a bandwidth of up to 11 Mbps, whereas FHSS can transmit at only 3 Mbps.

KEY TERMS

access point (AP) — A device that acts as both the base station and bridge for a wireless network.

ad hoc — A mode in which wireless stations communicate directly among themselves without using an access point; also called *peer-to-peer mode* or *Independent Basic Service Set (IBSS)*.

American Standard Code for Information Interchange (ASCII) — An arbitrary coding scheme that uses the numbers from 0 to 255 to represent letters, numbers, and other characters.

amplitude modulation (AM) — Commonly used modulation for transmitting conventional radio station signals between 535 KHz and 1,700 KHz.

antenna — A copper wire or similar device used to transmit radio signals that has one end exposed and the other end connected to the ground.

bandwidth — The transmission capacity of a network.

Barker code — A bit pattern used in a DSSS transmission; also called *chipping code*.

base 2 — The numeric system used by computers that represents any number by using just two digits, 0 and 1; also known as *binary code*.

Basic Service Set (BSS) — A WLAN mode that consists of wireless stations and one access point; also known as *infrastructure mode*.

binary code — A code used by computers that can represent any number by using just two digits, 0 and 1. Binary code is the same as the *base 2* numeric system.

carrier signal — A transmission over a single radio frequency that carries no useful information.

chipping code — A bit pattern used in a DSSS transmission; also known as *Barker code*.

detector — A device on light-based infrared WLAN systems that receives a signal.

diffused — An infrared transmission that relies on reflected light to send and receive signals.

directed — An infrared transmission that requires that the emitter and detector be aimed directly at one another.

direct sequence spread spectrum (DSSS) — A spread spectrum technique that uses an expanded, redundant code to transmit each data bit.

electromagnetic waves — Waves through which light and heat travel.

emitter — A device on light-based infrared WLAN systems that transmits a signal.

ether — A medium that early scientists theorized was the means through which light and heat traveled.

Extended Service Set (ESS) — A WLAN mode that consists of wireless stations and multiple access points.

Federal Communications Commission (FCC) — The U.S. governmental agency responsible for establishing how radio frequencies should be used in the United States.

frequency — A measurement of radio waves that is determined by how frequently the device that generates the waves moves or cycles.

frequency hopping spread spectrum (FHSS) — A spread spectrum technique that uses a range of frequencies and changes frequencies during the transmission.

frequency modulation (FM) — Commonly used modulation for transmitting conventional radio station signals between 88 MHz and 108 MHz.

gigahertz (GHz) — One billion hertz.

handoff — A change in association from one access point to another.

hertz (Hz) — The number of cycles per second.

hopping code — The sequence of frequencies used in an FHSS transmission.

Independent Basic Service Set (IBSS) — A mode in which wireless stations communicate directly among themselves without using an access point; also called *ad hoc* or *peer-to-peer mode.*

Infrared Data Association (IrDA) — A specification for a 115 Kbps directed transmission that is used for data transmissions between laptop computers and printers.

infrared light — Invisible light on the light spectrum that has many of the same characteristics as visible light.

infrastructure mode — A WLAN mode that consists of wireless stations and one access point; also called *Basic Service Set (BSS).*

kilohertz (KHz) — One thousand hertz.

light-based WLAN — A wireless local area network that transmits data using light.

light spectrum — All the different types of light that travel from the sun to the earth.

line of sight transmission — A transmission that requires that the sender and receiver be aimed directly at each other.

megahertz (MHz) — One million hertz.

modulation — Adjustment of the carrier signal so it can also carry information.

narrowband — Transmissions that send all of their power in a very narrow portion of the radio frequency spectrum.

network interface card (NIC) — A device, installed or built into a computer that is connected to the network, that plays a critical role in sending and receiving data between the computer and the network.

orthogonal FHSS — A set of hopping codes that never use the same frequencies at the same time.

packets — Small blocks of data.

peer-to-peer mode — A WLAN mode in which wireless stations communicate directly among themselves without using an access point; also called *ad hoc* mode or *Independent Basic Service Set (IBSS).*

radiotelephony (radio) wave — A wave created when an electric current passes through a wire and creates a magnetic field in the space around the wire.

remote wireless bridge — A device used to connect network segments using radio-based technology.

roaming — Movement of a mobile wireless user through different access points and areas of coverage.

spread spectrum — A technique that spreads a narrow signal over a broader portion of the radio frequency band.

voltage — Electrical pressure.

REVIEW QUESTIONS

1. The arbitrary coding scheme that uses the numbers from 0 to 255 to represent letters and other characters is called _____.

    a. American Standard Code for Information Interchange (ASCII)

    b. FHSS

    c. DSSS

    d. CHIP

2. Computers are based upon binary code, which can represent any number by using just the digits _____.

    a. 0 and 1

    b. 0 and 2

    c. 1 and 2

    d. 2 and 0

3. _____ light is next to visible light on the light spectrum and has many of the same characteristics as visible light.

    a. X-ray

    b. Ultraviolet

    c. Infrared

    d. Violet

4. An emitter in a light-based infrared WLAN is usually a _____.

    a. relay

    b. light emitting diode

    c. transponder

    d. capacitor

5. Infrared transmission in WLANs can be either directed or _____.

    a. diffused

    b. dispersed

    c. chipped

    d. spread

6. Because directed WLANs use a line-of-sight principle, it is impractical for mobile users to use a directed WLAN. True or false?

2

7. Emitters are usually pointed at the floor and use the floor as the reflection point. True or false?

8. Infrared light does not interfere with other communication signals but can be affected by other signals. True or false?

9. When an electric current passes through a wire, it creates a magnetic field in the space around the wire. As this magnetic field radiates or moves out, it creates a radio electromagnetic wave. True or false?

10. Frequencies are measured in the number of cycles per second, but the term *megahertz* is used instead of *cycle*. True or false?

11. The wave measured as 710,000 Hz would also be listed as _____ KHz.

12. In the United States, the _____ is responsible for establishing how frequencies should be used.

13. A single radio frequency known as the _____, by itself carries no useful information.

14. _____ mode, also known as BSS, consists of wireless stations and one access point.

15. _____ transmissions send all of their power in a very narrow portion of the radio frequency spectrum.

16. Explain how spread spectrum works.

17. What are three advantages of spread spectrum?

18. Explain how FHSS works.

19. What does *orthogonal* mean in relation to WLANs?

20. Explain how DSSS works.

HANDS-ON PROJECTS

1. Write a one-page paper on the Infrared Data Association (IrDA) specification. Why has it been selected to be standard equipment for laptop computers instead of Bluetooth? What are its advantages and disadvantages? What future prospects are there for increasing its bandwidth?

2. Locate a television remote control unit that operates on infrared technology and a garage door opener that uses radio waves. Research these devices and answer the following questions: Does the device use diffused or directed technology? Does it use narrowband or spread spectrum? At what frequency does it operate? What new technologies are being used to prevent unauthorized users from "eavesdropping" on garage door opener frequencies? How can television remotes be improved?

3. Research how the Federal Communications Commission (FCC) allocates new radio frequencies by auction. What are the advantages and disadvantages? What problems have arisen? What new frequencies are going on the auction block? What is their projected price? Write a one-page paper on your findings.

4. What would be the transmission of the text "Hello, world" using a chipping code of 10110111011? Assume the arbitrary coding sequence is ASCII.

5. Research the specifications of three different vendors' remote wireless bridges. Compare these specifications by generating a table comparing these features:

   a. List price

   b. Bandwith

   c. Network interfaces

   d. Communication protocol

   e. PC Card or internal NIC

   f. Maximum radio channels

   g. Maximum bandwidth per channel

   h. Duplex scheme

   i. Configuration options

6. If possible, locate a wireless laptop computer. Determine how "mobile" you can be while using it. What is the approximate range? What type of object (wall, elevator, etc.) causes the most interference? How can its area of coverage be improved? If it is an ESS system, can you tell when you move from one AP to another? Write a paper on your findings.

7. If possible, locate a laptop computer and a printer both with an IrDA port. Use that port to print a one-page document of only text and then another document that contains graphics. Record the amount of time it takes for both to print. Then print those same documents using a standard connection. Write a paper describing how you set up the laptop, what problems you encountered, and how the print times differed. Include a recommendation regarding when an IrDA port should be used.

CASE PROJECT

Northridge Consulting Group

Your employer, Northridge Consulting Group (NCG), wants you to work with one of its new clients, a national distribution company, PAG. PAG has a large warehouse in your region and wants to invest in wireless technology on the warehouse floor. PAG has had visits from four different vendors, each of whom recommended different solutions. To compound the problem, an associate vice president is convinced that infrared light-based WLANs are the solution. This is because he uses the IrDA port on his laptop computer and is assured that the company's WLAN should be of the same type.

1. Write a report outlining the advantages and disadvantages of infrared light-based WLANs and radio-based WLANs. Be sure to include a comparison with IrDA.

2. PAG's information technology (IT) group wants more information regarding the differences between DSSS and FHSS. Prepare a report showing how these technologies function. Include advantages and disadvantages of each.

3. PAG wants to reduce its wide area network costs. Specifically, management wants to drop a leased telephone line between the warehouse and a smaller distribution center seven miles away. Management has asked you to provide information about the potential solutions that are available. Research remote wireless bridges and compare those costs to leased service from the local telephone carrier.

2

OPTIONAL TEAM CASE PROJECT

Cost is an issue with PAG. Management wants to know how much it would cost to set up a network of 25 mobile laptops and two access points. Create a team of three to four consultants. Each consultant should select a different WLAN vendor and create a cost sheet for setting up such a network. Be sure to include all costs, such as laptops, access points, wireless NICs, one network server, and the network operating system software.

3

IEEE 802.11 PHYSICAL LAYER STANDARDS

> **After reading this chapter and completing the exercises, you will be able to:**
> ♦ List the benefits and types of networking standards
> ♦ Explain the OSI model
> ♦ Discuss the history and the advantages of the IEEE 802.11 standard
> ♦ Describe the specifications for the IEEE 802.11 Physical (PHY) layer

Mention the word "standards" to someone who works in information technology and you'll likely receive a strong response—either pro or con. Some people in the industry believe that standards set for computer technologies stifle growth in this fast-paced field. They maintain that waiting for standards to catch up to the rapid changes in IT only slows everything down.

On the other hand, some in the industry just as fervently maintain that standards have proven to be a key element in the acceptance of new technology by users. They argue that nobody wants to go "out on a limb" with a new technology only to find six months later that everybody else has taken a different path and that they are now out on their own. Instead, users would rather invest in technology that is based on current industry standards that will ensure that what they buy today will not be obsolete tomorrow.

Although both camps have valid arguments, history indicates that standards have resulted in computer technologies being widely accepted without seriously slowing down growth. Standards have played and continue to play a vital role in information technology and particularly in computer networking. This chapter looks at such standards and how they apply to wireless LANs.

UNDERSTANDING STANDARDS

Standards for local area networks have been in place since the early 1980s. These standards have played an important role in the rapid growth of this technology and have demonstrated the benefits of standards in the marketplace.

The Need for Standards

Consider for a moment all of the different technologies associated with wireless LANs: light-based and radio-based WLANs, directed and diffused transmissions, narrowband and spread spectrum, FHSS and DSSS, and ad hoc mode and infrastructure mode, just to mention a few. What would happen if each WLAN vendor decided to choose from these different technologies to create its own unique WLAN? For example, Vendor A might develop and sell a light-based diffused transmission WLAN, whereas Vendor B might create and market a spread spectrum DSSS WLAN operating at the 2.1 GHz frequency. Vendor C designs a similar spread spectrum DSSS WLAN, but uses a completely different radio frequency. The result would be an almost endless variety of incompatible computer WLANs.

This would create serious problems. First, each vendor would have proprietary hardware and software for its own WLAN. This would result in a dizzying array of different types of WLANs. Buyers would face confusion and frustration in selecting the appropriate WLAN for their needs. Network consultants and installers would have to learn the intricacies of all the different types of WLANs in order to supply support. Computer merchandisers would be forced to market and stock an enormous amount of equipment for all the different types of available networks.

Another more serious problem would be that each wireless network would be incompatible with all other wireless networks. The users of one WLAN might not be able to communicate with users on another WLAN. Also, a user with a laptop computer might be confined to only the area supported by his or her "own" WLAN (Figure 3-1), rather than able to roam freely throughout the building. If different WLANs were made by different companies based on different technologies, the splintered market would seriously limit or even stall the growth of wireless computer networking.

The scenario just presented is precisely the situation that has occurred twice in recent years regarding computer networks. In the late 1970s and early 1980s, as computer local area networks (LANs) began to emerge, different vendors began to put together different combinations of technologies to create their own unique computer networks. Networks sold by competing vendors were unable to interoperate with one another. Although businesses recognized the potential for local area networks, they were reluctant to invest in a technology that lacked interoperability.

The lack of standards plagued local area networks in the 1970s, and it also stalled the growth of WLANs in the 1990s. The technology to implement wireless LANs has been available since the early 1990s. At that time, a few vendors created proprietary WLAN systems. The lack of standards made WLANs a curious oddity that businesses would not seriously consider, because they did not know where the marketplace was headed.

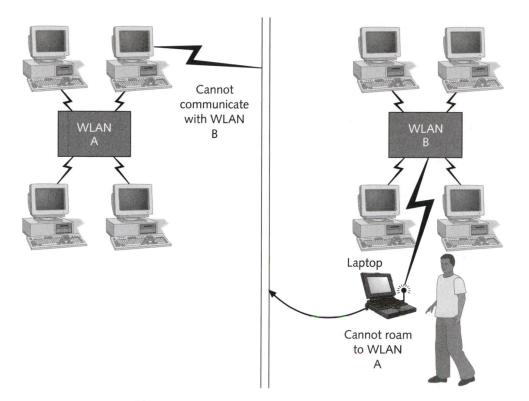

Figure 3-1   Incompatible WLANs

The introduction of LAN standards in the early 1980s and WLAN standards in the late 1990s has fueled the explosive growth in the networking market that continues today. These standards provided the framework needed to make it much easier for businesses to implement networks.

Benefits of Standards

There are several benefits of networking standards. First, standards ensure that WLAN devices from one vendor will interoperate with those from other vendors. As previously stated, WLAN devices that are not based on standards may not be able to connect and communicate with similar devices from other vendors. Standards ensure that a device purchased from Vendor A can be seamlessly mixed into a WLAN that contains devices from Vendor B. This is illustrated in Figure 3-2.

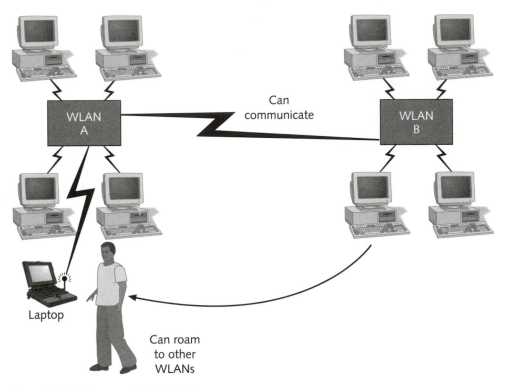

Figure 3-2   Compatible WLANs

A second benefit of standards is that they result in lower costs. A lack of standards forces a business to purchase its networking equipment from only one vendor to ensure interoperability of all components, as seen in Figure 3-3. However, this effectively eliminates price competition among vendors and may result in the prices remaining artificially high. The vendor has no benefit in reducing prices; instead, because there is a captive market, the vendor may in fact regularly raise prices.

However, standards encourage competition, because the vendors are all making similar products based on the same standards. To gain a larger portion of the market, vendors may reduce their prices, as seen in Figure 3-4. The competition among vendors, due to standards, usually results in lower costs to consumers.

3

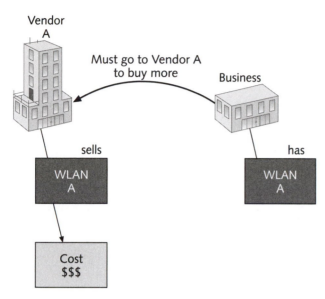

Figure 3-3 Lack of standards creates lack of competition

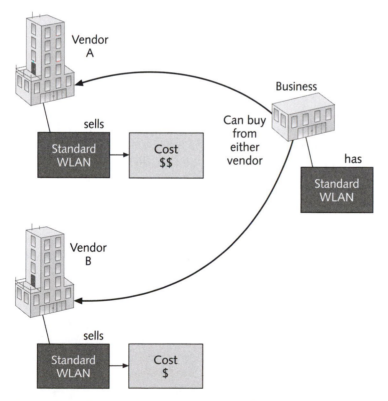

Figure 3-4 Standards encourage competition

A third benefit is that standards help protect the owner's investment in equipment. It is common for a vendor to phase out a product line. Without standards, a business has two choices: It can continue to support the now–obsolete ("orphan") product, or it can replace it with new equipment. Both choices are expensive: The costs of supporting obsolete equipment will dramatically escalate as replacement parts become more difficult to locate and support specialists more difficult to find, and a new system can be very costly (Figure 3-5).

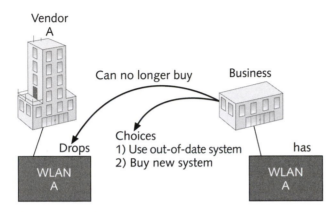

Figure 3-5   Orphan system

Standards, however, can help create an easier migration path. The body that is responsible for creating the initial standards will continue to incorporate new technologies into regularly revised standards. However, these new standards will almost always be backward-compatible. This means that standards reduce the number of orphan systems.

A final benefit of standards involves product development time and costs. Because standards have already paved the way, manufacturers do not have to invest large amounts of capital in research and development. Instead, they can use the standards as a blueprint for their manufacturing, thus reducing both their costs as well as the amount of time needed to get a product to the market.

Types of Standards

There are two types of standards. The first type is known as **official standards** (also called **de jure standards**). Official standards are those that are controlled by an organization or body that has been entrusted with that task. The process for creating these standards can be very involved. Generally the organization develops teams of industry experts to create the initial draft. The organization then publishes the draft and solicits comments from other organization members (these members may be developers, potential users, and other people having general interest in the field). The original committee then reviews the comments, which the organization may incorporate into the final draft. The entire organization reviews this draft before officially publishing the final standards.

3

Official standards organizations are often sponsored by industry consortiums or government.

De facto standards are not really standards at all. Rather, they are "common practices" that the industry follows for various reasons. The reasons range from ease of use to tradition to the practices of the majority of users. For example, most industry experts would agree that Microsoft Windows has become the de facto standard for PC and network server operating systems. This is because the overwhelming majority of users have elected to install and run Windows on their computers. No standards body proclaimed Windows as the standard; the widespread use of the operating system has created what has emerged as an unofficial standard.

Although Windows is the de facto standard for personal computers and network servers, UNIX is still the de facto standard for Internet Web servers. UNIX is found on almost 60% of Web servers, whereas Windows is installed only on about 30%.

De facto standards sometimes become official standards when they are approved by a standards committee. Ethernet is one example of a de facto standard that later became an official standard. However, official standards for computer networks have almost completely replaced de facto standards. Almost all local area networks and WLANs are based on official standards created by committees.

NETWORKING MODELS AND STANDARDS

Networking models and standards have proven to be the key for solidifying the WLAN market and spurring its dramatic growth.

Network Model: OSI

In the mid–1970s, an organization known as the **International Standards Organization (ISO)** began developing specifications for computer networks. The goal of the ISO was not to create an official physical standard for all computer networks, but to create an abstract model of networking. Completed in 1983, these conceptual specifications became known as the **Open Systems Interconnection (OSI) model**.

The International Standards Organization (ISO) is an organization based in Geneva, Switzerland. Started in 1947, its goal is to promote international cooperation and standards in the areas of science, technology, and economics. Today, groups from over 100 countries belong to the ISO.

The OSI model is made up of seven layers, as seen in Figure 3-6. Within each layer, several different networking tasks are performed. Each layer cooperates with the layer immediately above and below it by passing something to it or receiving something from it. Each layer does specific functions in order for the computer network to operate. The functions of the layers are outlined in Table 3-1.

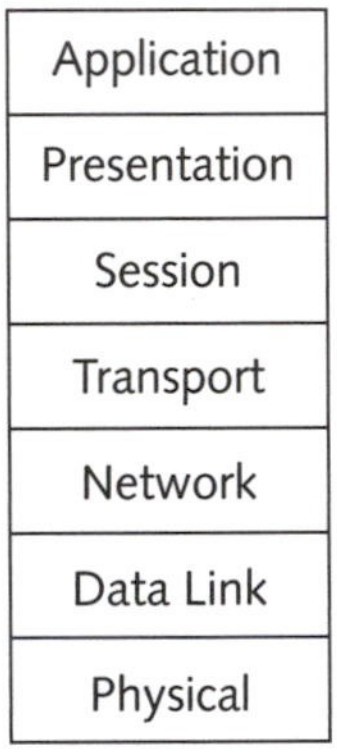

Application
Presentation
Session
Transport
Network
Data Link
Physical

Figure 3-6   OSI model

Table 3-1   OSI Layers and Functions

Layer	Function
Application (Layer 7)	Provides the user interface to allow network services. These services may include such things as sending and receiving e-mail and transferring files.
Presentation (Layer 6)	Handles how the data is represented and formatted for the user.
Session (Layer 5)	Permits the devices on the network to hold ongoing communications across the network. Handles session setup, data or message exchanges, and tear-down when the session ends.
Transport (Layer 4)	Ensures that error-free data is given to the user. It handles the setup and tear-down of connections.
Network (Layer 3)	Picks the route that packets take and addresses packets for delivery.
Data Link (Layer 2)	Detects and corrects errors. If data is not received properly, the Data Link layer requests that the data be retransmitted. Wireless NICs are included in this layer.
Physical (Layer 1)	Sends signals to the network or receives signals from the network. This layer includes wireless NICs and cables (for standard networks).

When sent, data flows down through the layers from Application to Physical, and when received, the data flows up through the layers from Physical to Application, as seen in Figure 3-7.

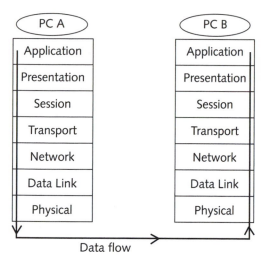

Figure 3-7 OSI data flow

There are several important items to note about the OSI model:

- Each layer performs specific functions in terms of networking.

- Because hardware or software may perform many jobs, they may be found in different layers. For example, a wireless NIC is found in both the Physical layer (sending and receiving messages by its transceiver) as well as the Data Link layer (dividing the data into packets).

- The flow between layers goes down when sending and up when receiving.

The OSI model gives a visual picture of how networking is done. Its purpose is to break the many complex functions of networking into seven basic layers, and to show how each layer provides specific services as it shares with the layers above and below it. It's important to remember that the OSI model is just that: It's a model of how networking is done. It is not a picture of an actual physical network, but a conceptual picture of how a network works.

Network Standards: IEEE Project 802

About the same time that the ISO was working on the OSI model, another group began work on networking specifications. The **Institute of Electrical and Electronic Engineers (IEEE)** started **Project 802** to ensure interoperability among network products.

 OSI and IEEE are not competing organizations. Rather, the two groups work together. In fact, IEEE is one of the members of the ISO.

 Project 802 received its name from the simple fact that the work was started in 1980 (80) during February, the second month (2).

Project 802 quickly expanded into several different categories, known as 802.1, 802.2, and so on, all the way to 802.14. Within these categories there are subcategories, such as 802.3u and 802.3z. Although the primary focus of Project 802 was network standards, it also includes standards for such things as cable television communications.

 Two of the most widely used Project 802 standards are the 802.3 (Ethernet) and 802.5 (Token Ring) networking standards.

It is important to remember the difference between how Project 802 and the OSI model are used. The OSI model is a *theoretical model* of how networking works. Project 802, on the other hand, sets *practical standards* for computer networking that are followed today. In short, the OSI model is theory, whereas Project 802 is the actual practice.

The IEEE's Project 802 used the OSI conceptual model as a structure for its specifications, with a couple of important differences. Project 802 subdivides the OSI model Layer 2, Data Link, into two sublayers, the **Logical Link Control (LLC)** and **Media Access Control (MAC)** layers. Also, the Project 802 standard abbreviates the Physical layer as PHY, as seen in Figure 3-8.

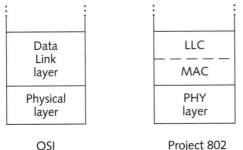

Figure 3-8   OSI model versus IEEE Project 802

IEEE 802.11 and 802.11b

In 1990, IEEE formed a committee to develop a standard for WLANs operating at 1 and 2 Mbps. The committee initially reviewed several different proposals before developing a draft. This draft went through seven different revisions that took almost seven years to complete. On June 26, 1997, the IEEE approved the final draft.

 All IEEE standards are subject to review at least once every five years.

The 802.11 standard defines a local area network that provides cable-free data access for clients that are either mobile or in a fixed location at a rate up to 2 Mbps. The 802.11 standard also

specifies that the features of a WLAN be transparent to the upper levels of the 802.11 standard. That is, the functions of the PHY and MAC layers provide full implementation of all of the WLAN features so that no modifications are needed at any other layers. This is illustrated in Figure 3-9. To accomplish this, however, the standard requires that some networking features that are usually associated with higher layers be performed at the MAC layer in WLANs.

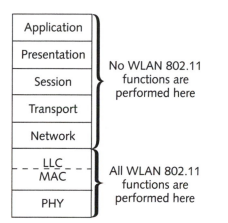

No WLAN 802.11 functions are performed here

All WLAN 802.11 functions are performed here

Figure 3-9   All WLAN functions are performed in the PHY and MAC layers

Because all of the WLAN features are isolated in the PHY and MAC layers, any network operating system or LAN application will run on a WLAN without any modification.

However, the limited bandwidth of only 2 Mbps for the 802.11 standard was not sufficient for most network applications. The IEEE body revisited the 802.11 standard shortly after it was released to determine what changes could be made to increase the speed. In September 1999, a new 802.11b High Rate was amended to the standard, which added two higher speeds (5.5 Mbps and 11 Mbps) to the original 802.11 standard. Vendors quickly chose to comply with 802.11b.

The 802.11b standard made changes only to the PHY layer of the original 802.11 standard.

Although the 802.11 and 802.11b standards were responsible for the explosive growth of the WLAN market, there have been some criticisms of the standards. Perhaps the most significant is that the standards do not define communications between access points. If a mobile client roams from the area served by one access point into the area served by another access point, no 802.11 standards define how this user can be "handed off," as seen in Figure 3-10. There are no such 802.11 standards because "handing off" is typically the job of the Network and Transport layers. As a result, vendors can use several different roaming options. It is up to the vendors of the access points to define the protocol for roaming.

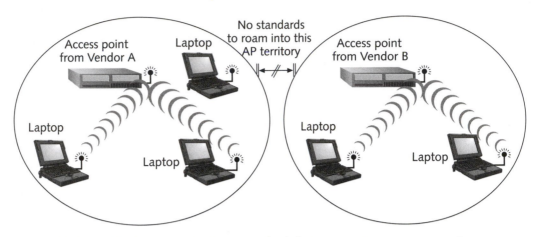

Figure 3-10   Lack of communications standards between APs prevents roaming

Because of a lack of 802.11 standards defining how a user is "handed off," some recommend that users purchase all access points from the same vendor to ensure their compatibility.

IEEE 802.11 PHYSICAL LAYER

The basic purpose of the PHY layer is to send the signal to the network and receive the signal from the network. However, two factors make the role of the PHY layer in a WLAN more complicated than in a standard wired LAN. First, WLANs are by nature more complex than standard wired LANs. For example, the 802.11 PHY standards support both the peer-to-peer mode Independent Basic Service Set (IBSS) as well as the infrastructure mode Basic Service Set (BSS). This means that a vendor's WLAN product that follows the IEEE 802.11 standards will allow a user to go from BSS to IBSS and back transparently, without any significant changes to hardware or software. This is illustrated in Figure 3-11. This flexibility to switch easily from peer-to-peer to infrastructure mode and back illustrates that the PHY layer of a WLAN is more complicated than that of a standard wired LAN.

The second reason that the PHY layer is more complex is that the 802.11 standards support three different transmission options: direct sequence spread spectrum (DSSS), frequency hopping spread spectrum (FHSS), and diffused infrared. A vendor's WLAN product that follows the IEEE 802.11 standards will allow a user to transmit using any of these options. Because the 802.11 standard supports all three options, the PHY layer is more flexible—and more complex.

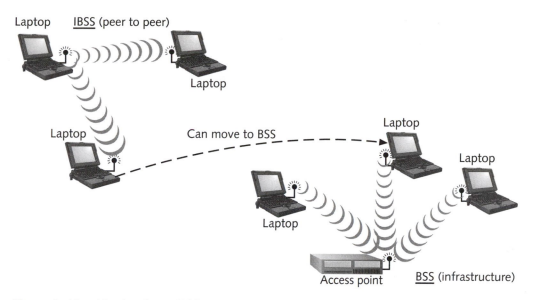

Figure 3-11   Moving from IBSS to BSS

 WLAN devices must use the same transmission option (FHSS, DSSS, or infrared) to interoperate. That is, an FHSS WLAN can communicate with another FHSS WLAN but not with a DSSS WLAN.

The 802.11 PHY layer is divided into two parts, as seen in Figure 3-12. The **Physical Medium Dependent (PMD) sublayer** includes the standards for the characteristics of the wireless medium (DSSS, FHSS, or diffused infrared) and defines the method for transmitting and receiving data through that medium. In practical terms, transmission and reception are accomplished by the transceiver found on the wireless NIC.

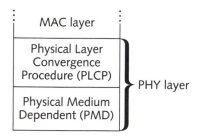

Figure 3-12   PHY sublayers

The second PHY sublayer is the **Physical Layer Convergence Procedure (PLCP) sublayer.** The PLCP performs two basic functions. First, when transmitting, it reformats the data received from the MAC layer into a packet (also known as a **frame**) that the PMD sublayer can transmit, as seen in Figure 3-13. Second, the PLCP "listens" to the medium to determine when the data can be sent.

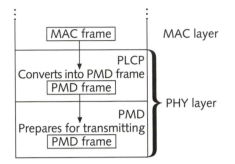

Figure 3-13   PLCP sublayer reformats MAC data

The characteristics of the Physical Medium Dependent (PMD) sublayer and Physical Layer Convergence Procedure (PLCP) sublayer are illustrated in Table 3-2.

Table 3-2   Summary of PMD and PLCP Sublayers

Function	Sublayer Performed
Establishes standards for the characteristics of the wireless medium	PMD
Defines method for transmitting and receiving data through the medium	PMD
Reformats data received from the MAC layer into a frame that the PMD sublayer can transmit	PLCP
Listens to the medium to determine when data can be sent	PLCP

Because the 802.11 standard supports three different transmission options—FHSS, DSSS, and diffused infrared—how the PMD and PLCP actually perform their functions differs based on which transmission option is being used. One way to understand how the PHY and its sublayers work is to consider it from the perspective of each transmission option.

Frequency Hopping Spread Spectrum PHY Specifications

Just as a language translator is responsible for translating text written in English into Italian, for example, the frequency hopping spread spectrum (FHSS) PHY layer translates data from the upper levels of the IEEE model into a format that can be sent over the network.

FHSS Physical Layer Convergence Procedure Standards

The primary function of the frequency hopping spread spectrum (FHSS) physical layer convergence procedure (PLCP) sublayer is to reformat the data received from the MAC layer (when transmitting) into a frame that the Physical Medium Dependent (PMD) sublayer can transmit. An example of an FHSS PLCP frame is illustrated in Figure 3-14. The frame is made up of three parts: the preamble, the header, and the data.

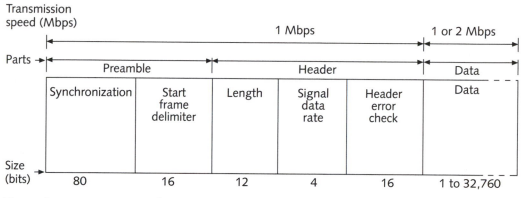

Figure 3-14   FHSS PLCP frame

The preamble alerts the receiving device to prepare for the rest of the frame. The preamble consists of two parts: the Synchronization field and the Start Frame Delimiter. The Synchronization field consists of alternating 0s and 1s to alert the receiver that a message is on its way. The receiving device then synchronizes with the incoming signal. The Start Frame Delimiter is always the same bit pattern and defines the beginning of a frame.

The Start Frame Delimiter for FHSS is always 0000110010111101.

The header provides information about the frame itself. The Length field indicates how long the frame is. The Signal Data Rate value determines the speed of the transmission. Table 3-3 illustrates the possible values for the Signal Data Rate field. The Header Error Check contains a value that the receiving device can use to determine whether the data was received correctly.

Table 3-3   FHSS Signal Data Rate Field Values

Signal Data Rate Values	Transmission Speed (Mbps)
0000	1.0
0001	1.5
0010	2.0
0011	2.5
0100	3.0
0101	3.5
0110	4.0
0111	4.5

The Data portion of the PLCP frame contains the actual information that is to be transmitted. The size of the data portion can be from 1 to 32,760 bits. It will be transmitted at the speed designated by the value in the Signal Data Rate field.

There are two items to note about the bandwidth of FHSS. First, the preamble and header of the PLCP frame are always transmitted at 1 Mbps. This allows for a slower sending device to talk to a faster receiving device because it is using the slowest speed, as seen in Figure 3-15. The disadvantage of using the lowest common speed is that two faster devices must still fall back to the 1 Mbps transmission rate for the preamble and header. However, the data can be sent at the faster rate.

 Note An advantage of the slower PCLP preamble and header transmission speed is that a slower signal can cover a larger area than a faster signal can.

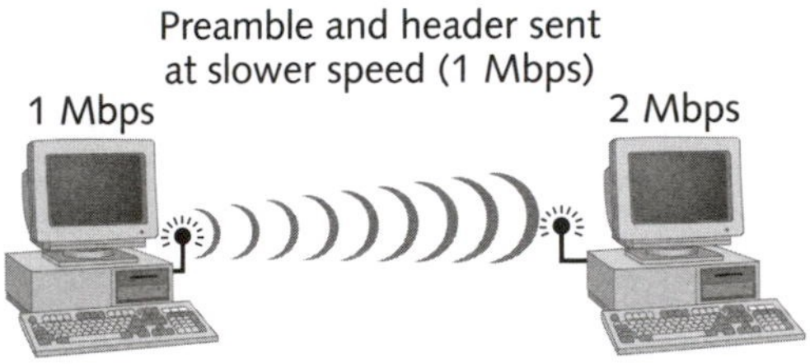

Preamble and header sent
at slower speed (1 Mbps)
1 Mbps   2 Mbps

Figure 3-15 Synchronization takes place at slower speed

A second notable item regarding bandwidth is that with FHSS the data can be transmitted only at either 1 or 2 Mbps based on the IEEE 802.11 standard. Although the Signal Data Rate values go as high as 4.5 Mbps, the 802.11 standard does not support speeds greater than 2 Mbps. Future standards may take advantage of the faster data rates.

FHSS Physical Medium Dependent Standards

Once the PLCP has created the frame, it then passes the frame to the Physical Medium Dependent (PMD) sublayer. The job of the PMD is to translate the binary 1s and 0s of the frame into radio signals that can be used for transmission.

Recall that frequency hopping uses a range of frequencies and changes frequencies during the transmission. A short burst is transmitted at one frequency, then a short burst is transmitted at another frequency, and so on, until the transmission is completed. The frequency at which FHSS transmits is part of the **Industrial, Scientific, and Medical (ISM) band**. This band of frequencies, approved by the Federal Communications Commission (FCC) in 1985, authorized wireless network products to use the ISM frequencies. An advantage of using the ISM frequencies is that this band of frequencies is unlicensed. That means it is not necessary to obtain a license from the FCC in order to transmit at these frequencies.

The unrestricted use of the ISM band is one of the factors that prompted the rapid development and deployment of WLANs.

The FCC approved three ISM frequencies for WLAN use: 902 MHz, 2.4 GHz, and 5.725 GHz, as seen in Figure 3–16. However, 2.4 GHz was the only unlicensed frequency available almost worldwide. Because of this, the IEEE 802.11 group decided that only the 2.4 GHz frequency would be the standard for WLAN transmission. (The lone exception to the availability of the 2.4 GHz frequency is France. Branches of the French military use part of this frequency to transmit secret communications.)

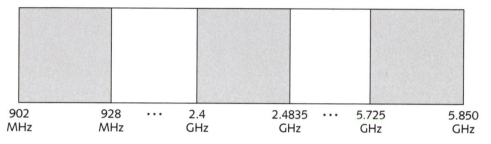

902
MHz

928
MHz

2.4
GHz

2.4835
GHz

5.725
GHz

5.850
GHz

Figure 3-16   FCC-approved Industrial, Scientific, and Medical (ISM) frequencies

Wireless devices that operate at the 5.7 GHz band can have a bandwidth of over 50 Mbps. The IEEE 802.11a subcommittee is currently working on this band as a future standard.

The 802.11 standard specifies a set of channels that are evenly spaced across the 2.4 GHz ISM band. Each channel is 1 MHz wide. The standard also sets the number of hopping sequences at 78 with a minimum hop distance of 6 MHz and a minimum hop rate of 2.5 hops per second.

The FHSS PMD transmits the data within the channel using a variation of the frequency. For transmissions at 1 Mbps, the standard specifies a two–level **Gaussian frequency shift key (GFSK)**. GFSK varies the frequency slightly within the channel to represent either a 0 (–160 KHz) or a 1 (+160 KHz). This is illustrated in Figure 3–17. For example, suppose an FHSS is transmitting at 2.402 GHz (equivalent to a frequency of 2,402,000,000 Hz). The center of that frequency would be 2,402,500,000 Hz (normally a transmission would take place as close to the center of the frequency as possible to minimize any interference from adjacent frequencies). A 1 would be transmitted at 2,402,660,000 Hz, and a 0 would be transmitted at 2,402,340,000 Hz:

Center of frequency	2,402,500,000
Transmit 1	+160,000
Transmission frequency for a 1	2,402,660,000
Center of frequency	2,402,500,000
Transmit 0	−160,000
Transmission frequency for a 0	2,402,340,000

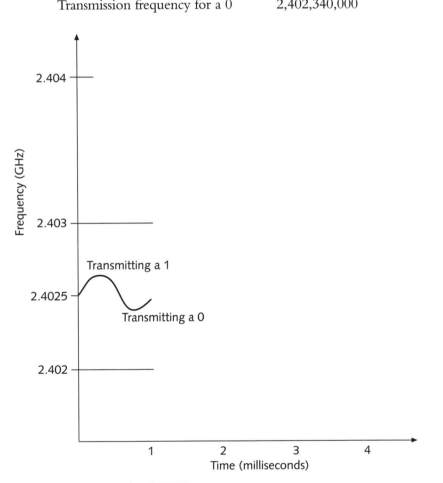

Figure 3-17   Two-level GFSK

For transmissions at 2 Mbps, a four-level GFSK modulation is used. Instead of having only two variations in frequencies for 0 and 1, the four-level GFSK has four variations in frequencies for four bit patterns. This is seen in Table 3-4.

Table 3-4   Four-Level GFSK Values

Bit Pattern	Four Level GFSK Values (KHz)
00	-216
01	-72
10	+216
11	+72

For example, suppose an FHSS is transmitting at 2.402 GHz (the center of the frequency is 2,402,500,000 Hz) and the two bits 10 were to be transmitted. The frequency for transmitting a 10 using the four-level GFSK would be 2,402,716,000:

Center of frequency	2,402,500,000
Transmit 10	+216,000
Transmission frequency for a 10	2,402,716,000

With four-level GFSK, two bits at a time are sent on a single frequency instead of just one bit. Although the actual transmission speed remains the same, twice as many bits are being sent, making the effective throughput 2 Mbps.

Direct Sequence Spread Spectrum PHY Specifications

Similar to the frequency hopping spread spectrum (FHSS) PHY layer, the direct sequence spread spectrum (DSSS) also translates data from the upper levels of the IEEE model into a format that can be sent over the network.

DSSS Physical Layer Convergence Procedure Standards

The DSSS physical layer convergence procedure (PLCP) sublayer, like the FHSS PLCP sublayer, must reformat the data received from the MAC layer (when transmitting) into a frame that the PMD sublayer can transmit. An example of a DSSS PLCP frame is illustrated in Figure 3-18.

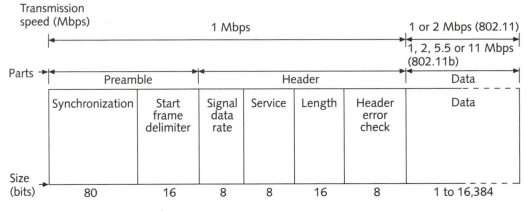

Figure 3-18   DSSS PLCP frame

There are many similarities between the FHSS PLCP frame and the DSSS PLCP frame. Both frames are made up of three parts (the preamble, the header, and the data) that perform the same type of functions. The Synchronization field and the Start Frame Delimiter field perform the same job in the DSSS PLCP frame as they do in the FHSS PLCP frame. The Signal Data Rate value indicates the speed at which the signal is being sent. Table 3-5 illustrates the possible values for the Signal Data Rate field in a DSSS PLCP frame. The Length field indicates how long the frame is, and the Header Error Check field contains a value that the receiving device can use to determine whether the data was received correctly. The size of the Data field can be from 1 to 16,384 bits. It will be transmitted at the speed indicated by the value contained in the Signal Data Rate field. However, as with the FHSS PLCP frame, the DSSS PLCP frame preamble and header are always transmitted at 1 Mbps.

Table 3-5   DSSS Signal Data Rate Field Values

Signal Data Rate Values	Transmission Speed (Mbps)
00001010	1.0
00010100	2.0

   The Start Frame Delimiter for DSSS is always 1111001110100000.

DSSS Physical Medium Dependent Standards

After creating the frame, the DSSS PCLC passes the frame to the PMD sublayer. Again, the job of the PMD is to translate the binary 1s and 0s of the frame into radio signals that can be used for transmission.

DSSS uses the ISM bands for its transmissions, as does FHSS. The 802.11 standard specifies 14 frequencies that can be used for DSSS transmissions, beginning at 2.412 GHz and incrementing by .005 GHz (except for channel 14). These are listed in Table 3-6.

Table 3-6   DSSS ISM Channels

3

Channel Number	Frequency (GHz)
1	2.412
2	2.417
3	2.422
4	2.427
5	2.432
6	2.437
7	2.442
8	2.447
9	2.452
10	2.457
11	2.462
12	2.467
13	2.472
14	2.484

The United States and Canada use channels 1–11; Europe, France, and Japan use channels 1–14.

The DSSS PMD can transmit the data in different ways depending on the speed of the transmission. For transmissions at 1 Mbps, a two-level **differential binary phase shift key (DBPSK)** is specified. You will recall that the GFSK used with FHSS varies the frequency slightly to represent either a 0 or a 1. DBPSK functions similarly except that the phase of the waveform being transmitted varies instead of the frequency. This is illustrated in Figure 3-19. Notice that the waveform for both 0 and 1 are identical. The difference is that the 1 wave shifts slightly to the right. This is known as the **phase change** and is measured in degrees. The phase change for DBPSK bit 0 is 0 degrees, whereas the phase change for bit 1 is 180 degrees.

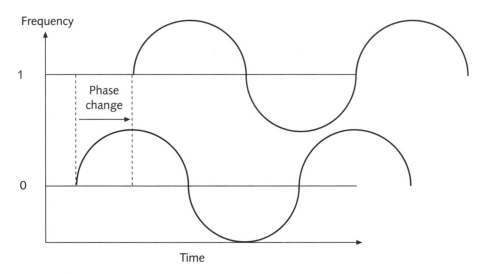

Figure 3-19   DSSS phase change

For DSSS transmissions at 2 Mbps, a four-level phase change is used. Instead of having only two variations in phases for 0 and 1, the four-level phase change has four variations in phases for the bits 00, 01, 10, and 11. This is known as a **differential quadrature phase shift key (DQPSK)**. The DQPSK values are seen in Table 3-7. With DQPSK, two bits are sent at a time instead of just one. Although the actual transmission speed remains the same, twice as many bits are sent, making the effective throughput 2 Mbps.

Table 3-7   DQPSK Values

Bit Pattern	DQPSK Values (degrees)
00	0
01	90
10	270
11	180

Recall that DSSS uses an expanded redundant code, called the Barker code, to transmit each data bit. The Barker code is used when DSSS is transmitting at 1 Mbps or 2 Mbps, according to the IEEE 802.11 standards. However, to transmit at rates above 2 Mbps, the IEEE 802.11b standards committee chose bit code other than the 11-bit Barker code. The 802.11b specifies that **Complementary Code Keying (CCK)** be used instead. CCK consists of a set of 64 eight-bit code words. As a set, these code words have unique mathematical properties that enable a receiver to distinguish them correctly from one another. The 5.5 Mbps rate uses CCK to encode four bits per carrier, whereas the 11 Mbps rate encodes eight bits per carrier. Both the 5.5 Mbps and 11 Mbps speeds use DQPSK as the modulation technique. These are summarized in Table 3-8.

Table 3-8   DSSS Transmissions

Data Rate (Mbps)	Bit Code	Modulation Technique
1.0	Barker	DBPSK
2.0	Barker	DQPSK
5.5	CCK	DQPSK
11.0	CCK	DQPSK

Diffused Infrared PHY Specifications

A diffused infrared WLAN does not require line-of-sight transmission but instead relies on reflected light. The emitters on a diffused WLAN network have a wide-focused beam and are usually pointed at the ceiling, which they use as the reflection point. When the emitter transmits an infrared signal, that signal bounces off the ceiling and fills the room. The PHY layer performs the functions of both reformatting the data received from the upper layers and transmitting the light impulses.

Diffused Infrared Physical Layer Convergence Procedure Standards

The diffused infrared PLCP has a function similar to that of the PLCP for FHSS and DSSS: It reformats the data received from the MAC layer (when transmitting) into a frame that the PMD sublayer can transmit. An example of an infrared PLCP frame is illustrated in Figure 3-20.

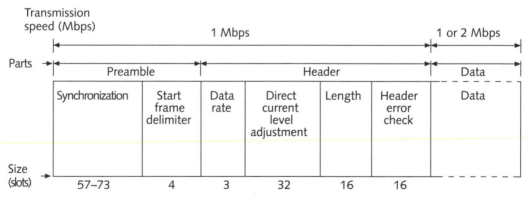

Figure 3-20   Infrared PLCP frame

Notice that the frame size is not measured in bits but in **slots** (also called **time slots**). You will recall that to transmit a 1, an infrared emitter increases the intensity of the current and sends a pulse using infrared light. Infrared WLANs send data by varying the intensity of the light wave instead of sending "on-off" signals of light (a higher impulse is a 1 and a lower impulse is a 0). The emitter transmits a pulse of infrared light at a specific time, known as the slot. In the Synchronization field of an infrared PLCP frame, the emitter may send between

57 and 73 pulses, each in its own time slot. The receiving device then synchronizes with the incoming signal. The Start Frame Delimiter is always the same bit pattern and it defines the beginning of a frame.

 The Start Frame Delimiter for infrared is always 1001, where 1 represents a high-intensity pulse and 0 is a lower-intensity pulse.

The Data Rate value determines the speed of the transmission. The Direct Current Level Adjustment field contains a pattern of infrared pulses that allows the receiving device to determine the signal level. Table 3-9 illustrates the possible values for these fields. The Header Error Check field contains a value that the receiving device can use to determine whether the data was received correctly, whereas the Length field indicates the number of microseconds needed to transmit the entire frame. The portion of the frame that contains the data consists of 1 to 20,000 time slots.

Table 3-9   Infrared Data Rate and Direct Current Level Adjustment Values

Transmission Speed (Mbps)	Data Rate Values	Direct Current Level Adjustment Values
1.0	000	00000000010000000000000001000000
2.0	001	00100010001000100010001000100010

As with the FHSS and DSSS PLCP frames, the preamble and header are always transmitted at 1 Mbps. Also, the IEEE 802.11 standard currently defines that the data can be transmitted only at either 1 or 2 Mbps.

Diffused Infrared Physical Medium Dependent Standards

After creating the frame, the PLCP then passes the frame to the PMD sublayer. The PMD translates the binary 1s and 0s of the frame into light pulses that can be used for transmission.

The infrared PMD transmits the data using a series of light impulses. For transmissions at 1 Mbps, a **16-pulse position modulation (16-PPM)** is specified. 16-PPM translates four data bits into 16 light impulses, which are then transmitted to the receiving device. This is illustrated in Table 3-10. For transmissions at 2 Mbps, a **4-pulse position modulation (4-PPM)** is used instead, as seen in Table 3-11.

Each time slot is one 250-billionth of a second, no matter which transmission speed is being used (1 Mbps or 2 Mbps). If each slot time is the same, how can the 4-PPM transmit at twice the speed? It is because four times the amount of data is contained in a 4-PPM transmission. Suppose that the data bits 0000 were to be transmitted. Using 16-PPM, it would take 16 time slots (0000000000000001). However, using 4-PPM to transmit the same data bits of 0000, would take only eight time slots (0001 and 0001). Thus 4-PPM can transmit at a maximum rate of 2 Mbps, whereas 16-PPM can transmit at only 1 Mbps.

Table 3-10   16-PPM Values

Data Bit	16-PPM Value
0000	0000000000000001
0001	0000000000000010
0011	0000000000000100
0010	0000000000001000
0110	0000000000010000
0111	0000000000100000
0101	0000000001000000
0100	0000000010000000
1100	0000000100000000
1101	0000001000000000
1111	0000010000000000
1110	0000100000000000
1010	0001000000000000
1011	0010000000000000
1001	0100000000000000
1001	1000000000000000

Table 3-11   4-PPM Values

Data Bit	Four-PPM Value
00	0001
01	0010
11	0100
10	1000

CHAPTER SUMMARY

❐ There are several benefits of networking standards. Standards ensure that WLAN devices from one vendor will interoperate with those from other vendors. Another benefit of standards is that they result in lower costs. Standards encourage competition among vendors. Standards also help protect the investment of equipment by creating backward - compatibility. New technologies are incorporated into regularly revised standards so that the technologies are compatible with equipment based on earlier standards. Standards also decrease product development time and costs. Because standards have already paved the way, manufacturers do not have to invest large amounts of capital in research and development.

❐ The OSI model is a conceptual model of network communications. It breaks the complex functions of networking into seven layers (Application, Presentation, Session,

Transport, Network, Data Link, and Physical). Each layer provides specific services and information to the layers above and below it. Within each layer, several networking tasks are performed. WLAN functions are performed only in the Data Link and Physical layers.

❑ The Institute of Electrical and Electronic Engineers (IEEE) publishes computer standards to ensure interoperability between vendor products. The standards for network interoperability are called Project 802. Two of the most widely known Project 802 standards are 802.3 (Ethernet) and 802.5 (Token Ring). In 1990, IEEE formed a committee to develop a standard for WLANs operating at 1 and 2 Mbps. In 1997, the IEEE approved the final draft. However, the slow bandwidth of only 2 Mbps for the 802.11 standard was not sufficient for network applications. The IEEE body revisited the 802.11 standard shortly after it was released to determine what changes could be made to increase the speed. In September 1999, a new 802.11b high rate was amended to the standard, which added two higher speeds (5.5 Mbps and 11 Mbps) to the original 802.11 standard. Although the OSI model is the conceptual model, Project 802 gives the specifications for putting the model into practice.

❑ The purpose of the IEEE 802.11 PHY layer is to send the signal to the network and receive the signal from the network. The PHY layer is divided into two parts. The Physical Medium Dependent (PMD) sublayer includes the standards for all three types of wireless media (DSSS, FHSS, or diffused infrared) and defines the method for transmitting and receiving data through each medium. The second sublayer of the PHY layer is the Physical Layer Convergence Procedure (PLCP). The PLCP reformats the data received from the MAC layer (when transmitting) into a frame that the PMD sublayer can transmit, and it "listens" to the medium to determine when the data can be sent.

Key Terms

4-pulse position modulation (4–PPM) — A modulation for diffused infrared 2 Mbps WLANs that translates two data bits into four light impulses.

16-pulse position modulation (16–PPM) — A modulation for diffused infrared 1 Mbps WLANs that translates four data bits into 16 light impulses.

Complementary Code Keying (CCK) — A code of 64 eight-bit code words used for transmitting DSSS at speeds above 2 Mbps.

de facto standards — Common practices that an industry may follow.

de jure standards — Standards controlled by an organization or body that has been entrusted with that task; same as *official standards*.

differential binary phase shift key (DBPSK) — A modulation used for DSSS transmission that varies the phase of the waveform slightly to represent a 0 or a 1.

differential quadrature phase shift key (DQPSK) — A modulation used for DSSS transmission that varies the phase of the waveform slightly to represent the bits 00, 01, 10, and 11.

frame — A packet of data.

Gaussian frequency shift key (GFSK) — A modulation used for FHSS transmission that varies the frequency slightly within the channel to represent different bits.

3

Industrial, Scientific, and Medical (ISM) band — An unlicensed band of frequencies approved by the FCC in 1985 for use by wireless network products.

Institute of Electrical and Electronic Engineers (IEEE) — A standards body that created computer network standards to ensure interoperability among vendors.

International Standards Organization (ISO) — A standards body that developed specifications for computer networks, among other things.

Logical Link Control (LLC) — A sublayer of the IEEE Project 802 Data Link layer (Layer 2).

Media Access Control (MAC) — A sublayer of the IEEE Project 802 Data Link layer (Layer 2).

official standards — Standards controlled by an organization or body that has been entrusted with that task; same as *de jure standards*.

Open Systems Interconnection (OSI) model — A conceptual model of computer networking that is based on layers, in which each layer does specific functions and cooperates with the layers immediately above and below it.

phase change — The variation of the phase of the waveform used in differential binary phase shift key (DBPSK) transmissions.

Physical Layer Convergence Procedure (PLCP) sublayer — A sublayer of the IEEE Project 802 PHY layer that reformats the data and determines when data can be sent.

Physical Medium Dependent (PMD) sublayer — A sublayer of the IEEE Project 802 PHY layer that defines the standards for the characteristics of the wireless medium and the method for transmitting and receiving data through that medium.

Project 802 — The standards created by the IEEE for computer networking.

slot — A time that a diffused infrared WLAN sends a pulse of infrared light; also called *time slot*.

time slot — A time that a diffused infrared WLAN sends a pulse of infrared light; also called *slot*.

REVIEW QUESTIONS

1. Which of the following is *not* a benefit of a standard?

   a. interoperability of network devices from one vendor with those from other vendors

   b. higher costs

   c. protection of the investment of equipment

   d. reduced product development time and costs

2. Official standards are also known as _____ standards.

   a. de facto

   b. de parte

   c. de jure

   d. di juriet

3. The International Standards Organization was responsible for creating the

   a. Project 802

   b. IEEE

   c. OSI model

   d. GFSK

4. The OSI model has _____ layers.

   a. five

   b. six

   c. seven

   d. eight

5. The layer that sends the signal to the network or receives the signal from the network is the _____ layer.

   a. Physical (PHY)

   b. Data Link

   c. Application

   d. Network

6. The flow in the OSI model between layers goes down from Application to Physical when the data goes out to the network, and up from Physical to Application when it is received from the network. True or false?

7. A wireless NIC is found only in the Data Link layer of the OSI model. True or false?

8. Project 802 subdivides the OSI model Layer 2, Data Link, into two sublayers, Logical Link Control (LLC) and Media Access Control (MAC). True or false?

9. The 802.11b standard defines a local area network that provides cable-free data access for clients that are either mobile or in a fixed location at a rate up to 2 Mbps. True or false?

10. The 802.11 standard also specifies that the features of a WLAN be transparent to the upper levels of the 802.11 standard. True or false?

11. The 802.11b high rate added two higher speeds of 5.5 Mbps and _____ Mbps to the original 802.11 standard.

12. The 802.11b standard made changes only to the _____ layer of the original 802.11 standard.

13. The 802.11 standard simultaneously supports _____ different transmission options.

14. The _____ sublayer consists of the standards for both the characteristics of the wireless medium and the method for transmitting and receiving data through that medium.

15. The _____ sublayer reformats the data received from the MAC layer into a frame that the PMD sublayer can transmit.

16. List and describe the functions of the three parts of the FHSS PLCP frame.

17. Tell what the FHSS Synchronization field does.

18. What are the advantages and disadvantages of the preamble and header transmitted at 1 Mbps in an FHSS PLCP frame?

19. Explain the Gaussian frequency shift key (GFSK).

20. Explain the difference between the GFSK and the two-level differential binary phase shift key (DBPSK).

HANDS-ON PROJECTS

1. The Complementary Code Keying (CCK) was a compromise between two different solutions proposed to the IEEE 802.11b committee. Write a one-page paper on this topic. What were the original solutions? What were their advantages and disadvantages? Why was a compromise necessary? What are the strengths and weaknesses of CCK compared to other options?

2. Write a one-page paper on the IEEE and the Project 802.11 and 802.11b subcommittees. Why did it take so long to ratify the standards? What other options were proposed? What future standards are being discussed today?

3. Select five different computer hardware or software technologies, such as operating systems, word processors, NICs, network cabling, universal serial ports, Firewire, and mouse ports. Determine which are the result of standards, and whether they are de facto standards or de jure standards. If they are de facto standards, what other products or technologies were originally introduced? Why did this standard win out? If they are de jure standards, what body set those standards? How were they determined? How often are they reviewed? Write a paper on your findings.

4. Draw a picture of the three different frames of FHSS, DSSS, and diffused infrared. Compare the fields that are different and explain why they are different. Identify the fields that are the same.

5. Draw a picture of the radio spectrum that includes the ISM band. What other devices use the ISM band? What devices use frequencies immediately adjacent to this band? What problems can WLANs encounter by using the ISM band?

6. Illustrate how the ASCII value *A* (01000001) would be transmitted using the following techniques:
   - Two-level Gaussian frequency shift key (GFSK)
   - Four-level GFSK
   - Two-level differential binary phase shift key (DBPSK)
   - Differential quadrature phase shift keying (DQPSK)
   - Sixteen-pulse position modulation (16-PPM)
   - Four-pulse position modulation (4-PPM)

CASE PROJECTS

Northridge Consulting Group

Northridge Consulting Group (NCG) has taken on an additional client and needs your services. The Low End, a music equipment retail franchise, is interested in moving its network in its corporate headquarters and distribution warehouse from wired Ethernet to a WLAN. However, a presentation from a vendor's salesperson to the Low End's Information Services (IS) group has the group members confused. The salesperson is attempting to sell the group a diffused infrared WLAN that does not meet 802.11 standards. The WLAN is being offered at a very low price, because the vendor is ready to come out with a new model, and thus is offering the Low End one last chance to buy the vendor's current model before prices go up. Many in the IS group feel that they should avoid a proprietary system, but the finance director is interested only in the lowest possible cost.

1. Make a presentation to the finance director about why a decision regarding WLANs should be based on standards. Create a PowerPoint slide presentation with a minimum of 20 slides that covers standards. Be sure to explain the reasons that standards are necessary, the advantages and disadvantages of standards, and the types of computer standards that are found today.

2. Make a separate presentation to the Low End's IS staff about IEEE 802 and 802.11 standards. Outline how these standards came about. Since the Low End has an Ethernet network already installed, use it to explain about IEEE and the Project 802. Finally, explain the differences between 802.11 and 802.11b. Create a PowerPoint slide presentation with a minimum of 20 slides.

OPTIONAL TEAM CASE PROJECT

The Low End has alerted NCG of something that the company just discovered. Its distribution warehouse is located in an office park that is just outside the perimeter of a military base. In addition, the warehouse across the street is used for testing and refurbishing medical imaging and diagnostic equipment. The Low End needs to know whether wireless signals from the military base and the medical warehouse could interfere with its proposed WLAN.

NCG needs your input. Create two teams of two or three consultants. One team should explore the ISM band regarding wireless transmissions from medical imaging equipment. The other team should look at military wireless transmissions. Which are most likely to interfere with a WLAN? Why? Can this interference be avoided? If not, can using a diffused infrared WLAN solve the problem? Write a paper on your findings.

4

IEEE 802.11 MEDIUM ACCESS CONTROL AND NETWORK LAYER STANDARDS

After reading this chapter and completing the exercises, you will be able to:

♦ Describe the ways that a WLAN can access the wireless medium

♦ Explain the steps necessary for a WLAN station to join the network

♦ List and discuss the actions needed for a station to remain connected to a WLAN

♦ Describe the MAC frame formats

♦ Tell how Mobile IP works

The IEEE 802.11 standard, which defines a local area network that provides cable-free data access for clients that are either mobile or in a fixed location, specifies that the features of a WLAN be "transparent" to the upper levels of the 802 standard above the PHY and MAC layers. This means that all WLAN features are implemented in the PHY and MAC layers.

There is an advantage to having the WLAN features isolated in the two bottom layers. Because no modifications are needed at any of the other layers, existing software designed to meet other 802.x standards will operate correctly on the new 802.11 standard. This means that any network operating system or LAN application will run on a WLAN without the need for changes.

However, isolating all of the WLAN functions in the bottom two layers of the IEEE 802.11 standard does not mean that new features cannot be added to the existing upper layers. A new feature can be added as long as it does not modify the standard. This is necessary so that all the features of mobile computing—something unheard of when the original IEEE 802 standards were designed back in 1980—can be incorporated into today's WLANs.

This chapter looks at the MAC layer of the IEEE 802.11 standard that provides the implementation of the WLAN features. The chapter also looks at new enhanced features in the Network layer that can provide additional benefits for mobile computing.

IEEE 802.11 MEDIUM ACCESS CONTROL LAYER

The 802.11 Data Link layer consists of two sublayers: the Logical Link Control (LLC) and Media Access Control (MAC) layers. The 802.11 standard specifies no changes to the LLC sublayer (the LLC remains the same as for wired networks). All of the changes for 802.11 WLANs are confined to the MAC layer.

The functions of the MAC layer in an 802.11 WLAN can be viewed from three perspectives: first, how a station can access the wireless medium itself; second, how a station can connect to the WLAN; and third, how a station can remain connected even while roaming.

Accessing a Wireless Medium

One of the primary responsibilities of the MAC layer is to govern how a wireless station can access the medium. Because the medium is shared by multiple stations, there must be a standard set of procedures to allow all stations access.

Topologies

In computer networking the word **topology** refers to the physical layout of the network. There are two basic types of computer topologies. In a **point-to-point topology**, each device is directly connected to all other devices. An example of a point-to-point topology is a local printer directly connected to a computer. This would require a parallel or USB connection on the computer and a cable to attach the printer. Adding a second printer would call for a second parallel or USB connection on the computer and another cable to attach to this second printer, as shown in Figure 4-1.

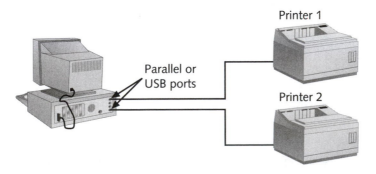

Figure 4-1   Printer connections

A point-to-point topology would not be feasible for a modern computer network. Each computer would need to have a separate connection point (such as a NIC) and medium (such as a cable in a traditional wired LAN) to connect to all of the other computers on the network. In a computer network of just five computers, each computer would need four separate connection points and mediums to connect to each of the four other computers, as shown in Figure 4-2. For a WLAN, such topology would require 29 wireless NICs and 29 different frequencies on which to send a signal. Because of this complexity, no LANs use point-to-point topology.

4

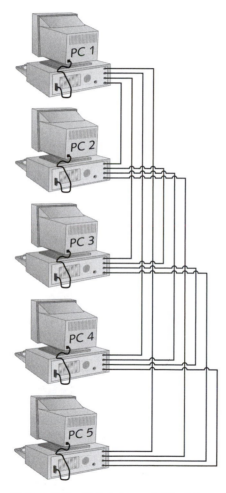

Figure 4-2   Point-to-point topology LAN

 A wired computer network of 500 computers using a point-to-point topology would require a total of 249,500 cables!

The other type of topology is **multipoint**. The key to a multipoint topology is sharing. Instead of requiring a separate connection point and medium to connect to every computer on the network, each computer has just one connection point and shares the medium. The single connection point and medium share the sending and receiving of messages across the network, as shown in Figure 4-3. All computer networks today use a multipoint topology.

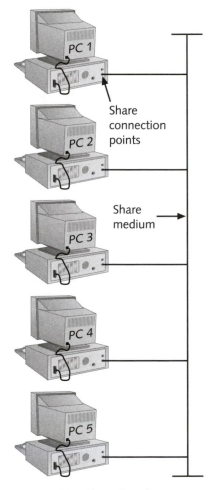

Figure 4-3   Shared multipoint topology LAN

Distributed Coordination Function

Because the medium is shared in a multipoint topology, there must be rules for cooperation among the devices that are sharing the medium. These rules ensure that the network can function effectively. The different ways of sharing are called **channel access methods**. One type of channel access method is known as **contention**. The philosophy of contention is that computers contend or compete with each other for use of the network. With contention, any computer can attempt to transmit a message at any time. However, if two computers send messages at the same time, a **collision** results and all the messages can become scrambled, as shown in Figure 4-4.

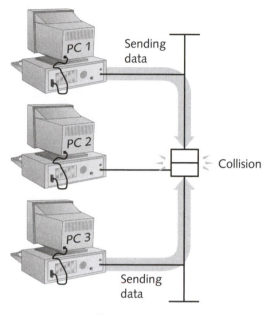

Figure 4-4   Collision

One way to prevent network collisions is to use the same principles as people use in polite conversation. First, listen to make sure no one else is talking. If someone is talking, then wait. If no one else is talking, then go ahead and speak.

The IEEE 802.3 Ethernet standard specifies contention with this "politeness" as its channel access method. It is called **Carrier Sense Multiple Access with Collision Detection (CSMA/CD)**. Under the CSMA/CD method, before a computer starts to send a message, it should first listen on the cable (called **carrier sense**) to see whether any other computer is transmitting. If the computer senses traffic, it should wait until that traffic is finished. If it senses no traffic, then the computer can send its message.

However, what if two computers simultaneously listen and hear nothing on the cable and then both start to send messages at exactly the same time? A collision would still result (see Figure 4-5A). CSMA/CD specifies that each computer must continue to listen while sending its message. If it hears a collision, each computer stops sending data and instead broadcasts a "jam" signal over the network (see Figure 4-5B). This signal tells all other computers to wait to send any messages. The two sending computers then pause a random amount of time (called a **backoff interval**) (see Figure 4-5C) before attempting to resend their messages (see Figure 4-5D).

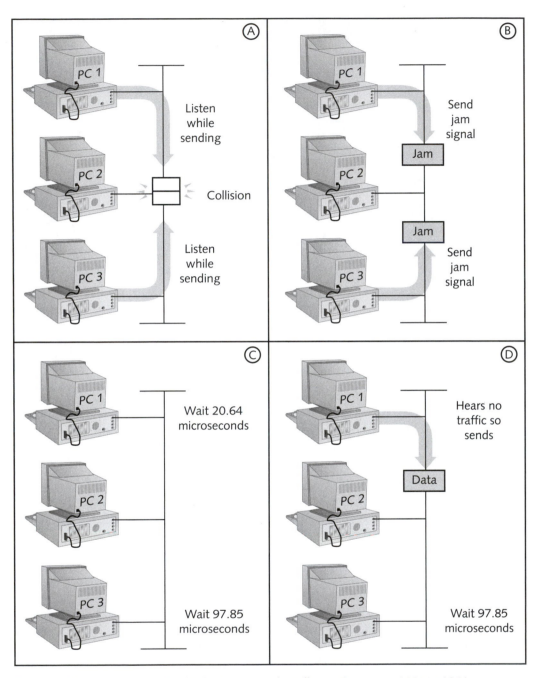

Figure 4-5   Carrier Sense Multiple Access with Collision Detection (CSMA/CD)

However, the 802.11 standard for wireless networks does not use CSMA/CD. This is due to the fact that collision detection is very difficult with wireless transmissions. With CSMA/CD, the stations must be able to transmit and listen at the same time. However, in radio systems, the signal from a transmitting station is so strong that it will overpower that same station's ability to receive a transmission simultaneously. In short, while it is transmitting, a station "drowns out" its own ability to detect a collision.

Another factor that makes collision detection so difficult with wireless transmission is that all stations would have to be able to detect transmissions from all other stations at all times. In a wireless environment that covers a large area, a station may not be in range of all other stations. In Figure 4–6, Stations A, B, and C are all within range of the access point but not within range of each other. Station B can detect a transmission from Station C but not from Station A. If Station B "listens" and hears no traffic, it may assume there are no transmissions taking place, whereas Station A actually is already transmitting. This is known as the **hidden node** problem.

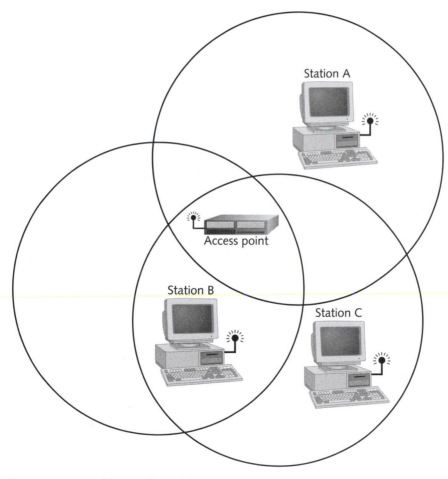

Figure 4-6   Hidden node problem

Instead of using CSMA/CD, the 802.11 standard uses an access method known as the **Distributed Coordination Function (DCF)**. The DCF specifies the use of a modified procedure known as **Carrier Sense Multiple Access with Collision Avoidance (CSMA/CA)**. Whereas CSMA/CD is designed to handle collisions when they occur, CSMA/CA attempts to avoid collisions altogether.

Consider for a moment a home that has only one telephone but several children. When will there be the most conflict over who gets to use the phone? Usually it will be immediately after someone talking on the phone has hung up. This is because everyone else has been forced to wait until that telephone conversation was over, and now the others all want to use the phone at the same time.

The same is true with a contention channel access method. When using this method, the time at which the most collisions occur is immediately after a station completes its transmission. This is because all other stations wanting to transmit have been waiting for the medium to clear so they can send their messages. Once the medium is clear, the stations all try to transmit at the same time, which results in more collisions and delays. CSMA/CD handles the collisions by having the two stations responsible for the collision wait a random amount of time (the backoff interval) before attempting to resend.

Think about the home with one telephone again. Suppose the parents create a reward system based on household duties to perform (cleaning a room, mowing a lawn, etc.) for the week. Each week the parents give each child a "Telephone Wait Time" number. The child who completes all of his or her duties may have a Telephone Wait Time of one minute, whereas a child who has not completed his or her duties may have a Telephone Wait Time of five minutes. Whenever the telephone becomes available, each child must wait his or her Telephone Wait Time before trying to use the phone. If both Ann and Ben want to use the phone, but Ann has to wait only one minute whereas Ben has to wait five minutes, Ann would obviously get to go first and Ben would be forced to wait until her call is completed. Because everyone's time is different, there is no contention for using the phone once it is available.

This same analogy is applied to WLANs. In wireless technology, Carrier Sense Multiple Access with Collision Avoidance (CSMA/CA) handles the situation differently than Carrier Sense Multiple Access with Collision Detection (CSMA/CD). Instead of making just the two stations responsible for the collision wait a random amount of time before attempting to resend after the collision, CMSA/CA has *all* stations wait a random amount of time after the medium is clear. This significantly reduces the number of collisions. CMSA/CA is illustrated in Figure 4-7.

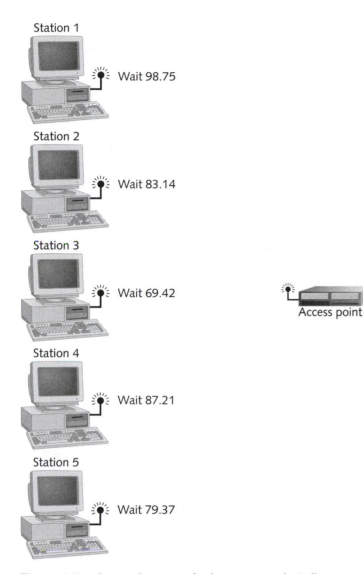

Figure 4-7   Carrier Sense Multiple Access with Collision Avoidance (CSMA/CA)

The amount of time that a station must wait after the medium is clear is measured in **slot time**. Slot times for WLANs, measured in microseconds, are shown in Table 4-1. Each station must wait a random amount of slot time as its backoff interval. For example, if the slot time for a type of WLAN is 50 and Station A's backoff interval is three slot times, then that station must wait 150 microseconds (50 microsecond slot time × 3) before attempting to transmit. With CMSA/CA, all stations wait a random amount of time after the medium is clear, which significantly reduces the number of collisions.

Table 4-1   Slot Times

Interframe Space (IFS)	DSSS	FHSS	Diffused Infrared
Slot time	20	50	8

The slot time for an 802.3 Ethernet 10 Mbps transmission is 51.2 microseconds.

CSMA/CA also reduces collisions by using explicit **packet acknowledgment (ACK)**. The receiving station sends an acknowledgment packet (or ACK) to the sending station to confirm that the data packet arrived intact. If the ACK frame is not returned to the sending station, either because the original data packet was not received or the ACK was not received intact, the sending station assumes a problem has occurred and retransmits the data packet after waiting another random amount of time. This explicit ACK mechanism handles interference and other radio-related problems.

Because packet acknowledgment (ACK) does add some overhead (time) that 802.3 Ethernet does not impose, an 802.11 WLAN will always have slower performance than an equivalent Ethernet LAN.

The 802.11 standard also defines three different **interframe spaces (IFS)** or time gaps. These are standard spacing intervals between the transmissions of the data frames. Instead of being just "dead space," these time gaps are used for special types of transmissions. One time gap, the **short IFS (SIFS)**, is used for immediate response actions such as ACK. Another time gap is the **Point Coordination Function IFS (PIFS)**. This is the time used by a station to access the medium after it has been asked and then given approval to transmit (PIFS is discussed in the next section). The **Distributed Coordination Function IFS (DIFS)** is the standard interval between the transmission of data frames.

The times of these space intervals, measured in microseconds, are shown in Table 4-2.

Table 4-2   Interframe Spaces (IFS)

Interframe Space (IFS)	DSSS	FHSS	Diffused Infrared
SIFS	10	28	7
PIFS	30	78	15
DIFS	50	128	23

Figure 4-8 illustrates a transmission by Station A using direct sequence spread spectrum (DSSS). Station A has been assigned three slot times. The amount of time that a station must wait after the medium is clear is given as the number slot times. The total amount of waiting time, known as the backoff interval, is calculated by multiplying the number of slot times by the length of each slot time, which is 20 microseconds.

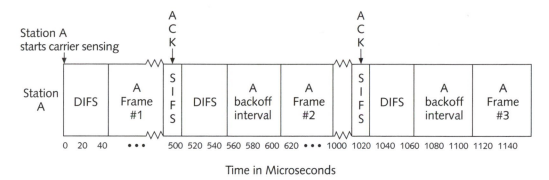

Time in Microseconds

Figure 4-8   CSMA/CA with one station transmitting

Station A starts listening (carrier sensing) before transmitting. If there is no traffic at the completion of the DIFS space (50 microseconds), Station A starts transmitting. When the transmission is over, the receiving station sends back an acknowledgment (ACK) in the SIFS gap, stating that the transmission was successful. Once this acknowledgement is received, the process starts all over again with Station A carrier sensing at the next DIFS. This time, if no traffic is detected, Station A starts its backoff interval of 60 microseconds (20 microseconds × 3 slot times). At the end of each slot time interval (20 microseconds), Station A again listens for traffic. If at the end of its backoff interval Station A still detects no traffic, then the station transmits its second frame. Once the ACK packet is received, the process resumes again.

When two stations are transmitting, the process becomes more complicated, as shown in Figure 4-9. Station A is using DSSS with three slot times, whereas Station B has only two slot times. Station A begins carrier sensing and then transmitting its first frame. Station B then begins carrier sensing while Station A's first frame is being sent. Because it detects traffic, Station B waits. Once Station A has received its ACK, both stations begin carrier sensing during the second DIFS. At the end of the second DIFS, Stations A and B begin their backoff intervals. Because the number of Station B's slot times is only 2, it will finish its backoff interval of 40 (20 microseconds × 2 slot times) before Station A finishes its backoff interval of 60 (20 microseconds × 3 slot times). Station B then begins transmitting its first packet.

Because each station continues to carrier sense at the end of each of its time slots, Station A detects that Station B is now transmitting. Station A "remembers" that it has already counted off two of its slot times. Station A must now wait until B's transmission and acknowledgment are complete and the next DIF begins. After the DIF gap time, Station A and B both begin their backoff intervals. However, this time Station A has to wait only one slot time. This is because Station A already waited for two of its slot times. If a station is "bumped" by another station from transmitting, it has to wait only the remaining number of time slots and not start all over again. This increases the probability that those stations that are waiting will transmit sooner than a new station will.

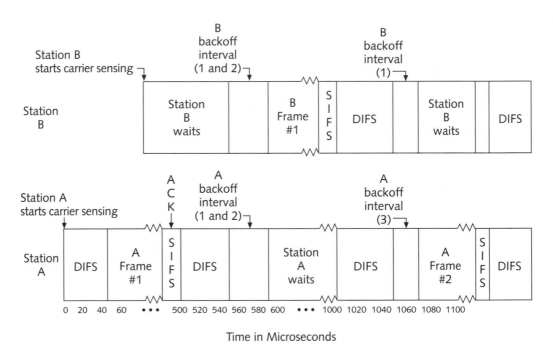

Time in Microseconds

Figure 4-9   CSMA/CA with two stations transmitting

Although CSMA/CA dramatically reduces the potential for collisions, it does not eliminate them altogether. CSMA/CA cannot solve the hidden node problem, which is the result of stations being out of range of each other without knowing that certain other nodes exist. The 802.11 standard provides an option that may be used when collisions occur due to a hidden node. That option is known as **virtual carrier sensing** or the **Request to Send/Clear to Send (RTS/CTS)** protocol. This option solves the hidden node problem and provides additional protection against collisions. In Figure 4–10, Station A and Station B are within the range of the access point. However, Station B cannot sense any transmissions from Station A, since Station A is outside of B's coverage area, shown in gray. Station C is not hidden from any other station.

Consider again the home with one telephone. Suppose that someone has just finished using the phone, and now Ann and Ben want to make a call. However, the mother announces that she is expecting a call from her business partner, so nobody should use the phone for the next hour until she receives the call (the household does not have call waiting). The mother has reserved the phone for a period of time for a special call.

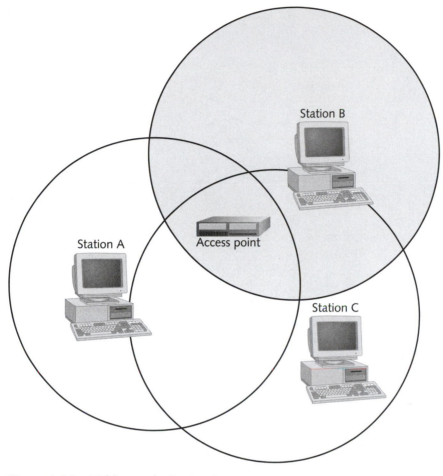

Figure 4-10   Hidden node Station B

This system is analogous to RTS/CTS, which also is the solution to the hidden node problem. Station B transmits request-to-send (RTS) frame (sent during the SIFS time gap). This frame contains a duration field that defines the length of time needed for both the transmission and the returning ACK frame. The access point as well as all stations that can receive Station B's signal will be alerted that Station B needs to reserve the medium for a specific period of time. Each receiving station stores that information in its **net allocation vector (NAV)**. No station can transmit if the NAV contains a value other than zero. The access point then responds to Station B with a clear-to-send (CTS) frame that alerts all stations that can hear the access point that the medium is now being reserved and that they should suspend any transmissions. After receiving the CTS frame, Station B can then proceed with transmitting its message. This is illustrated in Figure 4-11.

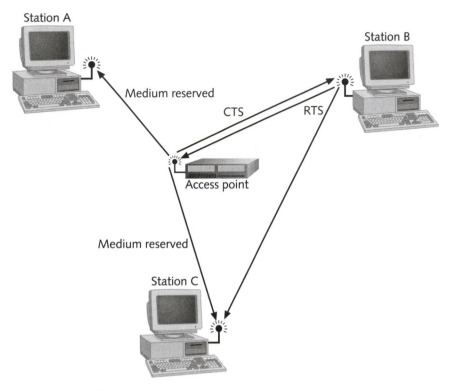

Figure 4-11   RTS/CTS

The RTS/CTS protocol imposes significant additional overhead upon the WLAN with the transmission of its RTS and CTS frames. The RTS/CTS protocol is especially taxing when short data packets are being transmitted. For this reason, the 802.11 standard specifies that when the RTS/CTS option is invoked, short data packets may still be transmitted without RTS/CTS. The size limit defining which packets can be transmitted without RTS/CTS is known as the **RTS threshold**. Only packets that are longer than the RTS threshold are transmitted using RTS/CTS.

The RTS/CTS protocol imposes additional overhead and is not used unless there is poor network performance due to excessive collisions. The first approach should be to move the stations or access point if possible so that the devices can sense each other's transmissions.

Point Coordination Function

The channel access method known as contention, in which any computer can attempt to transmit a message at any time, is the basis for CSMA/CA. Another type of channel access method is **polling**. With this method, each computer is polled or asked in sequence whether it wants to transmit. If the answer is yes, then the computer is given permission to transmit while all other devices must wait. If the answer is no, then the next device in sequence is polled. This method is a very orderly way of allowing each device to send a message when it becomes its turn, as shown in Figure 4-12. Polling effectively prevents collisions because every device must wait until it receives permission before it can transmit.

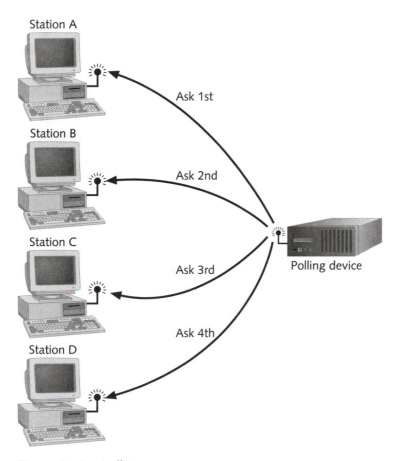

Station A

Ask 1st

Station B

Ask 2nd

Station C

Ask 3rd

Polling device

Ask 4th

Station D

Figure 4-12   Polling

The 802.11 standard provides for an optional polling function known as **Point Coordination Function (PCF)**. With PCF, the access point serves as the polling device or point coordinator. It queries each station in an orderly fashion to determine whether the station needs to transmit.

The point coordinator begins by sensing the medium, just as all other stations do, after a SIFS time gap during which an ACK was transmitted. However, whereas the other stations must wait through the duration of the distributed coordination function IFS (DIFS) time gap, the point coordinator has to wait only through the point coordination function IFS (PIFS) time gap. Because the PIFS time gap is shorter than the DIFS time gap, the point coordinator will gain control of the medium before any other stations, as shown in Figure 4-13.

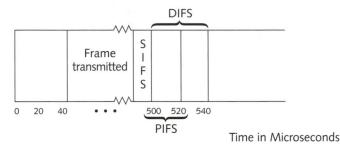

Figure 4-13   DIFS versus PIFS time gap

If the point coordinator hears no traffic at the end of the PIFS time gap, then it sends to all stations a frame known as a **beacon frame**. One field of this frame contains a value that indicates the length of time that PCF (polling) will be used instead of DCF (contention). After the stations receive this beacon frame, they must stop any transmission for that length of time. The point coordinator then sends out another frame to a specific station, granting it permission to transmit one frame to any destination. If the station has nothing to send, then it returns a **null data frame** to the point coordinator.

 Stations that receive the beacon frame store the value of the Length of Time field for PCF in their own NAV field.

Because each station can be told the length of time that PCF will be used instead of DCF, the 802.11 standard allows a WLAN to alternate between PCF (polling) and DCF (contention). Figure 4-14 illustrates how PCF and DCF frames can be intertwined. The point coordinator waits during the first PIFS and then sends a beacon frame, "reserving" the network for a specific amount of time. During this time, a station is polled and a PCF frame is transmitted. At the conclusion of that transmission, the time expires and the WLAN returns to the default DCF method, allowing another station to transmit based on contention. When that frame is completed, the point coordinator can again take control of the medium by sending another beacon frame.

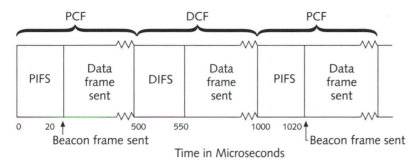

Figure 4-14   PCF and DCF frames

 PCF always has a higher priority than DCF.

PCF is most often used in WLANs that transmit time-sensitive frames. These types of transmissions, such as audio or video, depend heavily upon each frame arriving very quickly one after the other. Delays in transmission can result in a video that "freezes" on the screen or a conversation that has gaps of dead space. Data transmissions, on the other hand, are not as sensitive to time. DCF cannot distinguish between voice, video, and data frames. Using PCF or a combination of DCF and PCF allows for the smooth transmission of time-sensitive frames.

Fragmentation

In addition to PCF, another means of reducing collisions is **fragmentation**. This is also part of the 802.11 standard. Fragmentation involves dividing the data to be transmitted from one large frame into several smaller ones (see Figure 4-15). Sending many smaller frames instead of one large frame reduces the amount of time that the wireless medium is used and likewise reduces the probability of collisions.

If the length of a data frame to be transmitted exceeds a specific value, the MAC layer will divide or fragment that frame into several smaller frames. Each fragmented frame is given a fragment number (the first fragmented frame is 0, the next frame is 1, etc.). The frames are then transmitted to the receiving station. The receiving station receives the frame, sends back an ACK, and then is ready to receive the next fragment (a station can receive fragmented frames from up to three different senders). Upon receiving all of the fragments, the station reassembles them, based on their fragment numbers, into the original single frame.

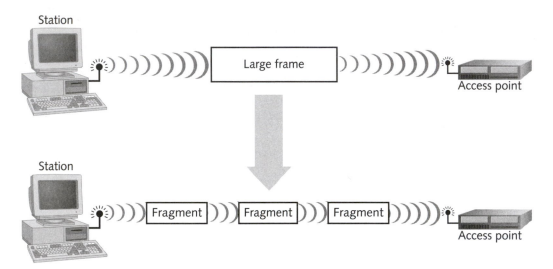

Figure 4-15   Fragmentation

The fragmentation frame size, which can be set by the WLAN administrator, is typically between 256 and 2,046 bytes.

Fragmentation can reduce the probability of collisions and may be considered an alternative to RTS/CTS. However, fragmentation does have additional overhead associated with it (it requires a separate ACK from the receiving station for each fragmented frame as well as additional SIFS time gaps). Because of the increased overhead RTS/CTS and fragmentation generate, under certain conditions these options may actually decrease the speed of the network. It is generally recommended that these options be turned on only when needed and that the network be monitored when they are functioning.

Fragmentation does not always have to be used separately from RTS/CTS. The 802.11 standard permits them to be used simultaneously.

Joining the Wireless Network

The MAC layer of the 802.11 standard also provides the functionality for a station to join a WLAN. The most important of these functions are association, authentication, and privacy.

Association

There are two different modes in which data can be sent and received in a radio-based WLAN. The Independent Basic Service Set (IBSS) mode defines wireless stations that communicate among themselves without using an access point. The Basic Service Set (BSS) mode consists of wireless stations and one access point, whereas the Extended Service Set (ESS) consists of two or more BSS wireless networks. However, no matter what mode is being used, a station must go through a process of initial communication with the other wireless stations or the access point before it can become accepted as part of the network. This process is known as **association**.

Association is accomplished by **scanning**. The station wanting to connect to the wireless network must scan the airwaves for information that it needs in order to begin the association process. There are two types of scanning. The first is called **passive scanning**. Passive scanning involves a station listening to each available channel for a set period of time (usually 10 seconds). The station listens for a beacon frame transmitted from all available access points. The beacon frame contains the necessary information for the station to begin a dialog with one access point regarding connecting to the WLAN. The information includes the time of the transmission, the frequency at which beacon frames are sent, the supported transmission rates of the network, and the access point's **Service Set Identifier (SSID)** number. The SSID is a unique identifier that has been assigned to an access point.

 SSIDs can be set by the WLAN administrator.

The second type of scanning is **active scanning**. In active scanning, the station first sends out on each available channel a special frame called a **probe** frame. The station then waits for all available access points to return an answer known as a **probe response** frame. Like the beacon frame, the probe response frame has the needed information for the station to begin a dialog with the access point.

 The primary difference between a beacon frame and a probe response frame is that a probe response frame omits the time of the transmission.

Once the station has the information from the access point by either active or passive scanning, it then begins to negotiate with one access point. The station sends to the access point an **associate request frame** that includes the station's own capabilities and supported rates. The access point will then send back an **associate response frame**, which contains a status code and station ID number for that station. At this point, the station becomes part of the network and can begin transmitting.

In an Extended Service Set (ESS) configuration with multiple access points, the station wanting to make an association may have many different access points from which to choose. The choice can be based on several criteria. Sometimes a station is configured to connect only to a specific access point. In this case, the station already contains the SSID of the access point with which it needs to connect. As it receives beacon frames or probe response frames from the different access points, the station compares their SSIDs with the SSID of the access point with which it needs to connect. The station will reject all access points until it finds a match, at which time it will then send an associate request frame to that access point. This is illustrated in Figure 4-16. If a station has not been configured to connect with a specific access point, it will connect with the access point from which it has received the strongest radio signal.

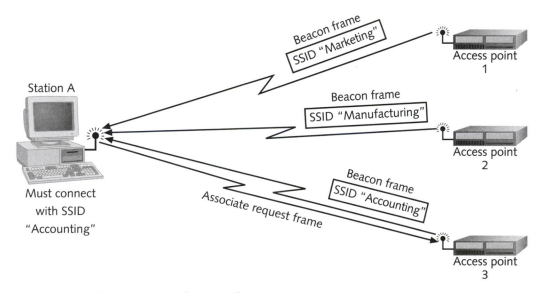

Figure 4-16   Connecting with a specific access point

Authentication

Authentication is a process that verifies that the user has permission to access the network. Authentication is critical with local area networks. It is considered even more important with WLANs due to the open nature of a wireless network. With a traditional wired LAN, an intruder must first gain access to a computer on the network in order to attempt to break into the network. However, with a wireless network, someone with a laptop computer sitting in a parked car outside a building could attempt to connect to the WLAN.

WLANs provide two means of authenticating potential users. First, each station can be given in advance the SSID of the access point or the network's **Extended Service Set ID (ESSID)**, a unique ID for the Extended Service Set. This number is transmitted to the access point when the station is negotiating with it for permission to connect to the network. Only those stations that transmit the appropriate the SSID or ESSID are allowed to connect to the network. The access point denies admission to wireless stations that do not send the correct ID.

The second method of authentication is to enter a list of approved users into a table in the access point. These users are designated by their **MAC address**. The MAC address is a unique number that is burned into the network interface card when it is manufactured. A list of approved MAC addresses can be entered into the **Access Control List** table in the access point. Only those stations on the Access Control List can be admitted. This is illustrated in Figure 4-17.

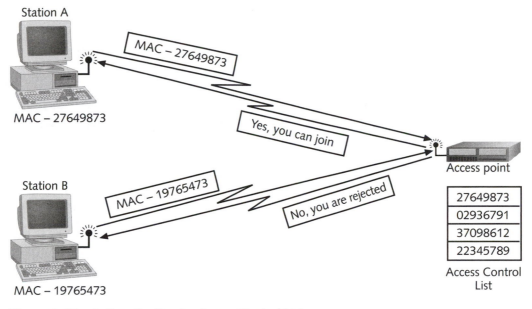

Figure 4-17   Authentication by Access Control List

A MAC address is a special number that is 48 bits long. The first 24 bits identify the company that markets the NIC, and the last 24 bits are randomly assigned.

Authentication by SSID and authentication by Access Control List are in addition to the authentication tools that are used by the particular network operating system (such as Microsoft Windows or Novell NetWare) that is running on the WLAN. These network operating systems use standard security measures such as login names and passwords. When these standard network security procedures are used with the WLAN tools, an unauthorized user will not be granted entrance to the network.

Privacy

Privacy is different from authentication. Authentication ensures that the user has permission to be part of the network. Privacy standards, on the other hand, make certain that transmissions are not intercepted and read by an unauthorized person. The 802.11 standard provides an optional **Wired Equivalent Privacy (WEP)** specification for data encryption between wireless devices to prevent eavesdropping.

Data encryption requires the use of mathematical keys to encrypt and decrypt messages. These keys have a numerical value that is used by an algorithm to scramble information and make it readable only to users who have the corresponding decryption key. Two types of keys are used in encryption. **Public key** cryptography uses matched public and private keys for encryption and decryption. One key is used to encrypt the message and a different key is used to decrypt it. The public key does not have to be kept secret; it can be openly distributed without revealing the private key. **Shared key** cryptography uses the same key to encrypt and decrypt the message. The key must be kept secret or the confidentiality will be compromised.

The strength of encryption rests not only on keeping the keys secret but also on the length of the key itself. The longer the key, the stronger the encryption because it is more difficult to break. The WEP standard specifies data encryption using a 40-bit shared key. However, it also allows proprietary privacy extensions by WLAN vendors. Several vendors, for example, offer their own 128-bit encryption mechanisms.

With today's faster and more powerful computers, it is easier to break keys and decrypt sensitive messages than it was just a few years ago. Keys that are 56 bits long have been broken in less than 22 hours.

Many experts recommend keys at least 75 bits long in order to provide adequate security.

The access point and each station can have up to four shared keys. Each key must be manually entered and must correspond to the same key position in each of the other devices. In Figure 4-18, the access point and Station 1 each have four keys defined. The access point can encrypt a message with Key-A and send it to Station 1. Because Station 1's Key-A is the same as the access point's Key-A, Station 1 can decipher the message received. However, the access point cannot send a message to Station 2 using Key-D because Station 2's Key-D is different than the access point's Key-D.

When WEP encryption is implemented, it can also be used for authentication. The access point can issue a challenge packet to any station attempting to associate with it. The station must use its key to encrypt a correct response in order to authenticate itself and gain network access. This process for authentication using WEP is shown in Figure 4-19. In Step 1, the requesting station sends an **authentication frame** to the access point. The access point then generates a message of random text and sends it back to the requesting station in Step 2. Upon receipt of the random text, the station encrypts the message with its appropriate key and then returns the encrypted message to the access point in Step 3. In Step 4, the access point decrypts the message and compares it to the original. If they are the same, then the station is accepted into the network.

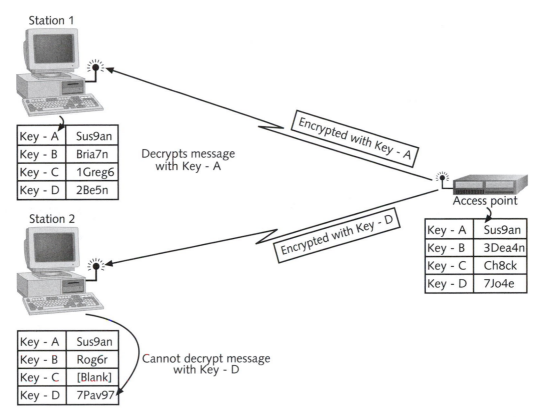

Figure 4-18   Encrypting and decrypting messages

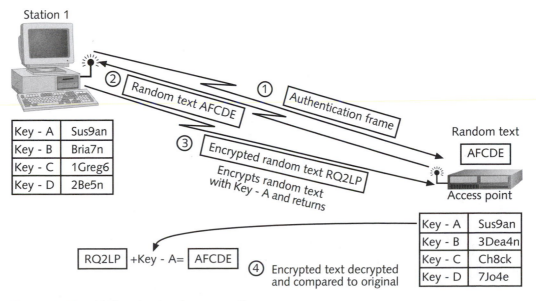

Figure 4-19   Authentication by encryption

WLAN 802.11 privacy measures, like the WLAN authentication provisions, can be used with the regular authentication tools used by a network operating system or application. Other types of encryption can enhance WEP. For example, **digital certificates**, which are issued by a trusted third party that validates the identity of a certificate holder and "signs" the certificate to attest that it hasn't been forged, are also used with WLANs. When these additional tools are used with the WLAN tools, an unauthorized user will not be able to access network data or services.

The tools for authentication and privacy can provide a secure WLAN system for users when they are properly implemented. These features are summarized in Table 4-3.

Table 4-3   Security and Privacy Summary

Function	Description	Source
Authentication	Predefined SSID or ESSID	WLAN
Authentication	Access Control List table	WLAN
Authentication	Username and passwords	Network operating system
Privacy	Shared key	WLAN
Privacy	Digital certificates	Third party

Access points can also be configured to accept encrypted data from stations with encryption enabled and accept unencrypted data from stations without encryption enabled. This allows stations that require security to use encryption without preventing others from using the network

Remaining Connected to the Wireless Network

Just as the MAC layer of the 802.11 standard provides the functionality for a station to connect to a WLAN initially, it likewise provides the features for a station to remain connected to the network, even if the station is roaming. These features include reassociation, synchronization, and power management.

Reassociation

Each station must go through a process of communicating with the other wireless stations or access points so that it can become accepted as part of the network. This process is known as association. However, once a station connects with a specific access point, it does not necessarily have to remain associated only with that access point. Rather, a station may drop the connection with one access point and establish a connection with another. This is known as **reassociation**.

There are several reasons that reassociation is necessary. A mobile station may roam beyond the coverage of one access point but into the coverage area of another access point, as seen in Figure 4-20. The mobile station must then sever its association with the original access point and reassociate itself with the new access point. Reassociation may also be necessary when the signal that a station receives from an access point becomes weak due to interference from another object that moves into the transmission path of the signal. The station would then begin the reassociation process to find an access point with a strong signal.

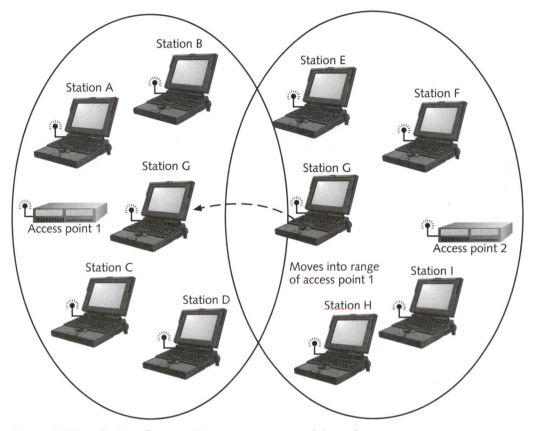

Figure 4-20   Station G roams into a new access point service area

When a station determines that the link to its current access point is poor, it begins scanning to find another access point. Alternately, a station can use information from previous scans that it performed to find a new access point. The station sends a **reassociation request frame** to the new access point. If the new access point accepts the reassociation request, it will send back a **reassociation response frame** to indicate its acceptance. The new access point will then send a **disassociation frame** to the old access point. This frame terminates the old access point's association with the station. This process is illustrated in Figure 4–21.

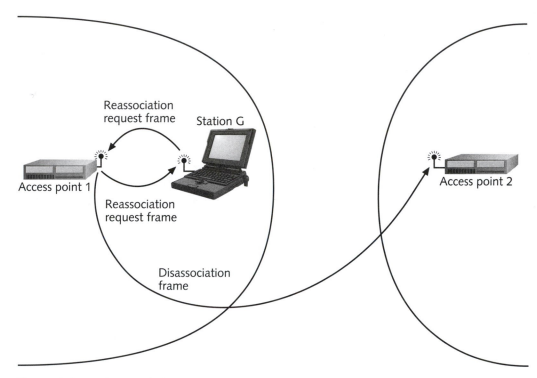

Figure 4-21   Reassociation process

    Reassociation is always initiated by the station and never by the access point.

Synchronization

The need for all stations and access points in a WLAN to be **synchronized** or "in step" with each other is critical. Stations need to be synchronized when the Point Coordination Function (PCF) option is being used to ensure that each station is queried at the right time. Synchronization is also necessary for frequency hopping spread spectrum (FHSS) to ensure that all stations "hop" at the same time as well as for direct sequence spread spectrum (DSSS) for the generation of the chipping code.

Every station maintains its own local timer. At regular intervals, the access point sends to all stations a beacon signal that contains a timestamp. When the stations receive this frame from the access point, they calibrate their local timers to be in synch with the access point.

Power Management

Most stations in a WLAN are portable laptop computers, freeing the users to roam without being tethered to the network by wires. These mobile laptop computers depend upon batteries as their primary power source. To conserve battery power, laptops go into **sleep mode** after a period of time, when the computer temporarily powers down some components (such as the hard drive and display screen). However, when that laptop is part of a WLAN, it must continue to remain "awake" in order to receive network transmissions. If a laptop is in sleep mode, it may miss important transmitted information or even lose the network connection altogether. The dilemma is how can the laptop power down into sleep mode during idle periods to preserve battery life, yet continue to be active to receive network transmissions?

4

The reason that a laptop must continue to remain awake in order to receive network transmissions is that the original IEEE 802 standard assumes that stations are always ready to receive a network message.

The solution to the dilemma is known as **power management** as defined by the 802.11 standard. Power management allows the mobile station to be off as much as possible to conserve battery life but not miss data transmissions. Power management is transparent to all protocols and applications so that it will not interfere with normal network functions.

The 802.11 power management function can be used only in infrastructure mode.

When a mobile 802.11 station goes into sleep mode, the access point is informed. The access point keeps a record of which stations are awake and which are sleeping. As the access point receives transmissions, it first checks its records to determine which station is in sleep mode. If a station is sleeping, the access point temporarily stores frames intended for that station (this storage process is called **buffering**).

At set times, the access point sends out a beacon frame to all stations. This frame contains a list, known as the **traffic indication map (TIM)**, of the stations that have buffered frames waiting at the access point. At that same set time, all stations that have been sleeping switch from sleep mode into active listening mode. This is possible because a station's local timer does not sleep. If a station learns that it has buffered frames waiting for it, that station can send a request to the access point to have those frames forwarded to it. If it has no buffered frames, the station can return to sleep mode. This is illustrated in Figure 4–22.

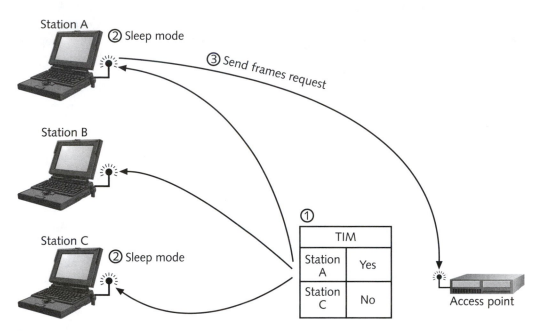

Figure 4-22   Power management

The amount of sleep time for a mobile station is generally 100 milliseconds, although the WLAN manager can change this parameter.

Power management is a means by which mobile laptops can conserve power but remain connected to the network. However, power management may make network response times slower. This is especially true if many of the stations are in sleep mode or if large files are being transmitted to a sleeping client.

MAC Frame Formats

The 802.11 standard specifies three different types of MAC frame formats. The first type is the **management frame**. Management frames are used to set up the initial communications between a station and the access point. The reassociation request frame, the reassociation response frame, and the disassociation frame are all management frames. The format of a management frame is illustrated in Figure 4–23. The Frame Control field contains information such as the current version number of the standard, whether power management is on, and whether encryption is being used. The Duration field contains the number of microseconds needed to transmit. This value will vary depending upon whether the mode being used is PCF or DCF. The Destination and Source Address fields contain the address of the sending station and the address of the receiving station. The Sequence Control field contains the sequence number for the packet and packet fragment number.

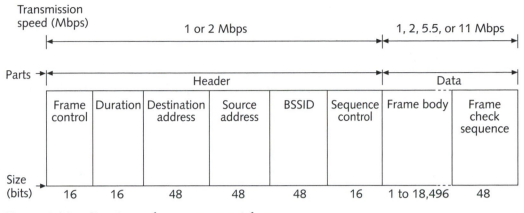

Figure 4-23   Structure of a management frame

The **control frame** is the second type of MAC frame. After the association and authentication among the stations and the access points are established, control frames assist in delivering the frames that contain the data. A typical RTS frame, which is a control frame, is illustrated in Figure 4-24.

Figure 4-24   RTS frame

The final type of MAC frame is the **data frame**, which carries the information to be transmitted to the destination station. The format of a data frame is illustrated in Figure 4-25. The fields Address 1, Address 2, Address 3, and Address 4 contain the address of the SSID, the destination address, the source address, the transmitter address, or the receiver address. Their contents vary depending upon the mode of transmission.

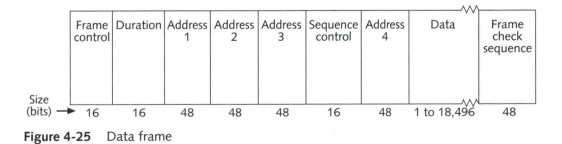

Figure 4-25   Data frame

The three different types of MAC frame formats play an important role in the transmission of data across a WLAN. These frame formats are summarized in Table 4-4.

Table 4-4   MAC Frame Formats

Frame Format	Purpose	Example
Management frame	Sets up initial communications between the station and access point	Reassociation request frame, reassociation response frame, disassociation frame
Control frame	Assists in delivering data frames	RTS frame
Data frame	Carries information to be transmitted	Data frame

IEEE 802.11 Network Layer

The IEEE 802.11 standard specifies that the features of a WLAN be confined to the PHY and MAC layers. However, at the Network layer, an enhancement is emerging that does not modify the existing standard yet extends mobility, especially to wireless users. This enhancement involves the standard protocol for sending and receiving network data, TCP/IP.

TCP/IP

In computer networking, **protocols** are rules for sending and receiving frames (packets). The modern standard protocol for local area computer networks (wired and wireless) is **Transmission Control Protocol/Internet Protocol (TCP/IP)**. TCP/IP is actually made up of several different protocols and computer programs, each performing different tasks. The IP protocol, which functions at the Network layer, is responsible for moving frames from one computer to another.

TCP/IP works on the principle that each device on the network (called a **host**) has a unique IP number. An IP number is 4 bytes (32 bits) long. Each byte is represented as a decimal number (from 0 to 255), and the four bytes are separated by periods, as in 198.146.118.20. IP numbers indicate the number of the computer network and the number of the host on that network.

IP numbers are used to locate a path to a specific host. When a frame is sent to a station on another network, a series of **routers** examine the network number and forward it toward its destination, as seen in Figure 4-26. The frame is addressed to the host with the IP number 198.146.118.20. The first three sets of numbers indicate the network (198.146.118), and the last number (20) is the host number. The first router examines the number and forwards it to the router on the 146 network. The next router sends the frame on to the 118 network router, which then directs the frame to its destination at host 20.

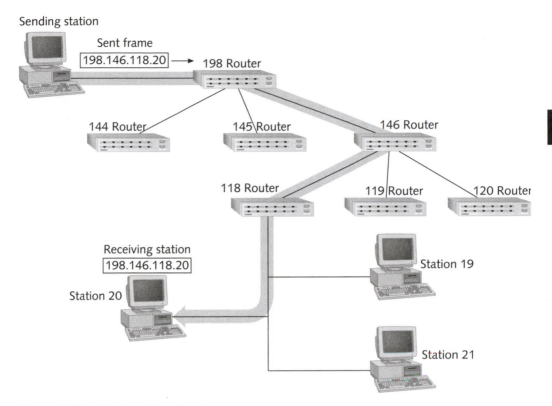

Figure 4-26   Routers directing frames

Because IP numbers are used to locate a specific host based on the network number, a mobile user cannot switch from one network to another network and use the same IP number. If a user's laptop were connected to the network as 199.106.98, the user could not move to the network 202.10.14 and use the same IP number. The user who wanted to roam would have to be given a new IP number for each network to which he or she is connected.

Mobile IP

Because standard TCP/IP cannot handle users roaming from one network to another without changing IP numbers, a new standard is being proposed. It is called **Mobile IP**. Mobile IP provides a mechanism within the TCP/IP protocol to support mobile computing. It does not replace TCP/IP but rather provides additional services.

With Mobile IP, computers are given a **home address**, which is a static IP number, on their **home network**. The computer also has a **home agent**. A home agent is a forwarding mechanism that keeps track of where the mobile computer is located.

A home agent can be a router, firewall, or gateway.

When the computer roams to another network (called the **foreign network**), a **foreign agent** provides routing services to the mobile computer, as Figure 4-27 shows. The foreign agent assigns the mobile computer a new (but temporary) IP number. This new IP number is known as the **care-of address.** The computer then registers the care-of address with its home agent, as shown in Figure 4-28.

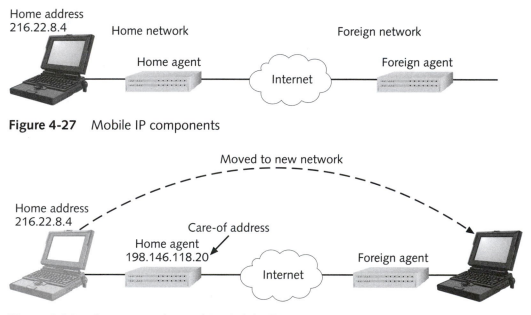

Figure 4-27   Mobile IP components

Figure 4-28   Computer relocated in Mobile IP

When a frame is sent to the computer's home address, the home agent intercepts the frame. It then **encapsulates** (or **tunnels**) that frame into a new frame with the care-of address as the destination address. It then redirects the frame to the foreign agent, which sends the frame on to the computer now located on the foreign network. This process is shown in Figure 4-29.

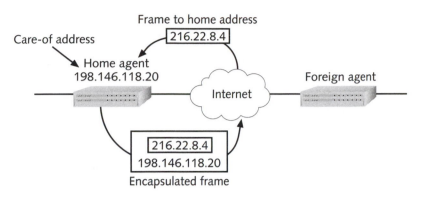

Figure 4-29   Encapsulated Mobile IP frame

 To respond to the original sender, the mobile computer uses traditional IP routing instead of tunneling back toward its home agent.

Mobile IP enables a host to be identified by a single IP number even as it moves from one network to another. This movement is seamlessly achieved without the intervention or the knowledge of either the mobile user or the sending computer. Mobile IP is the first protocol to offer such transparent mobility. Although Mobile IP is not restricted to wireless applications, it is likely to be deployed first in this arena.

CHAPTER SUMMARY

- In the multipoint topology, the medium for sending and receiving signals is shared. The different ways of sharing are called channel access methods. One type of sharing is known as contention, in which computers compete with each other to use the network when it is available. However, if two computers start sending messages at the same time, a collision results. The 802.11 standard uses an access method known as the Distributed Coordination Function (DCF). The DCF specifies the use of Carrier Sense Multiple Access with Collision Avoidance (CSMA/CA), which attempts to avoid collisions. CSMA/CA reduces collisions by using explicit packet acknowledgment (ACK) and the Request to Send/Clear to Send (RTS/CTS) protocol.

- Another type of channel access method is polling, in which each computer is asked in sequence whether it wants to transmit. The 802.11 standard provides for an optional polling function known as Point Coordination Function (PCF), in which the access point serves as the polling device. PCF is most often used in WLANs that transmit time-sensitive frames such as audio or video. In addition to PCF, another means of reducing collisions is fragmentation, which involves dividing the data to be transmitted from one large frame into several smaller ones.

❑ The process that a station must go through to become accepted as part of the network is called association. Association is accomplished by scanning. The station wanting to connect to the wireless network must scan the airwaves for information that it needs in order to begin the association process. Authentication verifies that the user has permission to access the network. The 802.11 standard provides different means of authenticating potential users. Privacy makes certain that unauthorized persons do not intercept and read transmissions. The 802.11 standard provides an optional Wired Equivalent Privacy (WEP) specification for data encryption between wireless devices to preserve privacy.

❑ A station may drop its connection with one access point and establish a connection with another access point. This is known as reassociation. The need for all stations and access points in a WLAN to be synchronized or "in step" with each other is critical.

❑ Most stations in a WLAN are portable laptop computers. Power management allows such mobile stations to be off as much as possible to conserve battery life, but not miss out on data transmissions.

❑ The 802.11 standard specifies three different types of MAC frame formats. Management frames are used to set up the initial communications between a station and the access point, control frames provide assistance in delivering the frames that contain data, and data frames carry the information to be transmitted to the destination station.

❑ The standard protocol for local area computer networks is Transmission Control Protocol/Internet Protocol (TCP/IP). Static IP addresses are used to locate a specific host based on the network number, so a mobile user cannot switch from one network to another network using the same IP address. Mobile IP provides a mechanism to support mobile computing. It does not replace TCP/IP but rather provides additional services.

KEY TERMS

Access Control List (ACL) — A list of approved MAC addresses contained in the access point.

active scanning — The process of sending frames to gather information.

associate request frame — A frame sent by a station to an access point. The frame includes such information as the station's own capabilities and supported rates.

associate response frame — A frame returned to a station from the access point. The frame contains a status code and station ID number for that station.

association — The process of communicating with the other wireless stations or the access point so that the station or access point can become accepted as part of the network.

authentication — The process that verifies that the user has permission to access the network.

authentication frame — A frame sent to an access point by a station when WEP encryption is used for authentication purposes.

backoff interval — A random amount of time that two computers wait before attempting to resend.

4

beacon frame — A frame sent from the access point to all stations.

buffering — The process that the access point uses to temporarily store frames for stations that are in sleep mode.

care-of address — A temporary IP number assigned to a mobile station using Mobile IP.

carrier sense — The process of listening before sending in order to detect other traffic.

Carrier Sense Multiple Access with Collision Avoidance (CSMA/CA) — The IEEE 802.11 standard procedure used by WLANs to avoid collisions.

Carrier Sense Multiple Access with Collision Detection (CSMA/CD) — The IEEE 802.3 Ethernet standard that specifies contention with a backoff interval if a collision results.

channel access methods — The different ways of sharing in a multipoint topology.

collision — A conflict between packets sent by two computers that send messages at the same time.

contention — One type of channel access method in which computers compete with each other for the use of the network.

control frames — MAC frames that assist in delivering the frames that contain data.

data frames — MAC frames that carry the information to be transmitted to the destination station.

digital certificates — Electronic signatures that are issued by a trusted third party that validates the identity of a certificate holder.

disassociation frame — A frame sent by the new access point to the old access point to terminate the old access point's association with a station.

Distributed Coordination Function (DCF) — The default access method for WLANs.

Distributed Coordination Function IFS (DIFS) — The standard interval between the transmission of data frames.

encapsulate — In Mobile IP, to wrap a frame into a new frame and give it a different destination address; also called *tunnel*.

Extended Service Set ID (ESSID) — A unique ID for the Extended Service Set WLAN.

foreign agent — A forwarding mechanism that provides routing services to the mobile computer using Mobile IP.

foreign network — The remote network to which a computer relocates when using Mobile IP.

fragmentation — The division of data to be transmitted from one large frame into several smaller ones.

hidden node — A station in a WLAN that cannot be detected by all other stations.

home address — A static IP number given to a computer using Mobile IP.

home agent — A forwarding mechanism that keeps track of where the mobile computer currently is located.

home network — The original network of a computer using Mobile IP.

host — A device on a TCP/IP network.

interframe spaces (IFS) — Time gaps used for special types of transmissions.

MAC address — A unique number that is burned into the network interface card when it is manufactured.

management frames — MAC frames that are used to set up the initial communications between a station and the access point.

Mobile IP — An enhancement to the TCP/IP protocol that provides a mechanism to support mobile computing.

multipoint — A computer topology in which each computer has just one connection point and shares the medium.

net allocation vector (NAV) — Temporary storage space used by a station in a WLAN.

null data frame — The response that a station sends back to the access point to indicate that the station has nothing to send.

packet acknowledgment (ACK) — A procedure for reducing collisions by requiring that the receiving station send an explicit packet back to the sending station.

passive scanning — The process of listening to each available channel for a set period of time.

Point Coordination Function (PCF) — The 802.11 optional polling function.

Point Coordination Function IFS (PIFS) — A time gap interval that stations use when polling nodes that have a specific time requirement.

point-to-point topology — A computer topology in which each device is directly connected to all other devices.

polling — A channel access in which each computer is asked in sequence whether it wants to transmit.

power management — An 802.11 standard that allows a mobile station to be turned off as much as possible to conserve battery life but still not miss data transmissions.

privacy — Standards that assure that transmissions are not read by unauthorized users.

probe — A frame sent by a station point when performing active scanning.

probe response — A frame sent by an access point when responding to a station's active scanning probe.

protocols — Rules for sending and receiving frames.

public key — Cryptography that uses matched public and private keys for encryption and decryption.

reassociation — The process of a station dropping the connection with one access point and reestablishing the connection with another.

reassociation request frame — A frame sent from a station to a new access point asking whether it can associate with the access point.

reassociation response frame — A frame sent by an access point to a station indicating that it will accept its reassociation with that access point.

Request to Send/Request to Clear (RTS/CTS) — An 802.11 option that allows a station to reserve the network for transmissions.

router — A device that examines the network and host number in a TCP/IP network and forwards it toward its destination.

RTS threshold — A size limit that specifies that only packets longer than this value are transmitted using RTS/CTS.

scanning — The process that a station uses to examine the airwaves for information that it needs in order to begin the association process.

Service Set Identifier (SSID) — A unique identifier assigned to an access point.

shared key — Cryptography that uses the same key to encrypt and decrypt a message.

short IFS (SIFS) — A time gap used for immediate response actions such as ACK.

sleep mode — A power-conserving mode used by laptop computers.

slot time — The amount of time that a station must wait after the medium is clear.

synchronize — To set all stations and access points on the same time.

topology — The physical layout of the network.

traffic indication map (TIM) — A list of the stations that have buffered frames waiting at the access point.

Transmission Control Protocol/Internet Protocol (TCP/IP) — The standard protocol for local area computer networks.

tunnel — Used by Mobile IP, to wrap a frame into a new frame and give it a different destination address; also called *encapsulate*.

virtual carrier sensing — An 802.11 option that allows a station to reserve the network for transmissions.

Wired Equivalent Privacy (WEP) — An 802.11 standard that provides an optional specification for data encryption between wireless devices to prevent eavesdropping.

4

REVIEW QUESTIONS

1. The 802.11 standard specifies that the features of a WLAN will be confined to the PHY layer and the _____ layer.

   a. Network

   b. Application

   c. MAC

   d. Physical

2. In computer networking, the word _____ refers to the physical layout of the network.

   a. topology

   b. channel access

   c. point-to-point

   d. contention

3. In the _____ topology, each computer has just one connection point and shares the medium for sending and receiving messages.

   a. point-to-point

   b. multipoint

   c. network

   d. physical

4. If two computers start sending messages at the same time, a(n) _____ results and all the messages can become scrambled.

   a. access

   b. contention

   c. collision

   d. carrier sense

5. The IEEE 802.3 Ethernet standard uses

   a. Carrier Sense Multiple Access with Collision Detection (CSMA/CD)

   b. Carrier Sense Multiple Access with Collision Avoidance (CSMA/CA)

   c. Distributed Coordination Function (DCF)

   d. Point Coordination Function (PCF)

6. The 802.11 standard does not use CSMA/CD. True or false?

7. CSMA/CD is designed to handle collisions when they occur, whereas CSMA/CA attempts to avoid collisions altogether. True or false?

8. CSMA/CA has all stations wait a random amount of time after the medium is clear. True or false?

9. The amount of time that a station must wait after the medium is clear is measured in SISFs. True or false?

10. The 802.11 standard specifies seven different interframe spaces (IFS) or time gaps. True or false?

11. The _____ is the interval that stations use when polling nodes that have a specific time requirement.

12. The Request to Send/Clear to Send (RTS/CTS) protocol requires that a station first send a(n) _____ frame to the access point.

13. Only packets that are longer than the _____ threshold are transmitted using RTS/CTS.

14. The 802.11 standard provides for an optional polling function known as _____.

15. A frame sent to all stations is known as a(n) _____ frame.

16. Tell how PCF and DCF can be used simultaneously.

17. What is fragmentation and why is it used?

18. List and describe the two types of scanning.

19. Describe how authentication functions when using an Access Control List (ACL).

20. What is the difference between public key and shared key cryptography?

4

HANDS-ON PROJECTS

1. In addition to contention and polling, there are two other channel access methods known as token-passing and demand priority. Using the Internet and other textbooks on local area networks, research these two additional channel methods. Write a one-page paper explaining how all four types of channel access methods are used, and list their advantages and disadvantages.

2. Point Coordination Function (PCF), fragmentation, packet acknowledgment (ACK), and virtual carrier sensing are all meant to improve the transmission of frames in a WLAN. However, each carries with it additional overhead costs. Create a table listing the advantages and disadvantages of each of these. Give an example of the conditions under which each of these would be used.

3. Write a one-page paper about Mobile IP. What is its current status? How does the original message become encapsulated? What are the security concerns? What problems will it create with existing firewalls?

4. Locate a laptop computer and look at its sleep mode options. What parameters can the user set? What functions can be shut down entirely and after how long? What warnings are associated with using sleep mode? Is this laptop compatible with the 802.11 power management feature?

5. Compare public key and shared key cryptography. Which is considered more secure? What are the advantages and disadvantages of each type? What export controls are in place regarding sending this technology overseas? How do these types of cryptography compare to digital certificates? Write a one-page paper on your findings.

6. Research several other ways in which a user can be authenticated. Include biomechanical authentication techniques such as retinal scan, palm scan, and fingerprinting. Write a one-page paper about what you find.

CASE PROJECT

Northridge Consulting Group

You have been contacted again by the Northridge Consulting Group (NCG) to help the company with a new client. The Hull Group, a local stock broker investment firm, has recently purchased a large building in the historic section of the downtown region for its new offices. However, because the building is covered by local ordinances regarding historic buildings, the firm cannot run network cabling in the building. The Hull Group has turned to NCG to provide the firm with information about a WLAN.

1. The primary concern of the Hull Group regards authentication. The firm has heard that someone with a laptop computer sitting in a parked car outside a building with a WLAN could attempt to connect to the WLAN over radio waves. You have been asked to make a 15-minute PowerPoint presentation to the two executive vice presidents about WLAN authentication features. Neither of these executives has a background in information technology, so the presentation should not include technical networking terms. And because the time is so brief, your PowerPoint presentation should not include more than eight slides.

2. Your previous presentation was helpful to the executive vice presidents. However, the director of Computer Data Systems is skeptical about privacy. He feels that WLANs are not secure enough to be used by a brokerage firm such as the Hull Group. NCG has asked you to prepare a two-page summary of the privacy features of a WLAN. The director of Computer Data Systems is very well versed in privacy and serves as a technical advisor to the U.S. Securities and Exchange Commission (SEC). Your paper should be very technically detailed, covering public and private key encryption, digital signatures, and other technologies that can be used in a WLAN setting.

OPTIONAL TEAM CASE PROJECT

The Hull Group also wants to give to its brokers laptop computers that they can carry with them to a conference room upstairs or to one of the private rooms downstairs when working with individual investors. Because the brokers need to access the Internet quickly from either the conference room or a private room, they need the flexibility of Mobile IP or some similar technology.

NCG needs your help. Create two teams of two or three consultants. One team should explore the TCP/IP and how it functions in a traditional nonmobile environment. The other team should look at Mobile IP. How does Mobile IP differ from TCP/IP? How is it similar? What new features in IPv6 will assist or hinder the use of Mobile IP? Which competing technologies are being proposed that compete against Mobile IP? When will Mobile IP be fully implemented? Write a paper on your findings.

5

BUILDING AND SECURING A WLAN

After reading this chapter and completing the exercises, you will be able to:

♦ List the steps for planning a network

♦ Tell how to select a WLAN

♦ Explain the options for designing the layout of a WLAN

♦ Describe security options

♦ Explain how to provide user support

It is not uncommon for workers at a business or students at a college to leave on a Friday afternoon and return Monday morning to discover that a new network has been installed. To the casual observer, it might seem that building a LAN is easy. After all, how hard could it be just to connect computers to a server?

However, the complexity of building a LAN is frequently underestimated. Although a new network may magically "appear" on Monday morning, what the casual observer doesn't see are the many months that go into planning and designing a network and the ongoing process of maintaining the network and supporting users after the installation.

Building a WLAN can be even more challenging than building a wired LAN. Obviously, cabling issues do not have to be considered with a WLAN. However, that is not always an advantage. With a wired LAN, once the cable is installed and tested, if a problem arises, most troubleshooters assume that the cabling is not the primary culprit. With a WLAN, on the other hand, the transmission medium may be the primary suspect in a faulty installation. Coupled with the overall increased complexity of wireless compared to wired networks, building a WLAN is a more complicated adventure.

This chapter covers the steps involved in building a WLAN, from planning through support.

Planning for a New Network

"If you fail to plan, then you plan to fail." This familiar quotation is especially true in planning a network. The steps for planning a WLAN are similar to those for planning a wired network:

- Assessing needs
- Determining costs
- Gathering information
- Selecting a WLAN

There are also special wireless concerns that must be considered, such as compatibility and interoperability, which wireless standards to follow, and which wireless technology to use.

Assessing Needs

"Do we really need it?" is a question that organizations often ask too late in the planning process. In reality, it should be the first question that is asked. Sometimes changing a procedure or adding personnel may solve the problem, making an investment in a new computer network unnecessary. However, determining the need can sometimes be difficult because the solution may not be just to invest in technology but to assess a combination of several different resources.

Look at the Organization as a Whole

The first step in assessing the need is to look at the organization or business as a whole. Some questions to ask include:

- What is the purpose or mission of the organization?
- Is the current mission expected to change in the future?
- What is the size of the organization?
- How much growth is anticipated in the organization?

Although these questions may seem very basic, they often reveal a great deal that can help you assess needs. For example, a business that is rapidly losing market share and has changed presidents three times in the last six months may not be in a position to invest heavily in new networking technologies. On the other hand, a business that has captured a niche in the marketplace and currently has no serious competitors may be poised for rapid growth, and a new network may become the backbone of that growth. Obtaining a firm conceptual grip on the organization as a whole and its current status will reveal whether an investment today in technology is a wise step.

Look at Current Network Uses and Requirements

The next step in assessing the need for a wireless network is to look at how the organization or business uses its current network. For example, answer these questions:

- How does the current network support the organization's mission?

- What applications run on the network?

- How many users does it support?

- What are the strengths and weaknesses of the current network?

Some organizations, such as banks or brokerage firms, require networks that have a very high degree of security. Other organizations require networks to be completely fault-tolerant and cannot afford any downtime. How the network supports the organization is an important consideration. Examining the current status of the network, especially the applications that run on the network and the number of users, can reveal much of this information.

The question regarding the strengths and weaknesses of the network can begin to identify why a new network may be needed. If the current network can be upgraded or adapted to meet the current needs, then a new network may not be necessary. However, if the current network cannot support the anticipated future growth of the business or is based on a very old technology, then investing in a new network may be the answer.

Document the Current Network

This is a good time to document the current network in detail. It is sometimes surprising to see just exactly what the current network does. Documentation of the current network may include a table that summarizes information about the network. An example of such a table is shown in Table 5-1. Depending on the complexity of the network, a diagram of the network may also be necessary, as seen in Figure 5-1.

After assessing the needs and examining the network's current status and technical documentation, then you can decide whether to upgrade the network, replace it, or add a new network to meet the needs.

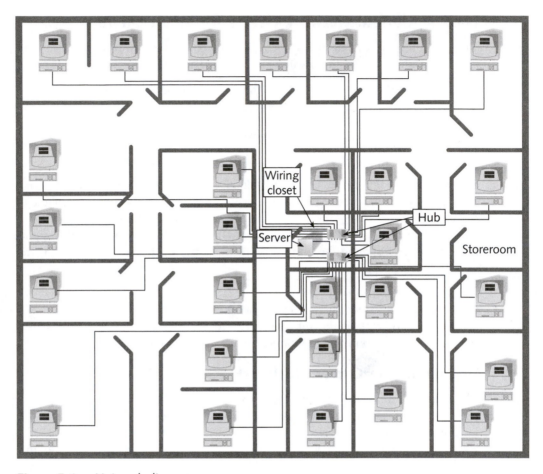

Figure 5-1   Network diagram

Table 5-1   Current Network Table

Number of clients	28
Types of clients	20 — Windows 2000 8 — Windows 98
Number of servers	1 — Windows 2000
Type of network	Ethernet 100 Mbps switched
Type of media being used	Category 5 enhanced
Types of devices connected to the network	6 laser printers; 1 scanner; hub connects to Gigabit Ethernet campus backbone

Determining Costs

"Can we afford it?" is the question that should be raised at this point of the process. It is senseless to spend hundreds of hours in planning a network if you have not assessed the costs and have not determined whether the project can be budgeted.

Hardware costs for a WLAN include purchasing access points and wireless NICs for all devices and computers. The number of access points depends on the coverage area, number of users, and types of services needed. Hardware costs may vary depending on such factors as performance requirements, coverage requirements, and bandwidth. Beyond assessing equipment costs, it is important to remember to take into account installation and maintenance expenses, as well as to include in the budget support and additional training for the technical staff.

Although a WLAN may seem expensive to purchase and install compared to a wired LAN, it is a viable alternative, and in many cases it is the only option. Many organizations pay thousands of dollars in electrical contracting and related fees to add new users as they expand wired networks or move to another location. These organizations are turning to wireless technology as a less expensive alternative to installing wiring, as well as a faster way to get the network up and running.

Gathering Information

Once it has been decided that a wireless network is the solution and it can be budgeted, the next step is to create a plan for implementing the network. Many organizations turn to outside consultants and vendors to provide information at this point. Some organizations may send out a **request for information (RFI)**. An RFI seeks to gain information about what a vendor may have to offer. RFIs are general in their scope. For example, a broad statement such as, "The vendor will install a wireless network on the second floor of the building to accommodate 45 users," may be enough to start things rolling. Vendors can then respond with information about the particular products that they sell that will meet the stated needs.

Once the RFIs have been returned, the organization examines each of them in detail. Generally a pattern will emerge from the RFIs. For example, if five vendors recommend a radio-based DSSS wireless network based on the IEEE 802.11 standard, whereas one vendor recommends its own infrared proprietary network, it becomes clearer which direction to take. However, additional work and research are still needed at this point. Basing a decision solely on information supplied by vendors may not be the wisest solution. The organization still must compare the RFI against industry standards and the requirements of the business.

SELECTING A WLAN

The process of deciding which type of WLAN to use, after examining all of the different vendors' responses to an RFI, can be challenging. There are several factors to consider.

Compatibility and Interoperability

If an existing network is in place and the WLAN is to be added to that network, the first question that is often raised focuses on the compatibility between the two systems. It is important to pick a WLAN, the thinking goes, that will be compatible with the existing network system.

Compatibility between a WLAN and an existing network should generally not be a problem. Almost all access points can connect to an Ethernet network (Figure 5-2) and some to a Token Ring network. This connection will allow the WLAN to seamlessly mesh into the existing network, as shown in Figure 5-3.

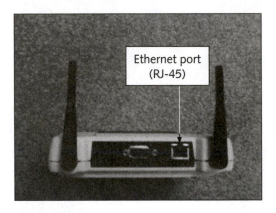

Figure 5-2   Access point interconnection

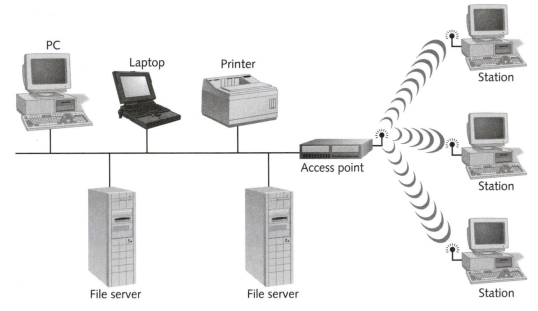

Figure 5-3   Adding a WLAN to wired network

Another fact that supports compatibility is that network operating systems recognize and support WLAN stations much like they recognize and support wired clients. Once the WLAN station is installed, the network treats it just like any other network device.

Although compatibility is not an issue between a WLAN and an existing network, the same is not always true for two WLANs. WLANs are not always interoperable, for several reasons. First, different WLAN technologies cannot interoperate. An FHSS WLAN cannot communicate with a DSSS or infrared WLAN. Second, systems using different radio frequency bands cannot communicate, even if they are both DSSS systems or both FHSS systems.

Finally, older WLAN systems from different vendors may not always interoperate, even if they are using the same technology (DSSS or FHSS) and the same frequency band. A wireless NIC from one vendor may have difficulty connecting to an access point from another vendor, because vendors may adjust their hardware or software to meet their own customization requirements and quality standards. However, the Wireless Ethernet Compatibility Alliance (WECA) now certifies WLAN vendors whose products are interoperable. The WECA seal (Wi-Fi Certification) guarantees that WLAN products from different vendors will work together out of the box. If interoperability is a concern, be sure to check that the vendors' equipment carries the WECA certification.

Proprietary versus Standard

Another issue to consider when choosing a WLAN is what standard it follows. Should a WLAN be chosen because it follows the IEEE 802.11 standard, or is a vendor's proprietary WLAN satisfactory?

There are actually very few situations today in which a proprietary WLAN should be chosen over one that follows the IEEE 802.11 standard. The only reasons for choosing a proprietary WLAN are to add stations to an existing proprietary WLAN or to implement an infrared WLAN (see the next section). Even when you want to expand an existing WLAN, purchasing more stations and access points based on a proprietary WLAN might not be the best solution. A vendor's proprietary WLAN will eventually no longer be supported and will have to be replaced. WLANs that follow the 802.11b standard are now widely supported and will likely continue to be so. Replacing a proprietary WLAN with one that follows the IEEE standard is a more forward-looking choice.

Radio-Based versus Infrared

Because the 802.11b standard is radio-based, selecting a WLAN based on that standard means choosing a radio-based network. There are several excellent advantages to radio-based WLANs. Radio waves do not have the limitations of light and heat waves, and thus make an excellent medium for data transmission. Radio waves can travel great distances and can also penetrate nonmetallic objects.

However, in some specialized instances, a proprietary infrared WLAN might be chosen (see Figure 5-4). Because infrared light does not interfere with other communications signals and is itself not affected by other signals, an infrared WLAN may be the network of choice if the stations are near sensitive scientific or medical equipment. And, because infrared signals do not penetrate walls and the signals are kept inside the room, an infrared WLAN may be suited for a network that handles sensitive data, such as in government or military applications. However, for most WLAN applications, a radio-based system is the best solution.

Signal does not leave room

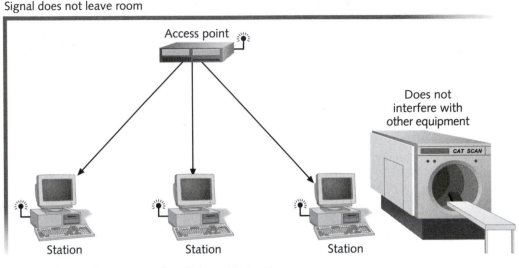

Figure 5-4   Advantages of an infrared WLAN

FHSS versus DSSS

As you learned in earlier chapters, frequency hopping spread spectrum (FHSS), instead of sending on just one frequency, uses a range of frequencies and changes frequencies during the transmission. Direct sequence spread spectrum (DSSS) uses an expanded redundant code to transmit each data bit. One of the most significant differences between DSSS and FHSS is bandwidth. FHSS transmits a short burst on one frequency that is typically only 1 MHz. DSSS transmits on a frequency that is 22 MHz. Because of this, FHSS can transmit at up to only 3 Mbps, whereas DSSS can transmit at up to 11 Mbps.

The original 802.11 wireless standard defines data rates of 1 Mbps and 2 Mbps via radio waves using either FHSS or DSSS. The enhanced 802.11b standard supports two higher speeds, 5.5 Mbps and 11 Mbps. Only WLANs using DSSS can transmit at the higher speeds. DSSS and the 802.11b standard should be chosen over FHSS and the 802.11 standard.

DSSS systems operating at 5.5 or 11 Mbps will interoperate with 1 Mbps and 2 Mbps 802.11 DSSS systems, but will not work with 1 Mbps and 2 Mbps 802.11 FHSS systems.

Requesting Vendor Proposals

The next step is for the organization to submit a **request for proposal (RFP)**. An RFP is a detailed planning document that the organization sends to vendors with precise specifications for the products and services that the organization intends to buy. RFPs are much more detailed than RFIs. An RFP may start with a statement such as, "The vendor will install a DSSS wireless network for 45 users in an area in which users are no more than 275 feet from the access point," and go on to include much more detailed information. The RFP should contain detailed information from the vendor regarding what will be installed and how much it should cost. Once the RFPs have been returned and analyzed, the organization can make a final decision.

The process for planning and selecting a WLAN is summarized in the flowchart in Figure 5-5.

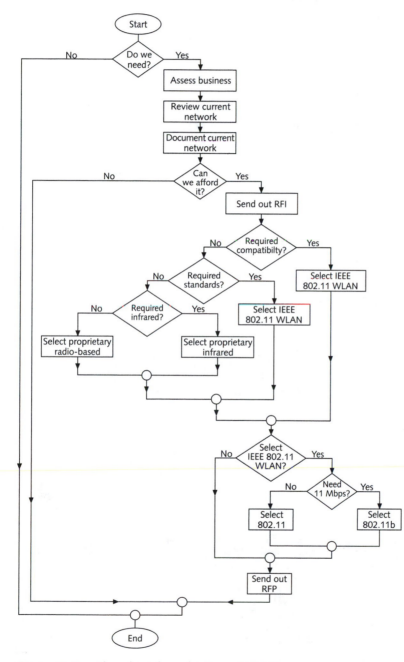

Figure 5-5   Flowchart for selecting a WLAN

DESIGNING THE WLAN LAYOUT

After deciding which type of WLAN to install, the organization must consider several issues about the layout of the stations, including the mode (topology) of the WLAN, the coverage area, the number of users, network utilization, the number and type of physical obstructions, and noise levels.

Peer-to-Peer versus Infrastructure Mode

As you learned in earlier chapters, radio-based WLANs can be set up in one of two modes: peer-to-peer or infrastructure. In peer-to-peer mode, the wireless stations communicate directly among themselves without using an access point. Peer-to-peer mode is also known as ad hoc mode or Independent Basic Service Set (IBSS). In infrastructure mode, wireless stations communicate through one or more access points. A network using just one access point is known as a Basic Service Set (BSS); two or more BSS wireless networks with multiple access points can be combined to form an Extended Service Set (ESS).

The decision regarding whether to configure the WLAN for peer-to-peer or infrastructure mode should be based upon the purpose of the network. Peer-to-peer mode (IBSS) should be used when wireless stations need to communicate only with each other. This mode is good for a wireless network that must be installed quickly where a network does not already exist, such as in a hotel room or convention center. However, IBSS wireless stations can communicate only among themselves, and there is no access to a larger network or to the Internet.

A Basic Service Set (BSS) WLAN should be used when one access point can cover the service area for the stations and users cannot roam beyond this area. However, if the service area is too large for one access point or users must roam outside of this area while still maintaining a network connection, then multiple access points should be used. Such a station thus calls for an Extended Service Set (ESS) WLAN.

Coverage Area

Determining the size of the coverage area is an important first step in designing the layout of the WLAN. The maximum distance that stations can be apart varies depending upon the setting. Table 5-2 summarizes those distances for DSSS.

Table 5-2   Coverage Areas for Various Settings

Setting	Description	Maximum Distance
Mostly closed indoor environment	Office environment with doors and walls	300 ft. (90 m.)
Semi-open indoor environment	Work space divided by shoulder-height, hollow walls	375 ft. (115 m.)
Open	Outdoors	1000 ft. (304 m.)

The differences are due to the wide range of factors that affect wireless transmissions. In a typical semi-open indoor environment, the maximum distance is about 375 feet (115 meters), whereas in a truly open environment it can be as far as 1000 feet (304 meters). This is true for both WLANs that use an access point (infrastructure mode), as shown in Figure 5-6, and those that do not (peer-to-peer mode), as shown in Figure 5-7.

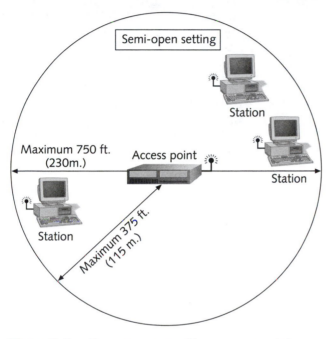

Figure 5-6 Coverage area with an access point

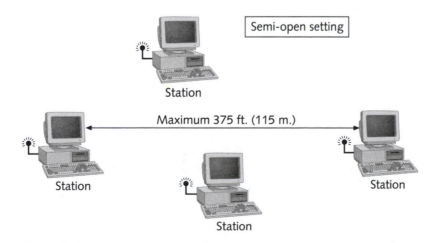

Figure 5-7 Coverage area without an access point

Several factors can reduce this distance. Physical obstructions such as walls and doors can limit the range. Table 5-3 shows examples of different building materials and their effect on radio transmissions.

Table 5-3   Materials and Their Effects on Radio Waves

Type of Material	Use in a Building	Impact on Radio Waves
Wood	Office partition	Low
Plaster	Inner walls	Low
Glass	Windows	Low
Bricks	Outer walls	Medium
Concrete	Floors and outer walls	High
Metal	Elevator shafts	Very high

Another factor that can reduce the distance of signals is interference from other devices emitting signals, as shown in Figure 5-8. Some of the most common sources of interference are microwave ovens, fax machines, and elevator motors.

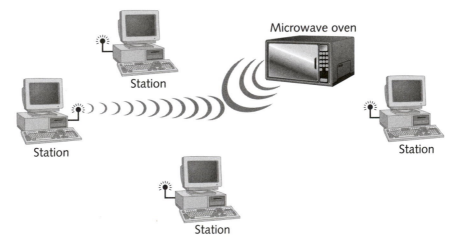

Figure 5-8   Interference reduces signal distance

When designing the layout for the stations, it is very important to note that the distance between the stations directly affects the speed of the network. Table 5-4 illustrates typical speeds in a semi-open environment, which is defined as workspace divided by shoulder-height, hollow walls.

Table 5-4 Areas of Coverage and Bandwidth

Distance between Stations (feet)	Distance between Stations (meters)	Speed (Mbps)
165	50	11
230	70	5.5
300	90	2
375	115	1

A station with an 11 Mbps wireless NIC can communicate with other clients up to a distance of 375 feet (115 meters) in a semi-open environment. However, only stations within the first 165 feet (50 meters) can communicate at 11 Mbps. Stations that are between 300 to 375 feet (90 to 115 meters) away will communicate at only 1 Mbps. This is illustrated in Figure 5-9 for a WLAN that uses an access point (infrastructure mode) and in Figure 5-10 for a network that does not (peer-to-peer mode).

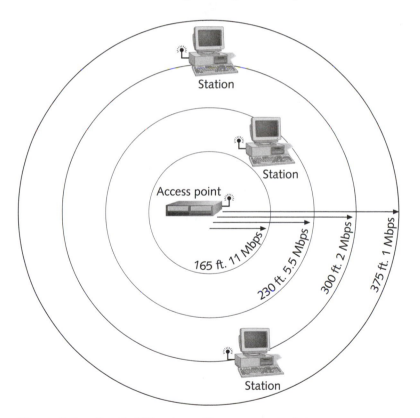

Figure 5-9 Bandwidth rates with an access point

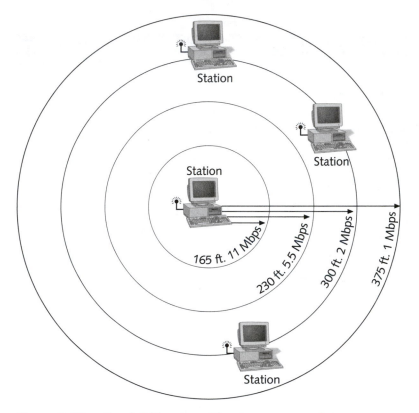

Station

Station

Station

165 ft. 11 Mbps

230 ft. 5.5 Mbps

300 ft. 2 Mbps

375 ft. 1 Mbps

Station

Figure 5-10   Bandwidth rates without an access point

This ability to adjust the data rates automatically to compensate for the changing nature of the radio signal is known as **dynamic rate shifting**. Users close to the access point or another station would connect at the full 11 Mbps rate. However, if a station roams beyond the optimal range for 11 Mbps operation or if there is interference from another source, the station will transmit at lower speeds (5.5, 2, or 1 Mbps). When the station moves closer, the connection will automatically speed up again.

When designing the layout, it is important to position stations as close as reasonably possible to either an access point (infrastructure mode) or other stations (peer-to-peer mode). Physical obstructions must also be taken into consideration.

Number of Users

Some WLAN vendors advertise that their products can support between 250 and 300 users in a single network. However, in actual practice, the number will be fewer. The main reason for this is the impact that distance has on bandwidth: stations that are farther away suffer a decrease in the speed of transmission. Although it would be ideal for all stations to have a bandwidth of 11 Mbps, it would be difficult to design the layout of a WLAN so that 300 users were all squeezed to within 165 feet (50 meters) of an access point. And, as more users are added to the network, the amount of network traffic increases, which again has a negative impact on bandwidth.

There is no "magic number" for the number of users in a WLAN. All of the various factors—such as the number of users, the area of coverage, and the necessary network bandwidth—must be weighed and then managed so that each user can use the network efficiently.

Designing Peer-to-Peer WLANs

Designing a peer-to-peer network involves three main considerations. First, the stations must be arranged so that they are all within the proper distance limits. Second, all stations must send and receive signals on the same transmission frequency. And finally, the hidden node problem must be avoided so that each station can communicate with all other stations. In Figure 5-11, Stations B, C, and D are all within Station A's range. However, Stations B and D are not within the range of one another and thus cannot send and receive messages. These two stations would have to move closer together in order to communicate.

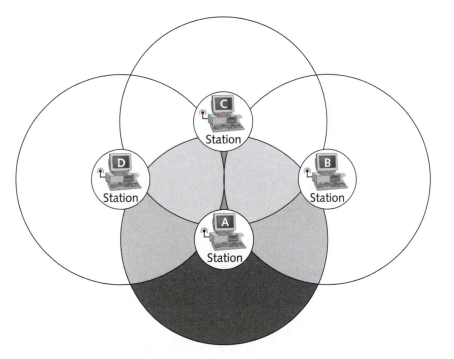

Figure 5-11   Hidden node problem

 Most wireless NICs have a factory-set default frequency. However, some vendors do not allow this setting to be changed, which could lead to interoperability issues between vendor products.

Designing Infrastructure Mode WLANs

The most important questions in the design of an infrastructure mode WLAN are how many access points are needed and where they will be located. Other design decisions for infrastructure WLANs include whether to set up access points as "cells" within the same network or as separate networks, and how to handle "handing off" users from one access point to another or from one network to another.

Access Points

The number of access points needed depends upon many different factors, including:

- Area of coverage
- Number of supported users
- Network utilization
- Physical obstructions or radio interference

As with peer-to-peer networks, stations that are farther away from an access point will have slower transmission speeds, as shown in Figure 5-12. Adding additional access points will decrease the distance between stations and the access point, which will in turn provide users with higher bandwidth. This is illustrated in Figure 5-13.

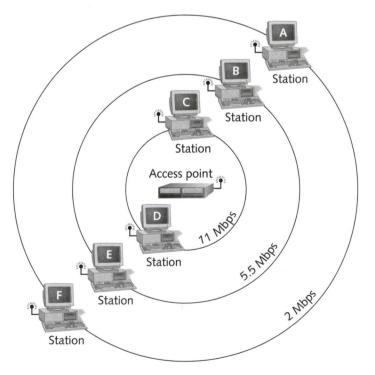

Figure 5-12   One access point

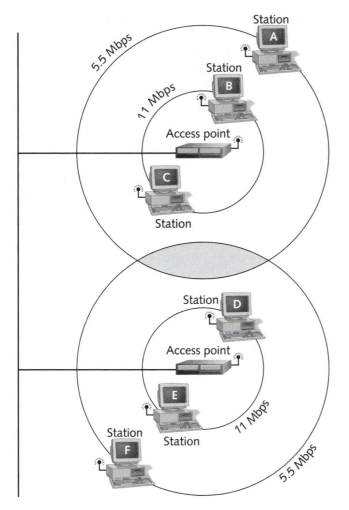

Figure 5-13   Additional access points

A second factor is the number of supported users. Although a single access point can support between 250 and 300 users, in actual practice the number should be fewer. Adding more access points will increase the throughput of the WLAN because fewer users will be contending for access.

Another factor is the network utilization. Frequently transferring large files over the WLAN would result in heavy utilization, whereas accessing e-mail would be light utilization. Heavily utilized networks will perform much better if more access points are added.

Finally, the number and type of physical obstructions and the noise levels in the radio frequencies can reduce the coverage area. Adding more access points can create broader areas of coverage.

Just as important as how many access points are used is where they will be located. A single access point should be placed as close as possible to the center of the planned coverage area. If it is necessary to install the access point in an obstructed location, an optional range extender antenna can usually be mounted to extend the coverage area. This is illustrated in Figure 5-14.

Figure 5-14   Optional range extender antenna

 A range extender antenna should also be used if the access point needs to be installed in a closed location (such as a closet) for security reasons.

 Some access points receive their electrical power over the same cable that connects the access point to the wired network. This feature eliminates the need to run a power wire to the access point that may be located on the wall or ceiling, making the installation quicker and less costly.

When selecting locations for multiple access points, it is important to remember that each coverage area must overlap another coverage area to allow roaming for the stations. The amount of overlap depends on the number of users in a coverage area and the utilization of the network. If one coverage area has more users or heavier network utilization than other coverage areas, overlap of the adjacent coverage areas may be increased by moving the access points closer together. In Figure 5-15, the access points are an equal distance from each other and overlap the same amount. However, if more users move to the area covered by access point 2, then shifting access point 3 to cover some of that additional area will spread out the load because some stations will now connect to access point 3 instead of access point 2. This is shown in Figure 5-16.

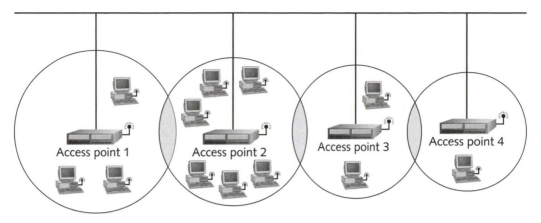

Figure 5-15   Access points with equal coverage areas

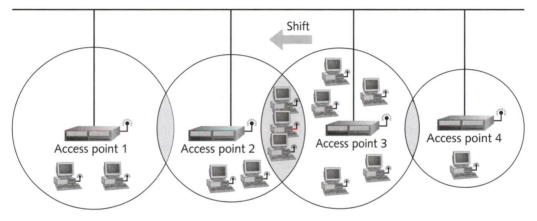

Figure 5-16   Access point 3 shifted

 It is also important to be aware of potential hidden station problems. Stations should be arranged to minimize or prevent any two clients from being within range of the access point but out of range of each other.

Most WLANs have a software utility known as a **site survey** that assists in the placement of access points. It will display such information as the signal level, the outside noise level, and the **signal-to-noise ratio (SNR)**, which indicates how much of the signal is being affected by noise. Some site survey tools use color-coded bars to indicate when the communication is poor, fair, good, or excellent (see Figure 5-17).

Using a laptop computer on which the site survey software is running, a user roams through the coverage area. A low signal level indicates that the access points may be too far apart. The solution may be to relocate or add access points. If the noise level is high, a user can walk through the area, monitoring the noise level indicator to determine the exact location of the source of interference. It may be necessary to switch off the source of the interference or relocate it.

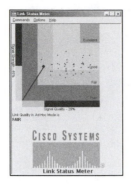

Figure 5-17   Site survey software

 Site survey tools may be used when initially installing the access points. They may also be used on a regular basis to determine whether the coverage areas change due to new obstructions or new sources of radio interference.

Separate Networks versus Cells

In an ESS network, all access points use the same frequency, which allows users to roam freely between cells, as shown in Figure 5-18. As an alternative to using these multiple cells in an ESS single network, separate networks can be created. Each access point (network) has a unique frequency, and each user is configured to use only one of the networks, as shown in Figure 5-19. The coverage areas of access points in different networks can overlap without interference as long as they use different channels.

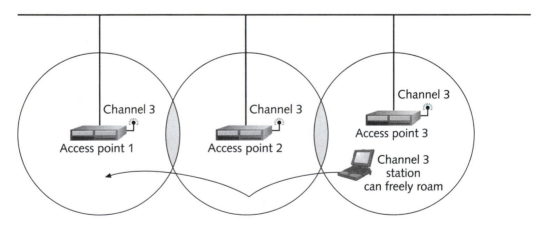

Figure 5-18   Multiple cells (access points) with the same frequency

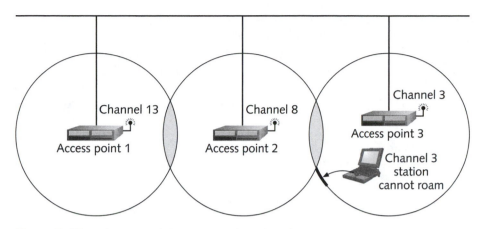

Figure 5-19 Access points as separate networks

The 802.11 standard specifies 14 frequencies that can be used for WLANs, beginning at 2.412 GHz and incrementing by .005 GHz (except for Channel 14). Most vendors assign a channel number to each frequency to make it easier to set the wireless NIC to the correct setting. For example, instead of setting a NIC to 2.412 GHz, the user would set it to channel 1.

Setting up access points as separate networks can prevent too many users from roaming to a particular coverage area and help to balance the load among the access points. It also allows a secure network and a general network to coexist. For example, on a college campus, the faculty can use a WLAN that uses encryption whereas students use another WLAN that does not use encryption.

When creating separate networks, the access points should use channels that are at least five channels apart.

Mobility

Although 802.11b defines how a station associates with an access point, it does not define how access points track users as they roam between two access points on the same network or to another network.

The IEEE committee will likely propose standards to address roaming between access points.

Many vendors have created their own protocols for handing off between access points. However, these protocols may vary in performance. If the protocol is not efficient, packets might be lost as the user roams from one access point to another.

When a user roams to another network, handing off becomes more complicated. One solution is to use the **Dynamic Host Configuration Protocol (DHCP)** across the network. DHCP "loans" IP numbers to users when they connect to the network and then takes the IP numbers back when the users log off. For mobile stations, DHCP allows users to shut down or suspend their portable laptops before crossing over to a new network, and to obtain a new IP address automatically upon resuming or turning on the laptop.

 Another solution to roaming to another network is to implement the Mobile IP protocol, as described in Chapter 4.

DETERMINING SECURITY

All too often, security issues are decided upon after the network is already in place. However, an organization should consider security while planning a WLAN. WLANs offer many security options for authentication and privacy, which are summarized in Table 5-5.

Table 5-5   Types of Security

Type of Security	Source	Method
Authentication	WLAN	Provide the station with the SSID of the access point
Authentication	WLAN	Provide the station with the ESSID of the network
Authentication	WLAN	Enter the MAC address in the ACL
Authentication	Network operating system	Set up passwords
Authentication	WEP	Authenticate by encryption
Privacy	WEP	Use shared key cryptography
Privacy	Third party	Use public key cryptography
Privacy	Third party	Use digital certificates

An organization should integrate WLAN security into its overall network security strategy. WLAN security should not be considered as an "add-on." With all of the options available for WLAN security, it should not be a difficult task to integrate security for the wireless system with that of the wired network.

 Physical security is also important for a WLAN. Because the access point may be mounted in an open area and not locked in a server closet, it is important to ensure its security by mounting it high on a wall or on a ceiling to discourage tampering.

PROVIDING SUPPORT

Planning, selecting, designing, and installing a WLAN are of little value if the users don't receive the support they need to use the new system properly and effectively. Fortunately, user support is receiving more attention today than in the past, as organizations realize its value.

Training

Training provides users as well as network support specialists the knowledge to operate and support the new WLAN effectively. Training is vital to the use of a WLAN. Users must know how to use the hardware and software, and the support staff needs to know how to manage the network and diagnose problems. Training increases the effectiveness of the new WLAN because users have less of a learning curve. This, in turn, minimizes the drop in productivity that is normally associated with the installation of a new system. Also, well-trained users will have fewer questions and require less support after they start using the new system.

5

Support

Whereas training is primarily done before the new system is turned on, support involves continuing follow-up in answering questions and assisting users. User support functions can be organized in a variety of ways, including the following:

- Establishing informal peer-to-peer support groups
- Creating formal user support groups
- Maintaining a help desk center
- Assigning support to the information technology department
- Outsourcing support to a third party

Each of these options has its strengths and weaknesses. However, establishing and staffing an internal help desk has proven to be one of the most effective means of support. A **help desk** is a central point of contact for users who need assistance using the network. The help desk manages customer problems and requests, and then provides support services to solve the problem. Here are some suggestions regarding a help desk:

- Have one telephone number for the help desk
- Plan for increased call volume after the new network is installed
- Create a method to track problems effectively
- Use surveys to determine user satisfaction
- Periodically rotate network personnel to work at the help desk
- Use information from the help desk to organize follow-up training

CHAPTER SUMMARY

❑ When an organization plans for a network, the first step is assessing the need. Generally the organization as a whole is reviewed, particularly its current status. The next step in assessing the need is to look at how the organization or business uses its current networks. This assessment will reveal the strengths and weaknesses of the network to determine whether the current network can be upgraded or adapted or whether a new network is required. This is a good time to document the current network in detail. Once the assessment of the needs is completed, along with an examination of the current status of the network, then the organization can decide whether to upgrade the network, replace it, or add a new network to meet the needs. The final step is to determine whether the organization can budget the cost of the new network. Although the cost of a WLAN may be expensive, today it is considered a viable alternative to a wired network.

❑ When selecting a WLAN, there are several different choices to be considered. If an existing network is already in place and the WLAN is to be added to that network, compatibility between a WLAN and an existing network should not be a problem. However, different types of WLANs are not always interoperable with each other. There are very few situations in which a proprietary infrared WLAN should be chosen over one that follows the IEEE 802.11 standard. DSSS and the 802.11b standard should usually be chosen over FHSS and the 802.11 standard. The higher data rates alone make DSSS the system of choice.

❑ After deciding which type of WLAN to install, the organization must consider several issues regarding the layout of the stations. Determining the size of the coverage area is an important first step. Several factors affect the distance that a wireless station can transmit. Physical obstructions such as walls and doors can limit the range, as can interference from other non-network devices. When designing the layout for the stations, it is very important to note that the distance between the stations directly impacts the speed of the network.

❑ Although some WLAN vendors advertise that their products can support 250 to 300 users in a single network, in actual practice the number will be fewer.

❑ The peer-to-peer mode should be used when wireless stations need to communicate only with each other. To arrange the layout for an infrastructure mode WLAN, there are two crucial questions to be answered: How many access points are needed, and where will they be located?

❑ As an alternative to using multiple cells in an ESS network, separate networks can be created instead.

❑ Security issues are often decided upon after the network is already in place. However, security should be considered far in advance. WLANs offer many security options for both authentication and privacy. WLAN security should be integrated into an overall network security strategy.

❒ Training provides all users as well as network support specialists the knowledge to operate and support the new WLAN system effectively. Users must know how to use the new hardware and software, and the support staff needs to know how to manage the network and diagnose problems. Whereas training is primarily done before the new system is turned on, support is the continued follow-up for answering questions and assisting users.

KEY TERMS

Dynamic Host Configuration Protocol (DHCP) — Part of the TCP/IP protocol that temporarily distributes IP numbers to stations.

dynamic rate shifting — An 802.11b standard that adjusts data rates automatically to compensate for the changing nature of the radio signal.

help desk — A central point of contact for users who need assistance.

request for information (RFI) — A document sent to a vendor to gain general information about a vendor's products or solutions to a problem.

request for proposal (RFP) — A detailed planning document sent to vendors that provides precise specifications for the products and services that the organization intends to buy.

signal-to-noise ratio (SNR) — A measurement that indicates how much of the radio signal is being affected by noise.

site survey — A software utility that assists in the placement of access points.

REVIEW QUESTIONS

1. The first question that an organization should ask when planning a new network is
   a. Do we really need it?
   b. How much does it cost?
   c. What type of WLAN do we need?
   d. None of the above

2. Each of the following are valid questions that can be asked when reviewing the organization as a whole except
   a. What is the purpose or mission of the organization?
   b. Is the current mission expected to change in the future?
   c. What type of network does the organization need?
   d. What is the size of the organization?

3. Each of the following are questions that should be asked when reviewing how the current network is used except

   a. How does the current network support the organization's mission?

   b. What applications run on the network?

   c. How many users does it support?

   d. How much did it cost?

4. A(n) _____ seeks to gain information about what a vendor may have to offer and is general in its scope.

   a. RFI

   b. CGI

   c. RPF

   d. PFI

5. A(n) _____ is a detailed planning document that is sent to vendors that has precise specifications for the products and services that the organization intends to buy.

   a. PRI

   b. RFP

   c. PFP

   d. RPP

6. Compatibility between a WLAN and an existing wired network should usually not be a problem. True or false?

7. All WLANs are always interoperable with all other WLANS. True or false?

8. There are actually very few situations in which a proprietary WLAN should be chosen over one that follows the IEEE 802.11 standard. True or false?

9. A radio-based WLAN may be the network of choice if the stations are surrounded by sensitive scientific or medical equipment or if the network is to handle sensitive data. True or false?

10. Systems based on 802.11b will interoperate with 1 Mbps and 2 Mbps 802.11 DSSS systems, but will not work with 1 Mbps and 2 Mbps 802.11 FHSS systems. True or false?

11. Plaster and wood have a(n) _____ impact on radio waves.

12. In a typical DSSS, only stations within the first 165 feet (50 meters) can communicate at _____ Mbps.

13. The ability to adjust the data rates automatically to compensate for the changing nature of the radio signal is known as _____.

14. The _____ mode is good for a wireless network that must be installed quickly where a network does not already exist, such as in a hotel room or convention center.

15. _____ mode consists of wireless stations and one access point.

16. List and explain some of the factors that influence the number of access points needed in a WLAN.

17. Explain what an organization must take into consideration when determining where an access point will be located.

18. Tell how a site survey works.

19. Explain how separate networks can be set up with multiple access points instead of cells and when separate networks would be used.

20. How can DHCP help when a user roams to another network?

5

HANDS-ON PROJECTS

1. Select a business or organization in your area. Interview the management for the purpose of creating a network plan. The first step is to look at the organization or business as a whole. Some questions to ask include:

    ❑ What is the purpose or mission of the organization?

    ❑ Is the current mission expected to change in the future?

    ❑ What is the size of the organization?

    ❑ How much growth is anticipated in the organization?

    ❑ What is its current market share?

    ❑ Who are its competitors, and how are they faring?

    Write a one-page executive summary on your findings.

2. The next step in assessing the need is to look at how the organization or business actually uses its current network. Using either the same organization as in Project 1 or a different business, document the current network. Create both a current network table and also a diagram of the network. Be sure to answer such questions as the following:

    ❑ How does the current network support the organization's mission?

    ❑ What applications run on the network?

    ❑ How many users does it support?

    ❑ What are the strengths and weaknesses of the current network?

    ❑ How many clients does the network support?

    ❑ What types of clients does the network support?

    ❑ How many servers does the network support?

    ❑ What is the topology of the network?

❑ What media are being used?

❑ How well does the network perform?

❑ What types of devices are connected to the network?

3. Using the Internet and other sources, research the Wireless Ethernet Compatibility Alliance (WECA). Who established this organization? What is its purpose? How many members does it now have? Who can join? What tests are involved with the Wi-Fi Certification? Write a one-page paper on your findings.

4. Using the Internet or other sources, research RFPs and response documents. Local vendors may be willing to share RFPs that they have received and their response documents. What type of information is generally included in an RFP document? How much detailed information does it contain? What does a typical response from a vendor to an RFP include? How long is it? How detailed? Write a report on your findings.

5. The decision to dispose of an outdated system in order to take advantage of new technology is difficult and costly, but delaying that decision can be even more costly. Talk with the network manager at a college or a business. Ask how many times he or she has faced this dilemma and what circumstances were behind it. What were the costs involved? What swayed the decision? After your interview, write a paper that gives your suggestions for tackling such a problem.

6. Make an appointment to talk with the IT director at a local hospital or medical center. In the interview, ask about the organization's current networking configuration. Ask about how the organization is looking at wireless technology, and what impact it may have on sensitive scientific or medical equipment. Conduct your own research to determine what types of equipment might be affected by interference from radio waves. Write a one-page paper on your findings.

7. Secure at least two wireless laptops. Using several colleagues, a tape measure, and the appropriate software, determine the distance and data rates for a specific building or room. Document the type of environment (close, semi-open, or open) and the type of building materials that are used in it. Then move to a different type of environment and determine the distance and data rates again. Finally, go outdoors and measure distance and data rates. What differences did you find? What types of obstacles caused the most problems? What are your recommendations? Outline your findings in a one-page paper.

8. Locate a wireless laptop computer that has the site survey software installed. Roam through the coverage area, observing the signal and noise levels. If possible, have other users roam with their laptops and observe the signal and noise levels. What recommendations do you have for improving the layout of this WLAN?

CASE PROJECT

Northridge Consulting Group

PAG, a national distribution company with a warehouse in your region, has again called Northridge Consulting Group (NCG) and wants to retain you as a network consultant to assist the company with selecting appropriate wireless technology for its warehouse floor. Management has decided that a radio-based WLAN is best for the company, but doesn't know what brand or features the company needs.

1. Write a report outlining the different types of WLAN options. Be sure to discuss the following:

   ❐ Compatibility

   ❐ Interoperability

   ❐ Proprietary versus standard WLANs

   ❐ FHSS versus DSSS

2. PAG's IT group is concerned about the layout of the stations. The company needs fixed as well as mobile stations in the warehouse, which is constructed with metal and concrete. The IT group is looking for information regarding how the layout will be designed. Create a presentation that outlines the issues involved in locating stations and what problems PAG may encounter. Be sure to discuss how the group might use site survey software.

OPTIONAL TEAM CASE PROJECT

Training and support is a major issue for PAG. Currently the company does very little training in-house, but instead sends its employees to workshops and conferences in the area. PAG does not have a formalized help desk but instead relies upon the employees calling anyone in IT they can reach.

Create a team of three to four consultants. Each consultant should select a different aspect of training and support. Research that area and develop a recommendation. Be sure to cover such areas as in-house training, Web-based training, computer-based training, outsourcing support, and creating an internal help desk. Provide cost estimates also.

6

INSTALLING THE CISCO AIRONET 340

> **After reading this chapter and completing the exercises, you will be able to:**
> ♦ Describe the features of the Cisco Aironet 340 Series WLAN
> ♦ Explain how to create a Cisco ad hoc WLAN
> ♦ List the necessary steps for setting up a Cisco infrastructure stand-alone WLAN
> ♦ Tell how to implement a Cisco infrastructure networked WLAN

Installing a WLAN for the first time can be a daunting task, even for seasoned network administrators. This may be true for several reasons. First, although from the user's perspective a WLAN functions the same as a wired LAN, from a network administrator's viewpoint a WLAN functions in a completely different way. Directed and diffused transmissions, narrowband transmissions, spread spectrum, FHSS, and DSSS are just some of the technologies that an administrator must first master. Then the administrator must deal with planning considerations such as ad-hoc mode versus infrastructure mode, reassociation, synchronization, coverage areas, and separate networks or cells. New hardware components such as wireless NICs, access points, and remote wireless bridges must be installed and properly configured. Because WLANs are much different than wired LANs to plan, install, and configure, administrators who are familiar only with wired networks may feel uneasy about installing a WLAN.

A second reason for this feeling is that WLANs have a dizzying array of options that wired LANs do not. The channel frequency, the transmission speed, and SSIDs are all options that the administrator must set as basic first steps in creating a WLAN. And that's just the beginning of the options. Any one incorrect choice can bring the network to a screeching halt. The array of choices often makes installing a WLAN seem very intimidating.

The final reason that administrators might feel a little overwhelmed when faced with installing a WLAN is that tried-and-true troubleshooting techniques that work great when identifying a problem on a wired LAN may be of little value on a WLAN. The wireless NIC is installed, the TCP/IP addresses are in place, and the access point is plugged in, and everything should be working fine—but it's not. Now what? Checking the cable for a good connection is no longer a first step. The administrator must develop an entirely new set of troubleshooting procedures, which are often learned through trial and error. Working with a new WLAN without this knowledge can be frustrating.

To overcome this apprehension, an administrator should systematically and carefully walk through the steps of a WLAN installation, mastering the basics before moving on to the more complex processes. In this chapter, you learn how to do that in setting up a WLAN for the first time.

PRODUCT OVERVIEW

Cisco Systems, a vendor of best-selling WLAN products, is by no means a newcomer to the network market. Cisco has been the dominant force behind the Internet and networking hardware since the late 1980s. The WLAN products from Cisco are based on the IEEE 802.11b standard. They also are Wi-Fi compliant, meaning they have passed certification tests approved by the Wireless Ethernet Compatibility Alliance (WECA).

The Cisco Aironet 340 Series is a comprehensive family of wireless NIC client adapters and access points that enables organizations to integrate the freedom of WLANs into their network infrastructure. The Aironet 340 hardware is designed to meet the mobility, performance, security, management, and reliability requirements needed in a WLAN. It is designed for:

- IT professionals or business executives who want mobility within the enterprise, as an addition or alternative to wired networks
- Business owners or IT directors who need flexibility for frequent LAN wiring changes, either throughout the site or in selected areas
- Any company whose site is not conducive to LAN wiring because of building or budget limitations, such as older buildings, leased space, or temporary sites

The specifications of the Cisco Aironet 340 Series are summarized in Table 6-1.

Table 6-1   Cisco Aironet 340 Series Features

Feature	Description
Data rates	1, 2, 5.5, and 11 Mbps
Range	1 Mbps: 1,800 feet (550 meters) open environment; 350 feet (106 meters) indoors 11 Mbps: 400 feet (121 meters) open environment; 100 feet (30 meters) indoors
Operating channels	11 channels (U.S., Canada)
Network standard	IEEE 802.11 at all data rates
Operating systems supported	Windows 95, 98, NT, 2000, CE, ME; NetWare Client; Linux
Wireless medium	Direct sequence spread spectrum (DSSS)
Media access protocol	Carrier Sense Multiple Access with Collision Avoidance (CSMA/CA)

6

CREATING A CISCO AD HOC WLAN

The basic mode used by radio-based WLAN stations, called the peer-to-peer or ad hoc mode, allows stations to communicate directly among themselves without using an access point. Creating an ad hoc mode network requires a minimum of two stations with wireless NICs. Setting up an ad hoc network is a good first step before creating an infrastructure network by adding an access point. The basic steps to set up an ad hoc WLAN are repeated for each station on the network:

1. Install a wireless NIC adapter.

2. Load any necessary drivers and utilities.

3. Configure the Windows operating system for the network.

4. Configure the station using the Cisco Aironet Client Utility (ACU).

Installing the Wireless NIC Adapters

The first step in setting up a WLAN is to install wireless NICs into the stations. The appropriate driver software must be then installed along with any additional utility software. The driver and utility software usually comes with the NIC or can be obtained or updated from the vendor's Web site.

Hardware and Software Requirements

To add an additional peripheral or expansion card to a computer, generally there are minimum hardware requirements that are specified for RAM size, processor speed, and so on. However, adherence to such requirements usually is not necessary with a wireless NIC. The only hardware requirement for a wireless NIC is that the computer have an appropriate slot or interface in which to install one.

Wireless NIC adapters are available in two different configurations. The first and most popular is the PC Card, as shown in Figure 6-1 next to an access point. A **PC Card** is a peripheral the size of a credit card. PC Cards are available for use as modems, sound cards, and even hard drives.

Figure 6-1   Access point and PC Card

PC Cards slip into a small adapter interface found on laptop and other portable computers. The PC Card standard defines the slide-in interface for these expansion cards. One end of the card is a dual-row, 68-pin connector. This design allows for a PC Card to be inserted only one way into the slot. There are three different categories of PC Cards: **Type I**, **Type II**, and **Type III**. Type I cards can be up to 3.3 millimeters thick and are used primarily for adding additional RAM to a laptop. Type II cards can be up to 5.5 millimeters thick and are often used by modem cards and wireless NICs. A Type III card can be up to 10.5 millimeters thick, which is large enough to accommodate a portable disk drive.

 The PC Card standard replaces the earlier standard developed by the Personal Computer Memory Card Interface Association (PCMCIA). The original cards were called PCMCIA cards.

The second type of wireless NIC is the PCI card, as shown in Figure 6-2. A PCI card fits in the PCI slot inside a standard desktop computer and has an external antenna. PCI cards are not used for laptop computers; conversely, PC Cards are not ordinarily used with desktop computers.

6

Figure 6-2   PCI WLAN card with external antenna

Any desktop computer that has a PCI slot or a laptop that has a Type II or Type III PC Card can accept a wireless NIC and become a station on a WLAN.

 An ISA (Industry Standard Architecture) card is also available for the Cisco Aironet 340.

You can also choose from a broad range of operating system software on the client station. Any of the following operating systems can support a Cisco wireless NIC:

- Windows 2000

- Windows NT (with Service Pack 4 or 5)

- Windows ME

- Windows 98 or 98SE

- Windows 95 B

- Windows CE

 The Cisco Aironet 340 also supports Linux.

Inserting the Adapter

 Static electricity can ruin the wireless NIC. Discharge any static electricity by first touching a metal part of a grounded unit before removing the client adapter from its antistatic packaging.

When inserting a wireless NIC PCI card, it is necessary first to turn off the computer and all its components and then remove the computer cover. Take out the screw from the top of the CPU back panel above an empty expansion slot. This screw holds the metal bracket on the back panel. Tilt the client adapter to allow the antenna connector and LED lights to slip through the opening in the CPU back panel. Gently press the client adapter into the empty slot until its connector is firmly seated, then reinstall the screw to the top of the CPU back panel.

The PCI wireless NIC comes with an external antenna. With the unit powered off, attach the antenna to the connector on the wireless NIC, as shown in Figure 6-3. Positioning the antenna vertically will result in the best signal reception.

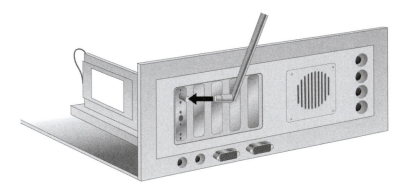

Figure 6-3   Attaching the antenna

When inserting a PC Card wireless NIC, it is important to examine the client adapter closely. One end is a dual-row, 68-pin client adapter connector. The other end contains an embedded antenna and will protrude from the laptop. Insert the adapter end into the PC Card adapter slot with the logo facing up. Apply just enough pressure to make sure that the adapter is fully seated.

 When installing a PC Card into a laptop that is running the Windows ME or Windows 98 operating system, turn the computer on before inserting the wireless NIC.

 The wireless NIC can be inserted into a Type II or Type III PC Card slot.

Do not force the client adapter into the PCI or PC Card slot. This could damage both the card and the slot. If the card does not go in easily, remove the card and try again.

Loading Drivers and Utilities

The next installation step is to load the appropriate drivers for the wireless NIC. There are variations to this, depending on the operating system. To install Cisco Aironet 340 drivers under the Windows ME or Windows 98 operating system, follow these steps:

1. Once the adapter is installed, it is automatically detected by Windows ME or Windows 98. A New Hardware Found window opens and data is collected for a driver information database. After the operating system gathers the needed information, the new hardware is ready to be configured.

2. Next, the Add New Hardware Wizard dialog box opens. At this point the new drivers for the client wireless NIC are to be installed. Click **Next** to display another dialog box asking how to locate the new driver. The best approach is to select **Search for the best driver for your device** and click **Next**.

3. The drivers for the Cisco Aironet 340 are on the installation CD-ROM. Insert it into the CD-ROM drive. Select **CD-ROM drive**, unselect all the other options, then click **Next**.

4. After the driver files are located, the message "Windows driver file search for the device: Cisco Aironet 340 Series Wireless LAN Adapter" appears. Click **Next** to copy the required files.

5. During the installation, dialog boxes may prompt you to enter a path to the required client adapter or Windows files. If the Windows files are installed on the computer, they will usually be located in the folder C:\Windows\Options\Cabs. Click **OK** to copy the required files. If the files are not on the computer, you will need to insert the Windows CD installation disk into the CD-ROM drive. If the CD-ROM drive is drive D, the path in the dialog box should be D:\WIN98. Click **OK** to copy the required files.

6. After the files are copied, the Add New Hardware Wizard window appears stating that the installation is complete. Click **Finish**. The wizard will ask, "To finish setting up your new hardware, you must restart your computer. Do you want to restart your computer now?" Remove the CD and click **Yes**.

7. After the computer restarts, Control Panel should automatically be launched. If it does not, double-click the **My Computer** icon on the desktop. In the My Computer window, double-click the **Control Panel** icon. In the Control Panel window, double-click the **Network** icon.

6

8. Select the **Cisco Systems 340 Series Wireless LAN Adapter**. Click **Properties**. On the client adapter Properties window, click the **Advanced** tab. In the Advanced window, select **Client Name**. Type your computer's unique client name in the Value dialog box. Click **OK** and close all windows to return to the desktop.

Installing Cisco Aironet 340 drivers under the Windows 2000 or Windows NT operating systems is similar to installing any new device on those systems, but the steps are slightly different from those for Windows ME/98. Use the following steps to install Aironet 340 drivers under Windows 2000 or Windows NT:

1. After inserting the wireless NIC adapter with the computer on, the Insert Disk window automatically opens. Insert the 340 series software and documentation CD for Windows 98 and Windows 2000 and click **OK**.

2. The Files Needed window may appear, indicating that the pcx500.sys file is needed. In the Copy files from dialog box, enter the letter of your CD-ROM drive (such as **D**) and click **OK**. If a Digital Signature warning message appears, click **OK** to continue.

3. In the Found New Hardware Wizard window, click **Finish**. If you are prompted to restart your computer, remove the CD and click **Yes**.

4. When the computer restarts, double-click the **My Computer** icon on the desktop. In the My Computer window, double-click the **Control Panel** icon. In the Control Panel window, double-click the **System** icon.

5. In the System Properties window, click the **Hardware** tab and then click **Device Manager**. In the Device Manager window, double-click **Network adapters**.

6. Right-click **Cisco Systems 340 Series Wireless LAN Adapter** and then click **Properties**. In the Properties window, click the **Advanced** tab.

7. In the Advanced window, select **Client Name**. Type your computer's unique client name in the Value dialog box. Click **OK** and close all windows to return to the desktop.

The Cisco 340 Series Software Installation CD-ROM also includes special utility software. There are three programs. The **Aironet Client Utility (ACU)** is a program that is used to configure the WLAN network. Another utility, **Link Status Meter (LSM)**, monitors the performance of the WLAN station. The **Client Encryption Manager (CEM)** utility program is used for setting security features. To install these utility programs, insert the CD designed for the Windows operating system running on the computer, click Start, then click Run. Type D:\utils\setup.exe, where *D* represents the CD-ROM's drive letter, then click OK. Follow the setup instructions on the screen to complete the installation. Three icons will be added to the Program menu, as shown in Figure 6-4.

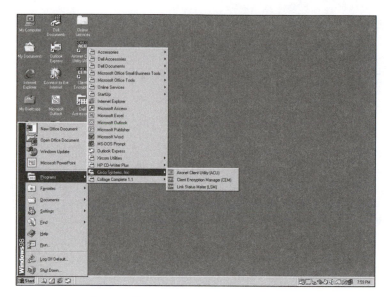

Figure 6-4   Cisco utility program icons

 The ACU, LSM, and CEM utilities are designed for the Windows family of operating system environments.

Configuring Windows for the Network

When setting up a Cisco Aironet 340 ad hoc network, you need to set several parameters in the Windows operating system as well as in the Cisco WLAN.

For Windows 2000, double-click **My Computer**, **Control Panel**, and **Network and Dial-up Connections**. Right-click **Local Area Connection** and click **Properties**.

For Windows 98 and 95, right-click **Network Neighborhood** and click **Properties** to display the Network dialog box, as shown in Figure 6-5.

Several settings are made through the Network dialog box:

- *Primary Network Login* — The Primary Network Login should be set to Client for Microsoft Networks. Click the Configuration tab to see this setting. If it displays Windows Logon, click the drop-down arrow and select Client for Microsoft Networks, as shown in Figure 6-6.

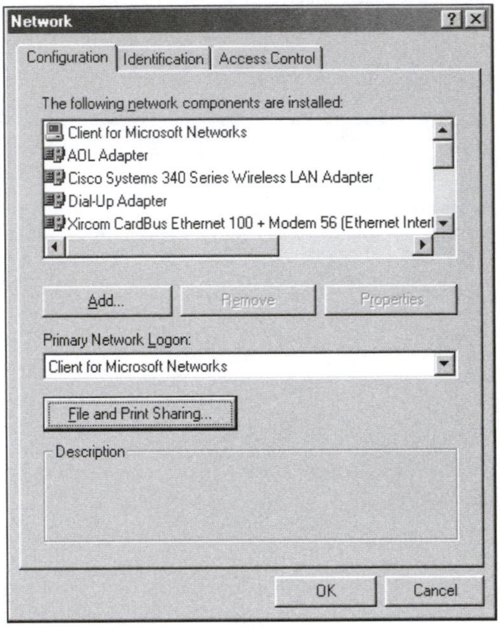

Figure 6-5 Network dialog box

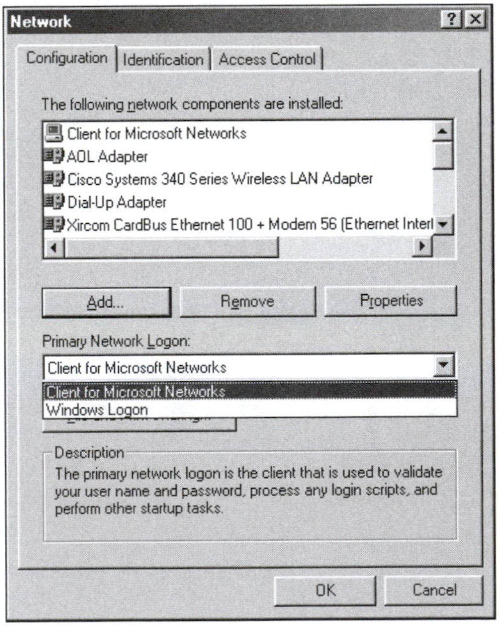

Figure 6-6 Client for Microsoft Networks

- *File and Print Sharing* — This option allows other WLAN stations to access the files or print capabilities on the laptop. Click this button to display the File and Print Sharing dialog box, as shown in Figure 6-7. Check the boxes for file sharing, print sharing, or both.

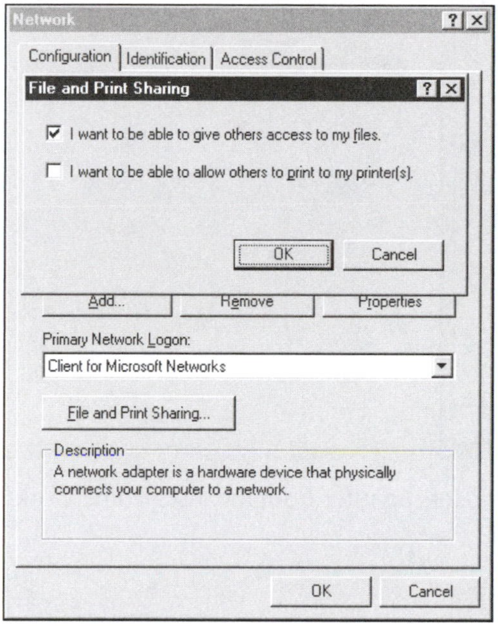

Figure 6-7   File and Print Sharing dialog box

- *Client Name* — This parameter was entered earlier, but now is a good time to check it. Click Cisco System 340 Series Wireless LAN Adapter from the list of network components installed, as shown in Figure 6-8. Then click the Properties button to display the properties of this adapter. Click the Advanced tab to view the settings. Select Client Name from the Property list to see the name of this computer, as shown in Figure 6-9.

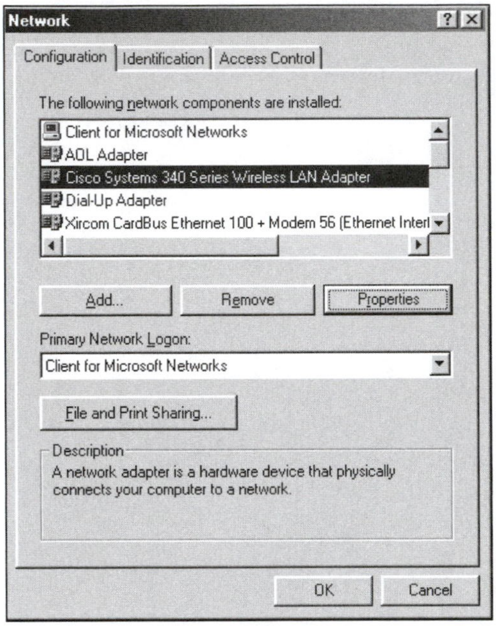

Figure 6-8   Selecting the Cisco 340 wireless adapter from the installed network components list

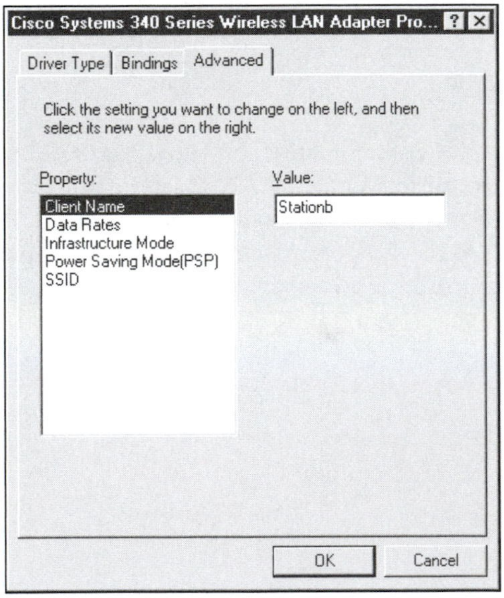

Figure 6-9   Selecting Client Name from the Property list

■ *IP Number* — The final Windows setting is the IP number of station (if one is not already assigned, either manually or by a DHCP server) on the configuration tab within the Network dialog box. Select TCP/IP -> Cisco System 340 Series Wireless LAN Adapter from the list of network components installed, click properties and then click the IP Address tab. Enter a valid IP number. Enter the subnet mask (ask your network administrator for the subnet mask). This is illustrated in Figure 6-10. Click OK.

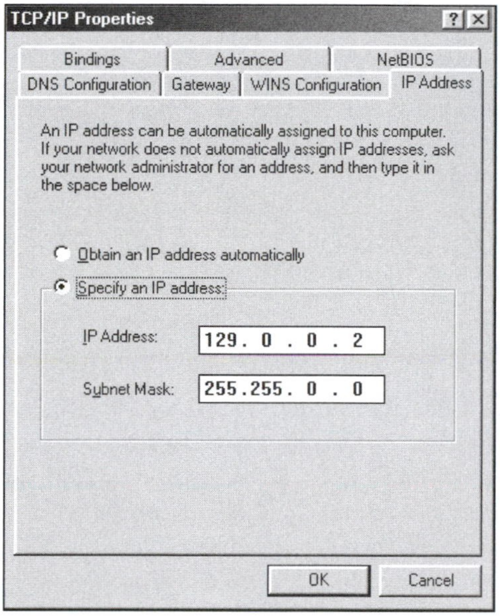

6

Figure 6-10   IP Address tab

When assigning IP numbers on an ad hoc network, it is recommended that any of these private network numbers be used: 10.*x.x.x*, 172.16.*x.x*, 172.31.*x.x*, 192.168.0.*x*, or 192.168.255.*x*, where *x* is any number between 0 and 255.

Configuring the Cisco WLAN

The next task is to set the WLAN System parameters on each station through the Cisco Aironet Client Utility (ACU). Click Start, point to Programs, point to Cisco Systems, Inc., and then click Aironet Client Utility to start the ACU program, as shown in Figure 6-11.

Version 4.11 of the ACU must be installed when configuring under Windows 2000. Check the Cisco Web site for the latest version.

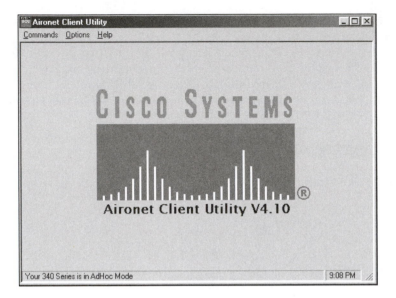

Figure 6-11   ACU

From the ACU screen, open the Commands menu and click Edit Properties. Click the System Parameters tab to display the 340 Series System Properties dialog box shown in Figure 6-12. On this tab, the client name should be the same as that entered earlier in the Network Adapter dialog box. Under Power Save Mode, the CAM (Constantly Awake Mode) radio button should be selected. Under Current Profile, Use Home Network Configuration should be selected. The Network Type option should be set to Ad Hoc.

 A **Home Network** is what Cisco calls an ad hoc network without an access point.

340 Series Properties   [×]

System Parameters | RF Network | Advanced (Infrastrucure) | Home Networking |

Client Name: | stationb |

SSID1: | |

SSID2: | |

SSID3: | |

Power Save Mode:
- ⦿ CAM (Constantly Awake Mode)
- ○ Max PSP (Max Power Savings)
- ○ Fast PSP (Power Save Mode)

Network Type:
- ○ Ad Hoc
- ⦿ Infrastructure

Current Profile
- ⦿ Use Enterprise Configuration
- ○ Use Home Network Configuration

Defaults

OK   Cancel   Help

Figure 6-12   340 Series System Parameters tab

Note

Because there is no access point to buffer transmissions, stations in an ad hoc network should not use the Max PSP or Fast PSP Power Save Mode settings.

Click the Home Networking tab to display the options for a Home Network, as shown in Figure 6-13. The Home Computer Name setting allows each station on the WLAN to have a unique name. The Home Computer Name should be the same as the Client Name set previously. Enter the value here for Home Computer Name. Home Radio Network Name is the SSID (Service Set Identifier) for the Home Network. Each device on a Home Network must use the same Home Radio Network Name. Enter the network name here and record that name; you must enter the name when setting up the other computers in the ad hoc network. The Home Encryption Key is the WEP key for the Home Network. Each device on a Home Network must use the same WEP key. Enter a value up to 10 digits and record that number, because you will need to enter the number on the other computers in the ad hoc network. The Home Data Rate setting should be set to Auto. The Home Network Type parameter specifies whether the Home Network uses a Base Station (the Home Network equivalent of an access point). Select No Base Station. Click OK when finished.

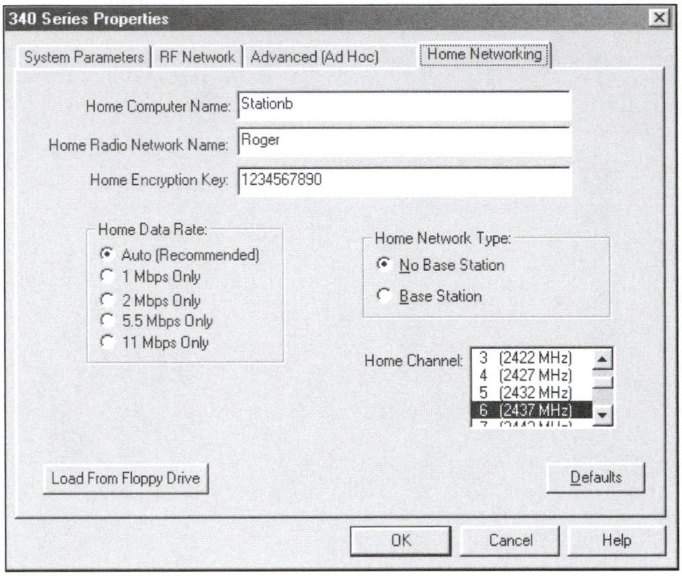

Figure 6-13 Home Networking tab

The Home Radio Network Name is case-sensitive.

In the Cisco 340 Series ad hoc mode, only one SSID and one WEP key can be used. In infrastructure mode, up to three SSIDs and four WEP keys can be set.

Completing the Ad Hoc Setup

The other stations that are to be part of the ad hoc network should also have a wireless NIC installed along with the drivers and utility software. Table 6-2 summarizes these settings.

Table 6-2 Summary of Cisco Ad Hoc WLAN Parameters

Parameter	Location	Station 1 Parameter	Station 2 Parameter
Client Name	Cisco Systems 340 Series Wireless LAN Adapter Properties	Different from other stations	Different from other stations
Primary Network Login	Cisco Systems 340 Series Wireless LAN Adapter Properties	Client for Microsoft Networks	Client for Microsoft Networks

Table 6-2   Summary of Cisco Ad Hoc WLAN Parameters (continued)

Parameter	Location	Station 1 Parameter	Station 2 Parameter
File and Print Sharing	Cisco Systems 340 Series Wireless LAN Adapter Properties	File and/or Print Sharing	File and/or Print Sharing
IP Number	TCP/IP -> Cisco System 340 Series Wireless LAN Adapter	Different from other stations	Different from other stations
Client Name	ACU — System Parameters tab	Different from other stations	Different from other stations
Power Save Mode	ACU — System Parameters tab	CAM (Constantly Awake Mode)	CAM (Constantly Awake Mode)
Current Profile	ACU — System Parameters tab	Use Home Network Configuration	Use Home Network Configuration
Network Type	ACU — System Parameters tab	Ad Hoc	Ad Hoc
Home Computer Name	ACU — Home Networking tab	Different from other stations	Different from other stations
Network Type	ACU — Home Networking tab	Ad hoc	Ad hoc
Home Radio Network Name	ACU — Home Networking tab	Same as other stations	Same as other stations
Home Encryption Key	ACU — Home Networking tab	Same as other stations	Same as other stations
Home Network Type	ACU — Home Networking tab	No Base Station	No Base Station

After configuring the settings for each station on the WLAN, you should reboot the stations. The connection is then established among all of the stations on the network. There are no obvious signs that a station is now part of the network. However, there are several ways in which to view the connection, depending on what function is to be performed:

- *Access another station* — Double-click Network Neighborhood or My Network Places to see all of the stations on the network, as illustrated in Figure 6-14. If permission was granted to share files, then double-clicking the icon of a station displays the drive and files.

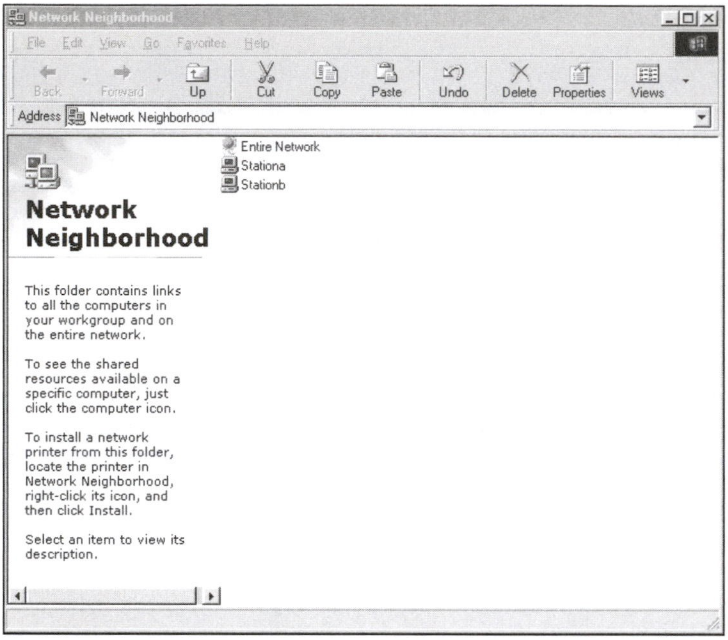

Figure 6-14   Network Neighborhood

Network Neighborhood will display the current station as well as all other stations in the WLAN.

If a station appears in Network Neighborhood but no drives or files are displayed, go to that station and double-click My Computer to display the drive that is to be shared. If the drive icon does not have a hand symbol under it, then the station is not set for sharing files. Select the drive by clicking it, then right-click to display the pop-up menu. Click Sharing to access the Sharing tab, where you can specify sharing for that drive.

- *View frame information* — To see information about the number of frames that are being sent and received, click Start, point to Programs, point to Cisco Systems, Inc., then click Aironet Client Utility to start the ACU program. Click the Commands menu and then Statistics to display the 340 Series Statistics window illustrated in Figure 6-15. The Statistics window shows the number of frames and errors that this station has sent and received.

- *Display signal strength and quality* — This software can display the relative signal strengths of the stations. Click Start, point to Programs, point to Cisco Systems, Inc., then click Link Status Meter to display the signal strength and quality status meter, as shown in Figure 6-16.

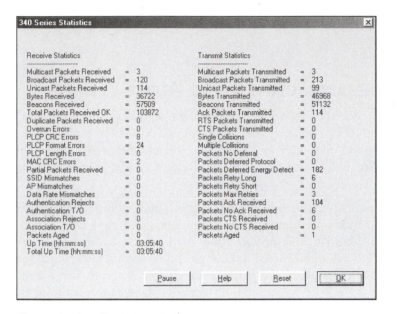

Figure 6-15   Statistics window

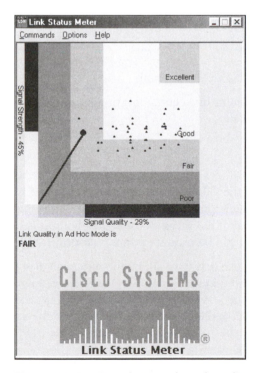

Figure 6-16   Signal strength and quality status meter

You can practice setting up and viewing an ad hoc WLAN in Hands-on Projects 2–5 near the end of the chapter.

CREATING A CISCO INFRASTRUCTURE STAND-ALONE WLAN

The second type of WLAN that can be created is the infrastructure mode, also known as the Basic Service Set (BSS). Infrastructure mode consists of wireless stations and one access point. If you need to add more users or increase the range of the network, you can create an Extended Service Set (ESS), consisting of two or more BSS wireless networks with multiple access points.

There are two types of Cisco infrastructure WLANs. The first is the infrastructure stand-alone WLAN, which uses an access point that is not connected to a wired network. Infrastructure stand-alone WLANs are sometimes used when a basic ad hoc network does not provide functions that are needed. For example, power-saving features are not available in an ad hoc network, but they are available in an infrastructure stand-alone WLAN. Infrastructure stand-alone WLANs can take advantage of these additional features.

Setting up an infrastructure stand-alone WLAN involves two steps beyond those of setting up an ad hoc WLAN. The first is to install the access point, and the second is to modify the configuration of the WLAN network.

Installing the Access Point

The following are the general steps to install an access point:

1. Temporarily position the access point in a central location among the stations.

2. Adjust the antennae.

3. Connect the power pack.

When installing the access point, it is a good idea to position the access point temporarily in a central location between the stations on the WLAN rather than to mount the access point permanently. This is because some configuration steps, such as communicating with the access point through a cable, may be difficult if the access point is already mounted. After the configuration is complete, the access point can be mounted on a pole or on the ceiling.

After you position the access point, the next step is to adjust the antennae. For maximum range, the antennae on the access point should point straight up or straight down, no matter where the access point is mounted. If the access point is on a table or desk, the antennae should be turned so they point straight up, as illustrated in Figure 6-17. If the access point will later be mounted on a wall or a pole, the antennae should be turned so they are vertical, even if the access point is on its side. Mounting the access point on the ceiling requires that the antennae point straight down.

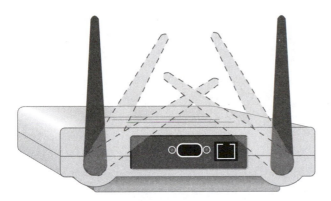

Figure 6-17 Extending the access point antennae

Once the antennae are adjusted, the final step is to connect the power pack. The power pack should be first plugged into a wall outlet or a power strip, and then the connector should be attached to the power receptacle on the back of the access point. Once the access point receives power, all three indicators on top of the access point will slowly blink amber, red, and green in sequence. During normal operation, the indicators will blink green.

Configuring the Network

The first step in configuring the network is to gather information about access point (AP) settings. To view these settings, you must connect the AP to a setup computer with a 9-pin, straight-through, male-to-female serial cable, as shown in Figure 6-18. The setup computer can be any computer, including a wireless laptop. One end of the cable is connected to the serial port on the computer and the other end to the RS-232 port on the back of the AP.

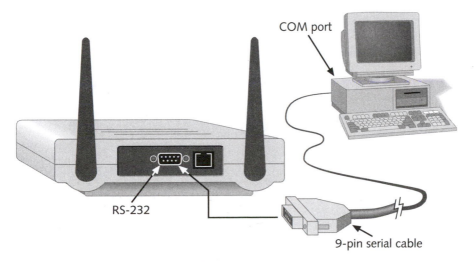

Figure 6-18 Connecting a cable to the access point

To set up an infrastructure stand-alone WLAN with a single access point, you usually can use the default settings of the access point. Once the cable is installed, a terminal-emulation program on the computer is used to communicate with the access point in order to view its settings.

> The steps for changing the default settings of the access point are covered later in this chapter.

HyperTerminal is a terminal-emulation program included with Microsoft Windows. The steps for opening HyperTerminal, connecting to the access point, and gathering information about the AP's default settings using Windows 95, Windows 98, or Windows ME are as follows:

1. Start the program by clicking **Start**, pointing to **Programs**, pointing to **Accessories**, pointing to **Communications**, and clicking **HyperTerminal**. The Connection Description dialog box appears. Enter a name for the connection, such as Access Point, and then click **OK**.

2. When the Connect To dialog box appears, use the text box drop-down arrow, if necessary, to change the Connect using setting to the communication port on the computer to which the serial cable is attached (for example, Direct to Com1). This is illustrated in Figure 6-19. Click **OK**.

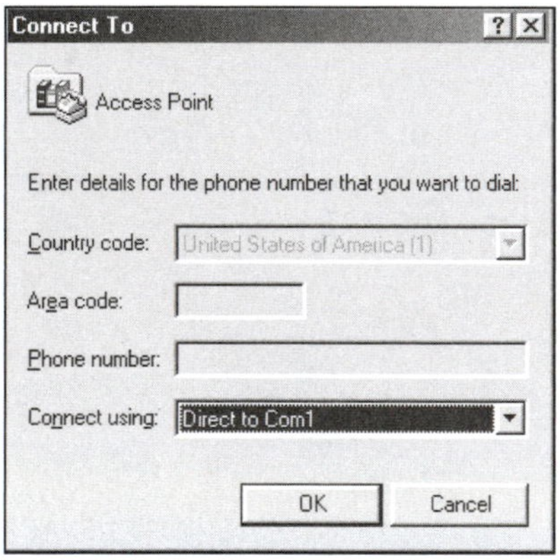

Figure 6-19   Connect To dialog box

3. The Communications Properties window appears. Configure the settings to the values shown in Table 6-3. Click **OK** after entering the settings.

4. The Express Setup screen appears in the HyperTerminal window. If text does not appear immediately, type the equals sign (=) or press **Enter**. This displays the default settings of the access point, as shown in Figure 6-20. Record the default IP address and Radio Service Set ID (SSID). Exit HyperTerminal.

Table 6-3   Communications Properties Settings

Setting	Value
Bits Per Second	9600
Data Bits	8
Parity	None
Stop Bits	1
Flow Control	Xon/Xoff

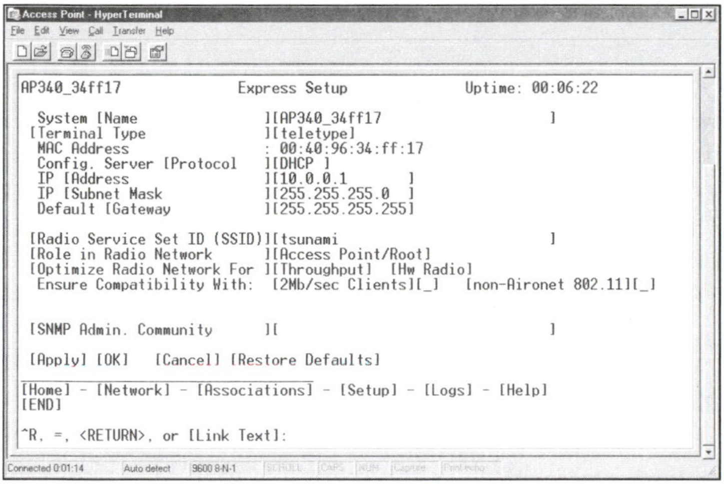

Figure 6-20   Access point default settings

After gathering the default access point information, you should configure the settings of the Cisco WLAN through the ACU. No settings need to be changed in Microsoft Windows. Table 6-4 summarizes the WLAN settings for an infrastructure stand-alone network.

Table 6-4   Summary of Stand-Alone Infrastructure Settings

Parameter	Location	Station 1 Parameter	Station 2 Parameter
Client Name	ACU — System Parameters tab	Different from other stations	Different from other stations
SSID1	ACU — System Parameters tab	Same as the access point	Same as the access point
Current Profile	ACU — System Parameters tab	Use Enterprise Configuration	Use Enterprise Configuration
Network Type	ACU — System Parameters tab	Infrastructure	Infrastructure

After you click OK in the ACU, the settings take effect; you need not reboot the station. The bottom of the ACU opening screen indicates the access point with which the station is now communicating, as shown in Figure 6-21.

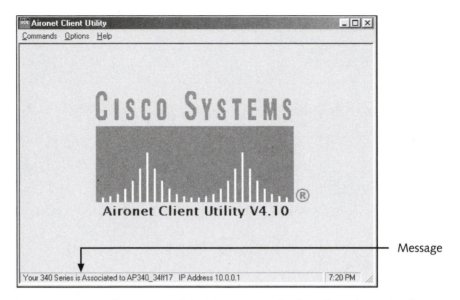

Message

Your 340 Series is Associated to AP340_34ff17   IP Address 10.0.0.1   7:20 PM

Figure 6-21   Infrastructure WLAN message displayed on the status line

You can practice setting up a Cisco infrastructure stand-alone WLAN in Hands-on Project 6 near the end of the chapter.

CREATING A CISCO INFRASTRUCTURE NETWORKED WLAN

The second type of Cisco infrastructure WLAN that you can create is an infrastructure networked WLAN. This WLAN uses an access point that is connected to a wired network. This connection allows the stations on the network to communicate among themselves as well as with clients on the wired network.

You first must install the wireless NIC adapters, drivers, and utility software. As with a stand-alone infrastructure WLAN, you should temporarily position the access point in a central location among the stations, and adjust the antennae on the stations. After the configuration is complete, the access point can be permanently mounted. In addition to requiring these steps, setting up an infrastructure networked WLAN involves configuring the access point settings and modifying the settings of the WLAN.

Configuring the Access Point

After installing the access point and adjusting the antennae, you can connect the access point to the wired LAN. Make this connection using a cable with an RJ-45 connector that inserts into the back of the access point. Connect the other end of the cable to the Ethernet network's hub. This is illustrated in Figure 6-22.

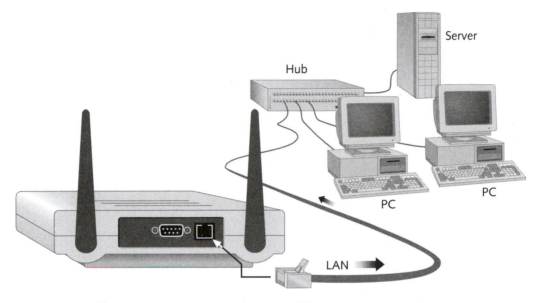

Figure 6-22   Connecting an access point to a LAN

 When connecting the access point to the wired LAN, make sure the AP is not powered up when you connect the network cable.

After installing the access point, you must adjust its settings. There are two ways to adjust the settings. The first and preferred method is to use a browser-based interface program that runs on the access point. The second technique is to use a terminal-emulation program as described earlier in the steps for creating a Cisco infrastructure stand-alone WLAN.

To use the browser-based interface, you first must identify the IP number of the access point. The way in which this is done depends on whether the network to which the access point is attached uses a DHCP server to assign IP numbers or whether these numbers are assigned manually.

Using a DHCP Server

If the network to which the access point is attached is using a DHCP server, then the server automatically assigns an IP number to the access point when it is connected to the network.

If access is available to the DHCP server, you can easily identify the IP number assigned to the access point.

However, if access is not available to the DHCP server, you can use a terminal-emulation program to identify the IP number on the access point. This is the same process as described for creating a Cisco infrastructure stand-alone WLAN. Attach a 9-pin, straight-through, male-to-female serial cable to the serial port on the computer and the other end to the RS-232 port on the back of the access point. Once the cable is installed, follow the steps in the "Configuring the Network" section earlier in the chapter to open HyperTerminal, connect to the access point, access the Communications Properties window, and configure the settings to those shown earlier in Table 6-3: Bits Per Second (9600), Data Bits (8), Parity (None), Stop Bits (1), and Flow Control (Xon/Xoff). Click OK after the settings are entered to display the Express Setup screen. If text does not appear immediately, type the equals sign (=) or press Enter to display the settings of the access point. Record the IP number and exit the program.

Manually Assigning an IP Number

If the network to which the access point is attached does not use a DHCP server, it is necessary to assign an IP number to the access point manually. To do so, you use the Address Resolution Protocol (ARP) and the Reverse Address Resolution Protocol (RARP). Both of these are part of the TCP/IP protocol.

The **Address Resolution Protocol (ARP)** associates a MAC address with an IP number. When a user needs to access an FTP server by using a command like *ftp ftpserver1*, the request first goes to a **Domain Name System (DNS)** server. This server contains a table that has the IP number of ftpserver1. The DNS server "resolves" this request by returning to the sender the IP number of ftpserver1. The sender can then send out frames to ftpserver1 that contain the correct IP number.

However, on an Ethernet network, the sender needs to know the MAC address of the recipient, not the IP number. When the IP number is known but the MAC address is needed, the ARP protocol steps in. ARP sends to all hosts on the network a message that says, "If this is your IP address, send back to me your MAC address." The host with that particular IP number then sends back a frame containing its MAC address. The sender can then send out frames to ftpserver1 that contain the correct MAC address. The ARP on the sender's computer then also stores that information for future use.

The **Reverse Address Resolution Protocol (RARP)** performs the opposite task. If a device knows its own MAC address but does not know its IP number, it sends to all hosts a broadcast frame that says, "This is my MAC address; if you know my IP number, send it back to me."

The Cisco Aironet 340 Series uses ARP and RARP to assign an IP number to an access point. The user creates an ARP entry on a client that is on the same network segment as the access point. This ARP command associates an IP number (such as 198.146.118.70) with the access point's MAC address (such as 00409634ff17). The access point then automatically queries the clients on the network with an RARP command asking for the IP number that corresponds with its MAC address. Upon receiving a response, the access point then stores and begins using that IP number. This is illustrated in Figure 6-23.

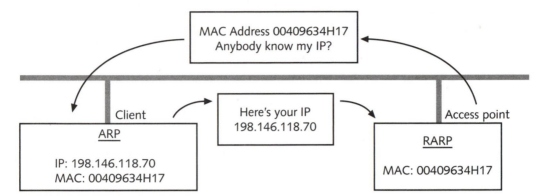

Figure 6-23   Access point receiving an IP number

To assign an IP number follow these steps:

1. Identify the MAC address of the access point. The MAC address is found on the label on the bottom of the access point. An example of a MAC address is 00409634ff17.

2. To make the association, open a Command Prompt window (click **Start**, point to **Programs**, then click **MS-DOS Prompt** in Windows 98/ME) on a computer that is on the same network subnet as the access point.

3. Enter the ARP command in the following format:

   arp –s *IP_number_for_access_point access_point_MAC_address*

   Then press **Enter**. For example, if the IP number that is to be assigned to the access point is 198.146.118.70 and its MAC address is 00409634ff17, then the ARP command would be as follows:

   arp –s 198.146.118.70   00-40-96-34-ff-17

Although a MAC address is often written with colons separating the numbers and letters (such as 00:40:96:34:ff:17), ARP requires that a dash be used instead (00-40-96-34-ff-17).

4. To verify that the ARP command was successful, enter the command **arp –a** to see a table of all associations.

The client computer and the access point must be on the same network segment in order for ARP to work. If the IP address of the client is 198.146.118.60, then the IP number assigned to the access point via ARP must be 198.146.118.*xx*.

If you cannot assign the IP address by using ARP, then another technique for configuring the access point is to use a terminal–emulation program such as HyperTerminal. To set the IP address and default gateway with HyperTerminal, follow these steps:

1. Attach the cable and run the HyperTerminal program to make the connection as described earlier in the chapter. The Express Setup screen appears in the HyperTerminal window. If the text does not appear immediately, type the equals sign (=) or press **Enter**.

2. Type **ad** (for address) and press **Enter**. Then type the IP number to assign to the access point and press **Enter**.

3. Next, type **g** (for gateway) and press **Enter**. Type the default gateway address and press **Enter**. (Default gateways are discussed in the "Assigning the Access Point Settings" section.)

4. Type **ap** (for apply) and press **Enter**.

5. Exit the terminal emulator program.

Testing the Connection

To test the connection, you can use the **ping** command. Ping sends a series of packets to an IP number and then listens for a response. To use ping, open a Command Prompt window and enter the ping command in the following format:

ping *access_point_IP_number*

If the connection is satisfactory, a message will return indicating that the ping frame was received. If the connection cannot be made, the message "Destination host unavailable" will appear.

Changing the Access Point Settings

To change the settings on the access point, you can use a browser-based interface program that runs on the access point. This is the preferred method. On the client, open an Internet browser such as Microsoft Internet Explorer or Netscape Navigator. Point to the access point by entering its IP number on the browser's address line (such as *http://129.0.0.2*) and press Enter. The Cisco Access Point's Summary Status page appears, as shown in Figure 6-24. From here you can change settings for the access point.

Cisco documentation also calls the Summary Status page the Express Setup page.

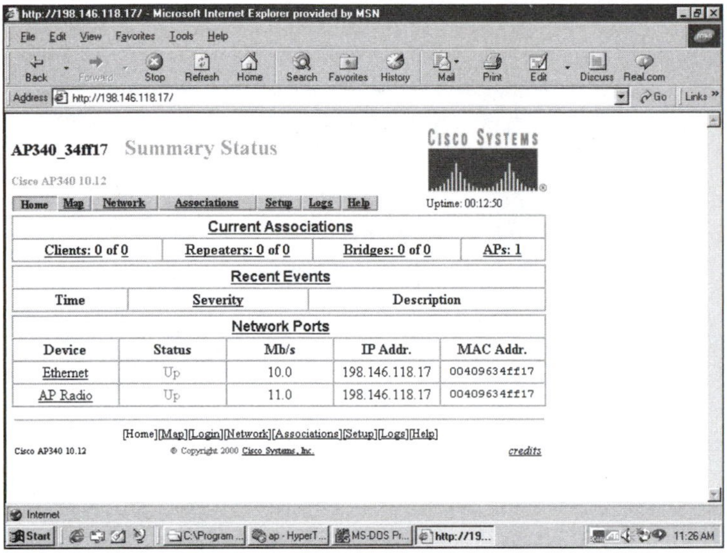

Figure 6-24   Summary Status page

One setting that you should configure is the Default Gateway parameter. The **gateway** is a computer or router that forwards network communications from one network to another. If you specify the IP number of the default gateway, a server can communicate with stations on another network. The IP number of the default gateway is for the subnet on which the access point will reside. To view the default gateway, click the Setup button to display the Setup page. Under the Services heading, click Routing.

Setting Up an Infrastructure Network WLAN

The WLAN settings for an infrastructure networked WLAN are the same as for those of an infrastructure stand-alone WLAN. These parameters, which are set by the ACU program, are summarized in Table 6-5.

Table 6-5   Summary of Network Infrastructure WLAN Settings

Parameter	Location	Station 1 Parameter	Station 2 Parameter
Client Name	ACU — System Parameters tab	Different from other stations	Different from other stations
SSID1	ACU — System Parameters tab	Same as the access point	Same as the access point
Current Profile	ACU — System Parameters tab	Use Enterprise Configuration	Use Enterprise Configuration
Network Type	ACU — System Parameters tab	Infrastructure	Infrastructure

You can practice setting up a Cisco infrastructure networked WLAN in Hands-on Project 7 near the end of the chapter.

CHAPTER SUMMARY

❐ The Cisco Aironet 340 Series is a comprehensive family of wireless NIC client adapters and access points. The Aironet 340 hardware is designed to meet the mobility, performance, security, management, and reliability requirements of enterprise-wide infrastructures. The WLAN products from Cisco are based on the IEEE 802.11b standard and are Wi-Fi compliant, having passed certification tests approved by the Wireless Ethernet Compatibility Alliance (WECA).

❐ When creating a Cisco ad hoc WLAN, the first step is to install the wireless NIC into the station. Wireless NIC adapters are available in two different configurations. The first and most popular is a PC Card, which is a peripheral the size of a credit card. The second type of wireless NIC is the PCI card. A PCI card fits into the PCI slot of a standard desktop computer and has an external antenna. The next installation step is to load the appropriate drivers for the wireless NIC. The operating system must also be configured for the WLAN. Special utility software is included on the Cisco 340 Series Software Installation CD-ROM: The Aironet Client Utility (ACU) configures the WLAN network; the Link Status Meter (LSM) assists in the placement of access points; and the Client Encryption Manager (CEM) utility program is used for setting security features.

❐ Infrastructure stand-alone WLANs use an access point, but that access point is not connected to a wired network. Setting up an infrastructure stand-alone WLAN involves two steps beyond those taken to set up an ad hoc WLAN. The first is to install the access point. The second is to modify the configurations of the WLAN network. When setting up a single access point, you usually can use the default settings of the access point. A 9-pin, straight-through, male-to-female serial cable is needed to view those settings of the access point. Once the default access point information is gathered, the settings of the Cisco WLAN need to be set through the ACU. No settings need to be changed in Microsoft Windows.

❐ Infrastructure networked WLANs use an access point that is connected to a wired network. Setting up an infrastructure networked WLAN involves both configuring the access point settings and modifying the settings of the WLAN. There are two different ways to adjust the access point settings. The first is by using a browser-based interface program that runs on the access point. To use the browser-based interface, you must first identify the IP number of the access point. The way in which this is done depends on whether the network to which the access point is attached uses a DHCP server to assign IP numbers or whether these numbers are assigned manually. The second technique is by using a terminal-emulation program. The WLAN settings for an infrastructure networked WLAN are the same as for those of an infrastructure stand-alone WLAN.

KEY TERMS

Address Resolution Protocol (ARP) — Part of the TCP/IP protocol that associates a MAC address with an IP number.

Aironet Client Utility (ACU) — A Cisco utility program that is used to configure the WLAN network and perform user-level diagnostics on the wireless NIC.

Client Encryption Manager (CEM) — A Cisco utility program that is used for setting security features.

Domain Name System (DNS) — Part of the TCP/IP protocol suite that associates an IP number with the name of a host.

gateway — A computer or router that forwards network communications from one network to another.

Home Network — Cisco's term for an ad hoc network without an access point.

Link Status Meter (LSM) — Cisco's site survey software that assists in the placement of access points.

PC Card — A peripheral the size of a credit card that is available for use as a modem, sound card, or hard drive.

ping — A program that sends a series of packets to an IP number and then listens for a response.

Reverse Address Resolution Protocol (RARP) — Part of the TCP/IP protocol that associates an IP number with a MAC address.

Type I — A category of PC Card that is a maximum of 3.3 millimeters thick and is used primarily for adding additional RAM to a laptop.

Type II — A category of PC Card that can be up to 5.5 millimeters thick and is often used by modem cards and wireless NICs.

Type III — A category of PC Card that can be up to 10.5 millimeters thick and is often used to accommodate a portable disk drive.

REVIEW QUESTIONS

1. The Cisco Aironet 340 Series WLAN supports each of the following operating systems *except* _____.

   a. Windows 95

   b. Windows 98

   c. Windows CE

   d. Apple Macintosh

2. A(n) _____ is a peripheral the size of a credit card.

   a. PC Card

   b. PCMPCA

   c. NIC CPA

   d. WLAN PC

3. _____ cards can be up to 5.5 millimeters thick and are often used by modem cards and wireless NICs.

   a. Type I

   b. Type II

   c. Type III

   d. Type IV

4. A(n) _____ wireless NIC card fits inside a standard desktop computer and has an external antenna.

   a. AMD

   b. SIA

   c. PCI

   d. Type III

5. Any laptop that has a(n) _____ can accept a wireless NIC and become a station on a WLAN.

   a. PCCI

   b. Type II PC Card

   c. Type IV PCMCIA Card

   d. SCSI

6. When inserting a wireless NIC PCI card, it is necessary first to turn off the computer and all its components. True or false?

7. The PCI wireless NIC comes with an external antenna. True or false?

8. When installing a PC Card into a laptop that is running the Windows ME or Windows 98 operating system, turn the computer on before inserting the wireless NIC. True or false?

9. The wireless NIC can be inserted into a Type II or Type III PC Card slot. True or false?

10. The drivers for the Cisco Aironet 340 come with Microsoft Windows NT and 98. True or false?

11. If the Windows files are installed on the computer, they will usually be located in the folder _____.

12. The _____ is a program that is used to configure the WLAN network and perform user-level diagnostics on the wireless NIC.

13. The _____ option will allow other WLAN stations to access the files or print capabilities on a station.

14. A(n) _____ is what Cisco calls an ad hoc network without an access point.

15. Because there is no _____ to buffer transmissions, stations in an ad hoc network should not go into a power save mode.

16. Explain how the SSID and WEP keys are configured for a Cisco ad hoc network.

17. Explain how the antennas on an access point should be positioned.

18. Explain the ways to adjust the settings on a Cisco access point.

19. Tell how to associate an IP number with the access point MAC address manually using ARP.

20. Explain what ping does and how it is used when associating an IP number with an access point.

HANDS-ON PROJECTS

1. Research Cisco Systems and its Aironet 340 Series of WLAN products. How did Cisco start? What are the greatest strengths of its product line? How was the Aironet 340 Series developed? How is it now being used? What do the reviewers say about it? Write a two-page paper on your findings.

2. Install wireless NICs and the driver software in two laptop computers. When installing a PC Card into a laptop that is running the Windows ME or Windows 98 operating system, turn the computer on before inserting the wireless NIC. When installing using Windows NT or 2000, insert the card while the computer is running. Carefully follow the steps to install the driver software for the wireless NICs. Also, install the ACU, LSM, and CEM utilities on each laptop.

3. For each of the two laptop computers from Project 2, set the Windows parameters for a Cisco Aironet 340 ad hoc network.

   a. Right-click **Network Neighborhood** and click **Properties** to display the Network dialog box. Configure the following settings:

      ❑ *Primary Network Login* — The Primary Network Login should be set to Client for Microsoft Networks. Click the **Configuration** tab to see this setting. If it displays Windows Logon, click on the drop-down arrow and change the setting to **Client for Microsoft Networks**.

      ❑ *File and Print Sharing* — Click the **File and Print Sharing** button to display the File and Print Sharing dialog box. On both laptops, select the box **I want to be able to give others access to my files**.

      ❑ *Client Name* — Click **Cisco System 340 Series Wireless LAN Adapter** from the list of network components installed and then click the **Properties** button. Click the **Display** tab and select the **Client Name** in the left pane to see the name of this computer. Is a name assigned? If a name is not already given, then enter a unique name for this laptop.

      ❑ *IP Number* — Click **TCP/IP -> Cisco System 340 Series Wireless LAN Adapter** from the list of network components installed, and then click **Properties**, then click the **IP Address** tab. Is there an IP number assigned? If an IP number is not already assigned, enter a valid IP number and subnet mask (you may want to check with the network administrator).

   b. Reboot the systems.

6

4. For each laptop, set the ACU parameters for a Cisco Aironet 340 ad hoc network:

   a. Click **Start**, point to **Programs**, point to **Cisco Systems, Inc.**, and then click **Aironet Client Utility** to start the ACU program.

   b. Click the **Commands** menu and then **Edit Properties**. Click the **System Parameters** tab to display the 340 Series Parameters dialog box.

   c. Enter a client name that is the same as that which was entered in the Network Adapter dialog box earlier.

   d. In the Power Save Mode panel, select the **CAM (Constantly Awake Mode)** radio button.

   e. Under Current Profile, **Use Home Network Configuration** should be selected. In the Network Type panel, select **Ad Hoc**.

   f. Click the **Home Networking** tab to display the options for a Home Network. The Home Computer Name setting provides a client name for the Home Networking configuration. Each computer on a Home Network must have a unique name. Enter your last name as the unique Home Computer Name (if two users have the same last name, then add a first initial to the name).

   g. Each device on a Home Network must use the same Radio Network Name. In the Home Radio Network fields for both computers in the ad hoc network, enter the network name **WIRELESS6**.

   h. The Home Encryption Key is the WEP key for the Home Network, and each device on a Home Network must use the same WEP key. In the Home Encryption Key field for both computers in the ad hoc network, enter the value **1234567890**.

   i. The Home Network Type parameter specifies whether the Home Network uses a Base Station. Select **No Base Station**. Click **OK** when finished and reboot the system.

5. View the ad hoc connections that you have now established.

   a. Double-click **Network Neighborhood** (for Windows 2000 double-click **My Network Places**) to see all of the stations on the network. Double-click the icon of the other station and display the drives and files. Copy a small file between the two computers.

   b. Click **Start**, **Programs**, **Cisco Systems, Inc.**, then **Aironet Client Utility** to start the ACU program. Click the **Commands** menu and then **Statistics** to display the 340 Series Statistics window. The Statistics window shows the number of frames and errors that this station has sent and received. What observations do you have about the transmissions?

   c. Click **Start**, point to **Programs**, point to **Cisco Systems, Inc.** and then click **Link Status Meter** to display the signal strengths on both laptops. While one station remains fixed, roam with the other station. At what point does the transmission begin to dip into the fair and then poor range? What are the reasons for this? Write a short paper on your observations.

6. Create a Cisco infrastructure stand-alone WLAN.

   a. Position the access point and adjust the antennas. Why did you select the location where you placed it?

   b. Connect one end of a 9-pin, straight-through, male-to-female serial cable: the cable to the serial port on the computer and the other end to the RS-232 on the back of the access point.

   c. Start the HyperTerminal program and enter the name **AP** for the connection. When the Connect To dialog box appears, change the Connect Using line to the communication port to which the serial cable is attached. Use the communications settings provided earlier in Table 6-3.

   d. The Express Setup screen appears in the HyperTerminal window. If the text does not appear immediately, type the equals sign (=) or press **Enter**. This displays the default settings of the access point. Record the default Radio Service Set ID (SSID). Exit HyperTerminal.

   e. Change the following parameters using ACU (System Parameters tab) on both laptops:

      ❑ SSID — Same as the access point

      ❑ Current Profile — Use Enterprise Configuration

      ❑ Network Type — Infrastructure

   f. The bottom of the ACU opening screen indicates the access point with which the station is now communicating. Click **Start**, point to **Programs**, point to **Cisco Systems, Inc.**, then click **Link Status Meter** to display the signal strengths on both laptops. While one station remains fixed, roam with the other station. What differences do you observe between the ad hoc network and the stand-alone infra-structure network? What are the reasons for those differences?

7. Create a Cisco infrastructure networked WLAN:

   a. If the network to which the access point is attached is using a DHCP server, then find the IP number assigned to the access point by going to the DHCP server. However, if access is not available to the DHCP server, use HyperTerminal to see the IP number on the access point. This is the same process as described for creating a Cisco infrastructure stand-alone WLAN. When the Express Setup screen appears in the HyperTerminal window, record the IP number and exit the program.

   b. If the network to which the access point is attached does not use a DHCP server, it is necessary to enter an IP number into the access point manually using the ARP command. Identify the MAC address of the access point from the label on the bottom of the access point. Enter the ARP command in the following format: **arp -s** *IP_number_for_access_point   access_point_MAC_address*

   c. Test the connection using the ping command in the following format: **ping** *IP_number_for_access_point.*

    d. Open an Internet browser such as Microsoft Internet Explorer or Netscape Navigator. Point to the access point by entering its IP number on the browser's address line preceded by *http://* and press **Enter**. Review the Cisco Access Point's Express Setup page.

    e. Enter the IP number of the default gateway for the subnet on which the access point resides. You will need to get this information from your network administrator.

    f. What are your observations about setting up these three types of networks? What difficulties did you have? What were the solutions? Record your responses and share them with other users.

CASE PROJECT

Northridge Consulting Group

The Northridge Consulting Group (NCG) has again asked you to assist the firm with a project. A local community college wants to create a WLAN for its Business Training Institute (BTI). BTI is responsible for providing college credit and noncredit offerings at area businesses. These classes and workshops are held at business sites instead of at the college. Classes can last anywhere from one afternoon to two weeks, and cover everything from basic applications, such as spreadsheets, to advanced network server administration.

The college has been carrying 15 laptop computers to the remote sites with a small hub and file server. However, this setup has several problems, most notably the complication of temporarily running cables between all of the clients. The college is now seriously considering purchasing a WLAN as an alternative.

Although the college's BTI is excited about the new technology, the school's Information Technology department has several concerns about WLAN. The department has compiled a series of questions, and NCG has asked for your help in answering the questions:

1. What are the advantages of the Cisco Aironet 340 Series over the competitor's products?

2. Which type of WLAN will be best: ad hoc, stand-alone infrastructure, or networked infrastructure? What if BTI wants to expand the lab from 15 stations to 30?

3. How long will it take to set up the WLAN?

4. What impact will running basic applications (word processing, spreadsheets, etc.) have on the response time of the network?

5. What are the typical problems that arise when setting up a WLAN in the field?

Write a one-page executive summary of WLANs for the IT department, and then a second page that addresses its concerns.

OPTIONAL .TEAM CASE PROJECT

The college's Information Technology department has developed its own proposal for the BTI portable lab. It recommends setting up a lab running Windows 2000 Terminal Server instead, using stripped-down network clients. These clients have no processing capability but rather send and receive screen images from the server, where all of the processing for the network takes place.

BTI has now made a counterproposal. It wants to set up a terminal server lab but still make it wireless by inserting wireless NICs in the network clients.

NCG needs your input. Create a team of three to four consultants. Each consultant should select a different aspect of proposal and counterproposal. Research that area and develop a recommendation. Be sure to cover such issues as cost, training, and bandwidth.

6

INSTALLING THE 3COM AIRCONNECT

> **After reading this chapter and completing the exercises, you will be able to:**
> - Describe the features of the 3Com AirConnect WLAN
> - List the necessary steps for setting up a 3Com infrastructure stand-alone WLAN
> - Tell how to implement a 3Com infrastructure networked WLAN

Like Cisco Systems, 3Com Corporation, another major vendor of WLAN products, is no stranger to networking. 3Com can trace its history back to the beginning of local area networks. Cofounded by Bob Metcalfe, who designed and even named the original Ethernet network, 3Com has been in the forefront of networking technologies for over 20 years. Its WLAN offering, known as the AirConnect, is likewise one of the leaders in wireless technology.

3Com's reputation as a leader in network innovation is also reflected in its AirConnect product. This can be illustrated in a recent 3Com venture. At 3Com Park (formerly known as Candlestick Park), home field of the San Francisco 49ers professional football team, 3Com is creating a wireless network to deliver a new spectator experience. Using 3Com AirConnect devices, 3Com is installing a WLAN at the stadium for 49er football fans attending a game. Fans will be able to access statistics from the 49ers game that they are watching as well as scores and statistics from other football games and sporting events in progress. They can also send e-mail and instant messages to friends who are either at the game or on the Internet.

And the application does not stop there. Soon streaming media features such as instant replays both of the live game and other games will be available. Fans can also order food and merchandise from their seats and have it delivered to them. They can even shop at their favorite grocery store at halftime, all through the AirConnect WLAN.

In this chapter, you will learn how to create infrastructure stand-alone and networked WLANs with the 3Com AirConnect product.

PRODUCT OVERVIEW

The 3Com AirConnect WLAN provides the high performance and throughput needed for bandwidth-intensive applications. Each AirConnect wireless LAN access point provides coverage within a radius of 300 feet (91 meters) for up to 63 simultaneous users. Up to three access points can cover the same physical space using different radio channels to support as many as 189 simultaneous users.

The AirConnect product has several advanced features:

- *Load balancing* — AirConnect WLAN NICs automatically switch to the best available access point when the current access point becomes congested or the signal weakens. To optimize performance during times of heavy network congestion, the AirConnect WLAN performs automatic load balancing among multiple access points. AirConnect network cards periodically check signal strength and packet error rates, and then automatically connect the user to the access point offering the best throughput. This provides uninterrupted access to network services at the highest possible data rates.

- *Bulk configuration* — The configuration of any access point can be automatically sent to all other access points on the same subnet.

- *Layer 3 security* — Wireless secure tunneling provides seamless and scaleable WLAN security. The company's wireless secure tunneling solution adds Layer 3 tunneling, authentication, and encryption to the 3Com AirConnect product to address the needs of commercial customers who must deliver secure wireless connectivity to hundreds or thousands of users.

- *Dual antennae* — Each AirConnect device is equipped with two antennae to provide signal diversity, so that each connected device has a choice of signals when confronted with a noisy environment.

3Com's Layer 3 security has several advantages designed for large networks with hundreds of users spread across multiple buildings. First, Layer 3 security uses private keys that are automatically negotiated and frequently changed, rather than manually entered shared keys as used with WEP. Also, it provides better security management than Access Control Lists (ACLs) based on MAC addresses because it utilizes the username and password facilities that already exist on the network and thus can automatically manage secure communications.

Table 7-1 summarizes the features of the 3Com AirConnect.

Table 7-1   3Com AirConnect Series Features

Feature	Description
Data rates	1, 2, 5.5, and 11 Mbps
Range	11 Mbps: 300 feet (91 meters) indoors
Operating channels	11 channels (U.S., Canada)
Network standard	IEEE 802.11 at all data rates
Security	40- and128-bit encryption and the RC4 algorithm
Wireless medium	Direct sequence spread spectrum (DSSS)
Media access protocol	Carrier Sense Multiple Access with Collision Avoidance (CSMA/CA)
Operating systems supported	Windows 95, 98, NT, 2000, CE, ME

7

CREATING A 3COM INFRASTRUCTURE STAND-ALONE WLAN

Infrastructure mode, also known as the Basic Service Set (BSS), consists of wireless stations and one access point. If more users need to be added or the range needs to be increased, an Extended Service Set (ESS) can be created consisting of two or more BSS wireless networks with multiple access points.

There are two types of 3Com infrastructure WLANs. The first is the infrastructure stand-alone WLAN, which uses an access point that is not connected to a wired network. The second type is the infrastructure networked WLAN, which uses an access point that is connected to a wired network. This connection allows the stations on the network to communicate among themselves as well as with clients on the wired network.

 The 3Com AirConnect does not support peer-to-peer (ad hoc) mode.

Setting up an infrastructure stand-alone WLAN involves five general steps:

1. Install the wireless NIC adapters, drivers, and utility programs.

2. Configure the wireless stations.

3. Configure Windows file and/or printer sharing.

4. Install the access point.

5. Configure the access point.

Installing the Wireless NIC Adapters

The first step in setting up a WLAN is to install the wireless NICs and the appropriate driver software into the stations. Then, you can install additional utility software.

Hardware and Software Requirements

Wireless NIC adapters for the 3Com AirConnect are available in two configurations. The first is a PC Card, which is a peripheral the size of a credit card. An illustration of a PC Card was shown in Figure 6-1. There are three different categories of PC Cards. Type I cards can be up to 3.3 millimeters thick and are used primarily for adding RAM to a laptop. Type II cards can be up to 5.5 millimeters thick and are often used by modem cards and wireless NICs. A Type III card can be up to 10.5 millimeters thick, which is large enough to accommodate a portable disk drive.

PC Cards slip into a small adapter interface found on laptop and other portable PC computers. The PC Card standard defines the slide-in interface for these expansion cards. One end of the card is a dual-row, 68-pin connector. This design ensures that a PC Card can be inserted only one way into the slot.

The second type of wireless NIC is the PCI WLAN card. An example of a PCI card was shown in Figure 6-2. A PCI card fits inside a standard desktop computer into the PCI slot and has an external antenna. PCI cards are not used for laptop computers, nor are PC Cards ordinarily used in desktop computers.

The minimum hardware requirements for a station to be connected to a WLAN are very basic. Any desktop computer that has a PCI slot, or a laptop that has a Type II PC Card can accept a wireless NIC and become a station on a WLAN.

  An ISA (Industry Standard Architecture) card is not available for the 3Com AirConnect.

Likewise, the operating system requirements for the client station are quite broad. Any of the following operating systems can support a 3Com wireless NIC:

- Windows 2000
- Windows NT (with Service Pack 4 or 5)
- Windows ME
- Windows 98 or 98SE
- Windows 95B
- Windows CE

  The 3Com AirConnect does not support Linux.

Inserting the PCI Adapter

When installing a 3Com AirConnect wireless NIC adapter, the sequence of events differs depending on whether you are installing a Type II PC Card in a laptop or a PCI adapter in a desktop computer. If you are installing a PC Card in a laptop, you should not insert the card into the system until you are prompted by the 3Com setup software (see the section that follows, "Loading Drivers and Utilities"). If you are installing a PCI wireless NIC in a desktop computer, you should install the NIC before running the 3Com setup software.

Static electricity can ruin the wireless NIC. Discharge any building static by first touching a metal part of a grounded unit before removing the client adapter from its antistatic packaging.

When you are inserting a wireless NIC PCI card, it is necessary first to turn off the computer and all its components and then remove the computer cover. Take out the screw from the top of the CPU back panel above an empty expansion slot. This screw holds the metal bracket on the back panel. Tilt the client adapter to allow the antenna connector and LED lights to slip through the opening in the CPU back panel. Gently press the client adapter into the empty slot until its connector is firmly seated, then reinstall the screw to the top of the CPU back panel.

The PCI wireless NIC comes with an external antenna. With the unit powered off, attach the antenna to the connector on the wireless NIC. Positioning the antenna vertically will result in the best signal reception.

Do not force the client adapter into the PCI or PC Card slot. This could damage both the card and the slot. If the card does not go in easily, remove the card and try again.

Loading Drivers and Utilities

The 3Com setup program guides the user through loading driver software and installing utility programs. If you have a laptop, the setup program also guides you through the process of inserting the PC Card wireless adapter. There are variations to this procedure depending on the operating system. To install the 3Com AirConnect under the Windows ME, 98, or 95 operating systems, follow these steps:

1. Turn on the computer and insert the End User Utilities CD in the CD-ROM drive. The setup program should start automatically. If it does not start, click the **Start** menu, click **Run**, and enter **D:\Setup.exe**, where D: is the letter of the CD-ROM drive. The 3Com AirConnect WLAN menu will appear, as shown in Figure 7-1.

2. Click **Installation for Windows**. This installation covers all Microsoft Windows products *except* Windows NT. The Windows installation screen appears, as shown in Figure 7-2.

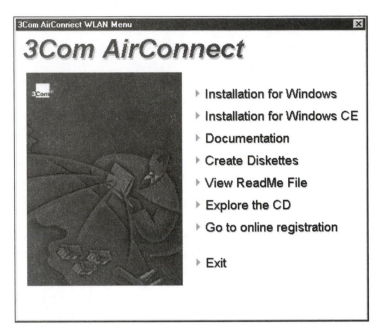

Figure 7-1   3Com AirConnect WLAN menu

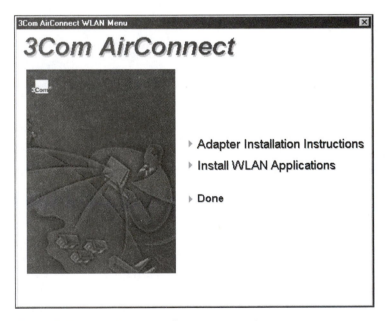

Figure 7-2   Windows installation screen

3. Click **Adapter Installation Instructions**. The instructions on the screen indicate that the wireless NIC should be installed in the PC Card slot now. When inserting a PC Card wireless NIC, it is important to examine the client adapter closely. One end is a dual-row, 68-pin client adapter connector. The other end contains an embedded antenna and will protrude from the laptop. Insert the adapter end into the PC Card adapter slot with the logo facing up. Apply just enough pressure to make sure that it is fully seated.

If the wireless NIC was already installed prior to running the setup utility, remove the card, wait five seconds, and then reinsert the card.

The wireless NIC can be inserted into a Type II or Type III PC Card slot.

7

4. Once the adapter is installed, Windows automatically detects it. The Add New Hardware Wizard dialog box then opens. At this point, the new drivers for the client wireless NIC will be installed. Click **Next** to display another dialog box asking how to locate the new driver. The best approach is to select the radio button **Search for the best driver for your device** and click **Next**.

5. The drivers for the 3Com AirConnect are located on the Installation CD-ROM. Select **CD-ROM drive**, unselect all the other options, then click **Next**.

6. After the driver files are located, the message "Windows driver file search for the device: 3Com AirConnect Wireless LAN PC Card" appears. Click **Next** to copy the required files.

7. After the files are copied, the 3Com AirConnect WLAN Easy Setup dialog box appears, as shown in Figure 7-3. Enter the name of the Wireless LAN Service Area of the wireless network to which your computer will connect. Click **OK**.

8. During the installation, dialog boxes may prompt you to enter a path to the required client adapter or Windows files. If the Windows files are installed on the computer, they will usually be located in the folder C:\Windows\Options\Cabs. Click **OK** to copy the required files. If the files are not on the computer, you will need to insert the Windows CD installation disk into the CD-ROM drive. If the CD-ROM drive is drive D, the path in the dialog box should be D:\WIN98. Click **OK** to copy the required files.

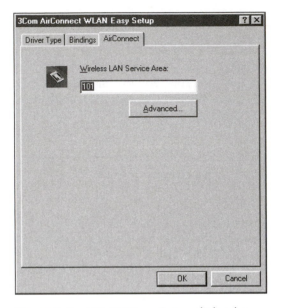

Figure 7-3   WLAN Easy Setup dialog box

The name of the Wireless LAN Service Area must match exactly the name assigned to the access point. Characters, capitalization, and spacing must all be identical.

9. The Add New Hardware Wizard window appears, stating that the installation is complete. Click **Finish**. The wizard then asks, "To finish setting up your new hardware, you must restart your computer. Do you want to restart your computer now?" Click **Yes**.

When you install 3Com AirConnect drivers under the Windows NT operating system, the steps are slightly different from Windows 95/98 or ME.

1. Turn the computer off and install the PC Card or PCI wireless NIC adapter.

2. Turn on the computer. Click **Select from list** for Network Adapters.

3. In the Select Network Adapters dialog box, click **Have Disk**. Put the End User Utilities CD in the CD-ROM drive. Make sure that the path to the CD-ROM drive is indicated and click **OK**.

4. When the Select OEM option dialog box appears, select the **3Com AirConnect WLAN PC Card** and click **OK**.

5. In the Windows NT Setup dialog box, click **Next** to continue.

6. When the Windows NT Setup dialog box appears, select the appropriate Network Protocols and Network Services. Follow the instructions on the screen to complete the installation.

Special utility software is also included on the AirConnect CD-ROM. There are five sets of programs:

- *3Com NIC Diagnostics* performs user-level diagnostics on the wireless NIC.

- *Mobile Connection Manager (MCM)* allows the user to configure specific parameters for different network settings.

- *Settings* displays the current WLAN settings.

- *Connection Monitor* is 3Com's site survey software that assists in the placement of access points.

- *Adapter Information* displays statistical data about the state of the WLAN and the wireless NIC adapter.

To install the utility software, follow these steps:

1. Insert the AirConnect Installation End User Utilities CD-ROM. If the menu does not appear, then click **Start**, click **Run**, and enter **D:\Setup.exe**, where D: is the letter of the CD-ROM drive. The 3Com AirConnect WLAN menu will appear.

2. Click **Installation for Windows** and then select **Install WLAN Applications**. The DynamicAccess Mobile Connection Manager Setup dialog box appears.

3. Click **Next** and accept the default settings to install the WLAN utilities.

4. The Automatic Start Option dialog box asks whether the DynamicAccess program should start each time the computer starts. Click **Yes**. Also click **Yes** when asked whether the user guides should be linked.

5. Reboot the computer when finished.

Configuring the Wireless Stations

To use a portable laptop computer to connect to several different WLANs in different locations, you must configure the laptop differently for each network. For example, when joining the WLAN in the downtown office, you may need to configure the laptop for Dynamic Host Configuration Protocol (DHCP) to allocate an IP number, for file sharing to be turned on, and for the default printer to be a color laser printer. However, the WLAN settings for your company's field office could be completely different. In this location, you may need to set the laptop with a specific IP number and gateway address, turn off file sharing, and configure the laptop for a black and white laser printer.

You could change each of these configurations manually whenever you connect the laptop to a different WLAN. However, 3Com offers a simpler solution. The 3Com **Mobile Connection Manager (MCM)** stores the information needed for each WLAN to which a mobile laptop might connect. These preferred settings are categorized by and stored in MCM profiles and configurations.

MCM Profiles

A **profile** contains information about how the laptop must be configured to communicate on a WLAN. This information includes details about the wireless NIC installed on the laptop, the IP number, default gateway, and the WLAN. Four types of profiles can be created:

- Dialing profiles
- Dial-Up networking profiles
- LAN profiles
- General Access profiles

 A given profile can be present in more than one configuration. If a profile is changed or deleted, all configurations using that profile are affected.

Dialing and Dial-Up profiles are used when connecting through a telephone line to a WLAN. For example, an MCM configuration can retrieve a telephone number from an electronic phone book on the laptop, set up the modem to dial without listening for the dial tone, and send credit card information to charge the long-distance telephone call.

LAN profiles contain information about how the computer must be configured to communicate on a WLAN. The LAN profile information includes the following:

- IP number
- Gateway address
- Domain Name Server
- WINS Server
- Information about the wireless NIC adapter
- WLAN settings

General Access profiles contain information about how resources on the computer are configured after it is connected to the network. The General Access profile information includes the following:

- Whether you want to share files or printers on your computer with other users on the network
- What printer you want to use as your default printer
- If you are using Internet Explorer as your Web browser, whether you want to configure it to use proxy servers
- Logon and NT domain information
- Workgroup identification information

MCM Configurations

A **configuration** is a collection of profiles. A configuration consists of a name, a description, and the associated profiles. An MCM configuration uses profiles to tell a computer how to configure itself for a specific WLAN. Two types of configurations can be created:

- Dial-Up configurations
- LAN configurations

When the 3Com driver and utility software is first installed, MCM automatically creates a General Access profile and LAN profile based on configurations already present on the laptop. For example, if an IP number had already been set for a 10/100 Mbps PC Card wired NIC, MCM would create a General Access profile and LAN profile based on that information. MCM would also create at least one configuration based on the profiles.

To view the default configuration and profiles, follow these steps:

1. Double-click the **3Com** icon in the Windows system tray on the lower–right portion of the screen. The 3Com Launcher opens, as shown in Figure 7-4.

Figure 7-4   3Com Launcher

2. Double-click the **MCM** icon, which is the second icon on the top row, to open the Mobile Connection Manager screen, as shown in Figure 7-5.

3. To view the profiles that were automatically created when the software was installed, click the **File** menu, then point to **Profiles**, and finally click **LAN Profiles** to bring up the LAN Profiles screen, as shown in Figure 7-6. Select a profile and click **View** to see the settings for that profile. Follow the same procedure to see the General Access profile.

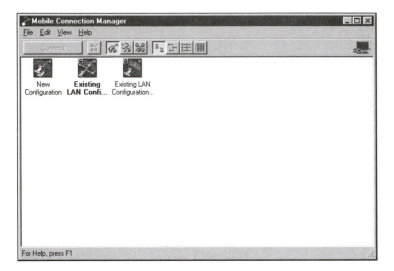

Figure 7-5   Mobile Connection Manager

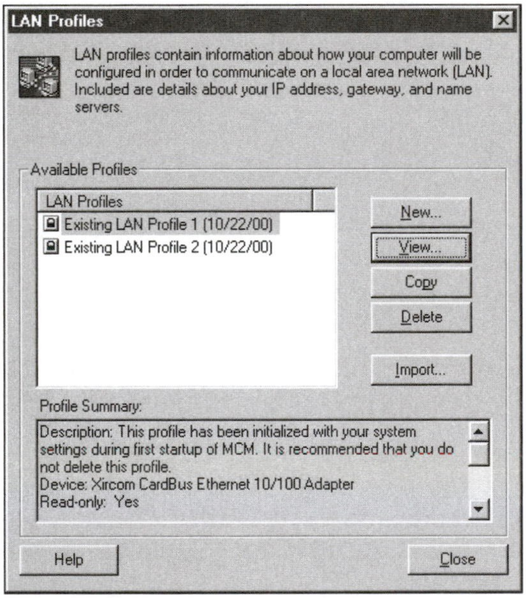

Figure 7-6   LAN Profiles screen

You can create, edit, copy, delete, or import profiles. However, 3Com recommends that you always use MCM to modify network settings for the NIC. Using the Control Panel to change the settings could cause MCM to be unable to apply the settings correctly.

You can practice configuring LAN profiles and General Access profiles in Hands-on Project 3 near the end of the chapter.

Configuring Windows File and Print Sharing

After installing the wireless NIC, loading drivers and utilities, and configuring the wireless stations, you must enable Windows print and file sharing to allow other WLAN users to access files and printers.

To configure file and print sharing for a laptop using Windows 98 and 95, follow these steps:

1. Right-click **Network Neighborhood** and click **Properties** to display the Network dialog box.

2. Select **3Com AirConnect Wireless LAN PC Card**, then click the **File and Print Sharing** button. Select the check boxes for file sharing, print sharing, or both. Click **OK**.

Installing the Access Point

7

When installing the access point, it is a good solution to position the access point temporarily in a central location among the stations on the WLAN rather than to mount the access point permanently. This is because some configuration steps, such as communicating with the access point through a cable, may be difficult if the access point is already mounted. After the configuration is complete, you can mount the access point on a pole or a ceiling.

Supplying Power

The next step is to connect the power pack. You should first plug the power pack into a wall outlet or a power strip, and then attach the connector to the power receptacle on the back of the access point. Once the access point receives power, the power indicator light-emitting diode (LED) will be a steady green color. The LED status indicators are summarized in Table 7-2.

Table 7-2   Access Point LED Status Indicators

LED Indicator	Off	On	Flash
Power	No power	Power on	During boot sequence
LAN	No power or no network connection	Link to hub but no network traffic	LAN traffic detected
WLAN	No power or no radio signal	No associated wireless stations	Radio traffic detected

As an option, the 3Com AirConnect can receive its power using an Ethernet cable and the **PowerBASE-T adapter**. The PowerBASE-T adapter is illustrated in Figure 7-7. You can use this option when an access point must be located in an area where access to an electrical outlet is limited.

Figure 7-7   PowerBASE-T adapter

To connect the PowerBASE-T, first connect the power adapter cable to the power supply, then connect the power adapter cable from the power supply to the PowerBASE-T module. Connect the power cord to the power supply and plug the power cord into a power outlet. When the PowerBASE-T module receives power, the green LED on top lights up. Connect an Ethernet cable from the Ethernet port to a network hub or switch. Connect an 8-wire Category 5 Ethernet cable from the PowerBASE-T module to the access point. When it receives power over the Ethernet cable, the access point starts its boot sequence and its LED lights up. This configuration is illustrated in Figure 7-8.

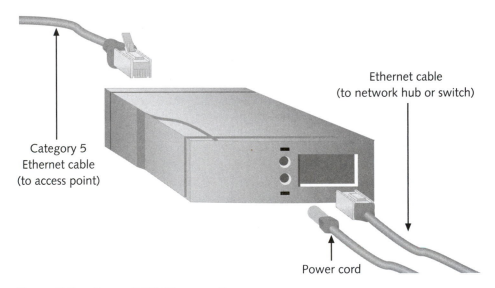

Ethernet cable
(to network hub or switch)

Category 5
Ethernet cable
(to access point)

Power cord

Figure 7-8   PowerBASE-T connections

Connecting to the Access Point

When setting up an infrastructure stand-alone WLAN with a single access point, you first must change the settings of the access point. To change these settings, you need the 9-pin, straight-through, female-to-female serial cable that is included with the 3Com AirConnect. One end of the cable is connected to the serial port on a setup computer and the other end to the RS-232 port on the back of the access point. The setup computer can be any PC, including a wireless laptop.

Once the cable is installed, a terminal–emulation program, such as HyperTerminal, on the computer is used to communicate with the access point. The 3Com Administration Utilities CD includes a script that will automatically start and correctly configure HyperTerminal to communicate with the access point through the serial interface.

To run the script, follow these steps:

1. Insert the Administration Utilities CD into the setup PC. When the 3Com Access Point main menu appears, select **WLAN Utilities**, and then select **Serial Connection**. HyperTerminal starts with a blank window.

2. Press **Enter** to see the AP default settings on the System Summary screen, as shown in Figure 7-9. After viewing the default settings, press **Esc** to return to the main menu (see Figure 7-10).

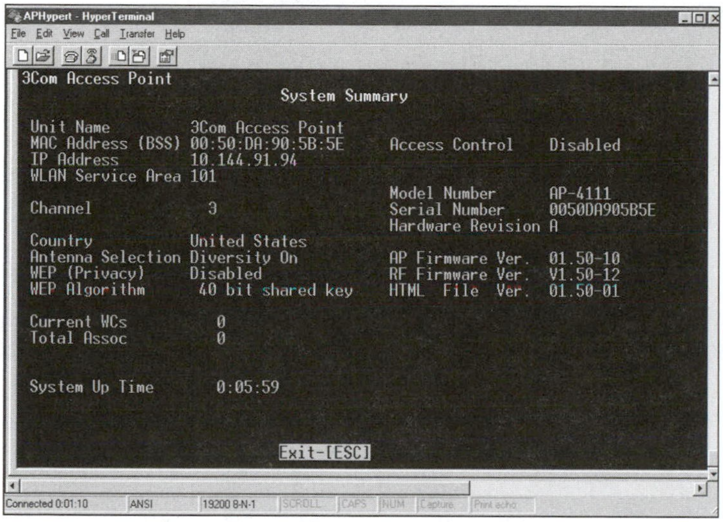

Figure 7-9 Default access point settings

Figure 7-10 Access Point main menu

If the HyperTerminal program is not available, you can use a similar terminal-emulation program instead. The configuration settings are shown in Table 7-3.

Table 7-3 Terminal-Emulation Configuration Settings

Setting	Value
Bits Per Second	19,200
Data Bits	8
Parity	None
Stop Bits	1
Flow Control	None

Configuring the Access Point

To configure the access point, from the 3Com Access Point main menu, choose AP Installation and enter the default administrative password (comcomcom). This will display the Access Point Installation screen. Enter the IP number and a Wireless LAN Service Area for this access point. Press F2 to save the settings and then reset the AP for the new settings to take effect.

One way to view the connections is to double-click the 3Com icon in the Windows system tray on the lower-right portion of the screen. This will open the 3Com Launcher. Double-click the AirConnect Monitor icon to view the signal strength, as shown in Figure 7-11.

 If you are running Windows 2000, make sure you are using AirConnect version 2.0.

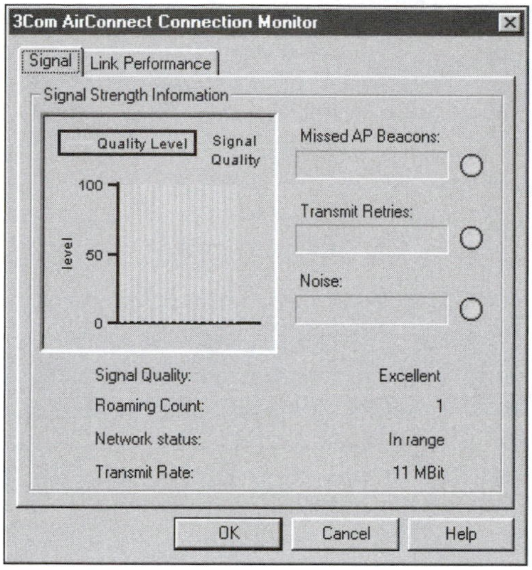

Figure 7-11   AirConnect Connection Monitor

CREATING A 3COM INFRASTRUCTURE NETWORKED WLAN

The second type of 3Com infrastructure WLAN that can be created is an infrastructure net-worked WLAN. Such a WLAN uses an access point that is connected to a wired network. This allows the stations on the network to communicate among themselves as well as with clients on the wired network.

Performing the Initial Setup

As with an infrastructure stand-alone WLAN, you first must install wireless NIC adapters, drivers, and utility software. You should temporarily position the access point in a central location among the stations. After you complete the configuration, you can mount the access point permanently. Then, after installing the access point and adjusting the antennae, you can connect the access point to the wired LAN. This connection requires a cable with an RJ-45 connector that inserts into the back of the access point. The other end of the cable connects to the Ethernet network's hub. In addition to requiring these steps, setting up an infrastructure networked WLAN involves configuring the access point settings.

Configuring the Access Point

When setting up an infrastructure networked WLAN, you must change the settings of the access point, using the same serial port connection and terminal-emulation software technique described in the section "Creating a 3Com Infrastructure Stand-Alone WLAN."

Once the serial cable is installed, a terminal-emulation program on the computer is used to communicate with the access point. You can use either the script found on the Administration Utilities CD or manually configure a similar terminal-emulation program.

Once either HyperTerminal or another terminal-emulation program has made the connection, a blank window appears. Press Enter to see the default access point settings. After viewing the default settings, press Esc to display the 3Com Access Point main menu shown earlier in Figure 7-10.

To configure the access point from the 3Com Access Point main menu, choose AP Installation and enter the default administrative password (comcomcom). This displays the Access Point Installation screen. Enter the IP number, the default gateway, and the subnet mask for this access point. However, if DHCP is being used, do not enter any of these three settings. Save the settings and then reset the AP for the new settings to take effect.

To view the connections, double-click the 3Com icon in the Windows system tray on the lower–right portion of the screen. This will open the 3Com Launcher. Double-click the AirConnect Monitor icon to view the signal strength.

CHAPTER SUMMARY

❑ The 3Com AirConnect WLAN provides high performance for bandwidth-intensive applications. The AirConnect access point provides coverage within a radius of 300 feet (91 meters) for up to 63 simultaneous users. A maximum of three access points can cover the same physical space using different radio channels to support as many as 189 simultaneous users. The AirConnect product has several advanced features, including load balancing, bulk configuration, and Layer 3 security.

❑ Creating a 3Com infrastructure stand-alone WLAN involves several steps. First, the wireless NIC adapters, drivers, and utility programs must be installed. Wireless NIC adapters are available in two different configurations: a PC Card, which is a peripheral the size of a credit card that fits in a laptop computer, and a PCI card, which fits inside a standard desktop computer and has an external antenna. The 3Com setup utility guides the user through the process of inserting the PC Card wireless NIC adapter, loading the driver software, and installing the utility programs. There are variations to this procedure depending on the operating system. The next step is to configure the wireless stations using the Mobile Connection Manager (MCM) software. After configuring the station, you must properly configure Windows file and/or printer sharing. Finally, the access point is installed and then configured.

❑ Infrastructure networked WLANs use an access point that is connected to a wired network. Setting up an infrastructure networked WLAN involves configuring the access point settings. The settings that must be entered include the IP number for the access point, the default gateway, and the subnet mask. However, if DHCP is being used, you can skip these steps. In addition, you also must enter the Wireless LAN Service Area for the access point.

KEY TERMS

configuration — Part of the 3Com MCM utility that is a collection of profiles.

Mobile Connection Manager (MCM) — A 3Com AirConnect utility that stores the configuration information needed for each WLAN to which a mobile laptop may connect.

PowerBASE-T adapter — A hardware device that provides power to a 3Com AirConnect access point over an Ethernet cable.

profile — Part of the 3Com MCM utility that contains information about how the laptop must be configured to communicate on a WLAN.

REVIEW QUESTIONS

7

1. Each AirConnect wireless LAN access point provides coverage for up to _____ simultaneous users.

   a. 53

   b. 63

   c. 73

   d. 83

2. The process by which AirConnect network cards periodically check signal strength and packet error rates and automatically connect to the access point that offers the best throughput is known as _____.

   a. bandwidth

   b. adoption

   c. load balancing

   d. NIC configuration

3. _____ configuration is a feature that distributes the configuration of any access point to all other access points on the same subnet.

   a. NIC

   b. WLAN

   c. AP

   d. Bulk

4. There are _____ different categories of PC Cards.

   a. two

   b. three

   c. four

   d. seven

5. A(n) _____ card fits inside a standard desktop computer and has an external antenna.

   a. PCI

   b. RPI

   c. RFP

   d. CPD

6. The 3Com AirConnect does not support peer-to-peer (ad hoc) mode. True or false?

7. PCI cards are not used for laptop computers. True or false?

8. An ISA card is available for the 3Com AirConnect. True or false?

9. When you are installing a PC Card, you should not insert the card into the system until the 3Com setup software prompts you to do so. True or false?

10. When you are installing a PCI wireless NIC, you should install the card before running the 3Com setup software. True or false?

11. The option Installation for Windows on the installation CD-ROM covers all Microsoft Windows products except _____.

12. Once the PC Card wireless NIC adapter is installed, Windows automatically detects it and opens the _____ dialog box.

13. The drivers for the 3Com AirConnect are located on the _____.

14. The _____ utility program performs user-level diagnostics on the wireless NIC.

15. 3Com's site survey software that assists in the placement of access points is known as _____.

16. Explain the difference between a profile and a configuration.

17. List the different types of profiles and configurations.

18. List some of the types of information that are found in a LAN profile.

19. Explain what the MCM does with default profiles and configurations when it is first installed on a computer.

20. Explain how to view LAN profiles.

HANDS-ON PROJECTS

1. Research 3Com and its AirConnect WLAN products. How did 3Com start? What are the greatest strengths of its product line? How was the AirConnect developed? How is it now being used? What do the reviewers say about it? Write a two-page paper on your findings.

2. Install wireless NICs and the driver software in two laptop computers. When installing a PC Card into a laptop, wait until you are prompted before inserting the wireless NIC. Carefully follow the steps to install the driver software for the wireless NICs.

Also, install the utilities on each laptop. After the files are copied, the WLAN Easy Setup dialog box appears. Enter the name **Local** for the Wireless LAN Service Area. Click **OK**.

3. Configure the wireless stations.

    a. Start the 3Com Launcher by double-clicking the **3Com** icon in the Windows system tray and then double-clicking the **MCM** icon.

    b. View the LAN profile that was automatically created when the software was installed by clicking the **File** menu, pointing to **Profiles**, then clicking **LAN Profiles** to bring up the LAN Profiles screen. Click the **View** button. The Existing LAN Profile Properties screen appears, as shown in Figure 7–12. Click each tab to view the default settings. Note any changes that need to be made. Click the **Close** button twice when finished.

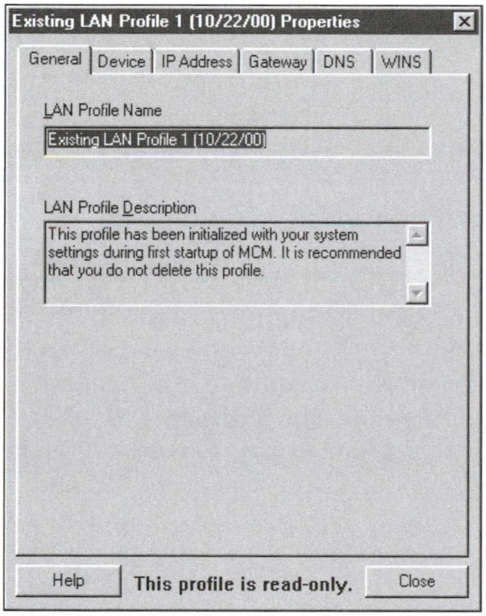

Existing LAN Profile 1 (10/22/00) Properties

General | Device | IP Address | Gateway | DNS | WINS

LAN Profile Name

Existing LAN Profile 1 (10/22/00)

LAN Profile Description

This profile has been initialized with your system settings during first startup of MCM. It is recommended that you do not delete this profile.

Help   **This profile is read-only.**   Close

Figure 7-12   Existing LAN Profile Properties

    c. View the General Access profile that was automatically created when the software was installed. To view this profile, click the **File** menu, point to **Profiles**, then click **General Access Profiles** to bring up the General Access Profiles screen. Click the **View** button. The Existing General Access Profile Properties screen appears, as shown in Figure 7–13. Click each tab to view the default settings. Note any settings that need to be changed. Click the **Close** button when finished.

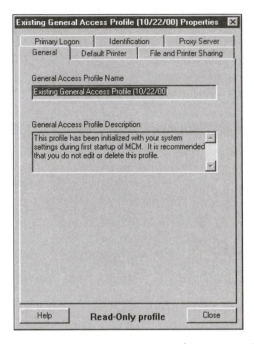

Figure 7-13 Existing General Access Profile Properties

d. If all of the settings of the LAN profile and General Access profile are acceptable, stop here. However, if you need to change any of the settings, you should create a new configuration with the modified profiles.

e. Click **File** and then **New Configuration** to start the New Configuration Wizard, as shown in Figure 7-14. Enter the name **Primary** and a description of the configuration, then click **Next**. Click **Local area network (LAN) Configuration** to indicate that this configuration will be a LAN and then click **Next**. The next screen, shown in Figure 7-15, gives the option of creating a new LAN profile or using an existing LAN profile. If the existing profile that you viewed is similar to the new one that you want to create, click **Use existing profile**, then select that profile from the drop-down box. The wizard prompts you to make the necessary modifications. If you want to create a completely different profile, click **Create new profile** and answer the questions as the wizard prompts.

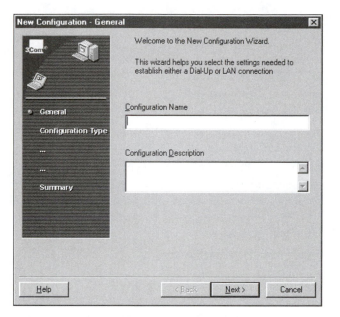

Figure 7-14   New Configuration Wizard

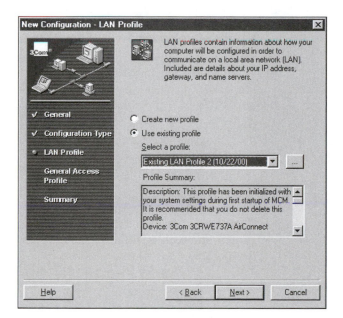

Figure 7-15   Creating a LAN profile

  f. The next screen allows you to create a new General Access profile or modify an
     existing profile. A series of screens appear asking questions regarding the necessary
     settings for this WLAN (default printers, print and file sharing options, proxy

servers, etc.). Set the computers for both file and print sharing. After answering the questions, click **Finish**. Then the new configuration icon will appear on the Configuration screen. Double-click that icon to apply the new configuration.

4. Configure the access point for a 3Com infrastructure stand-alone WLAN.

    a. Position the access point and adjust the antennae. Why did you select the location at which you placed the access point?

    b. Connect a 9-pin, straight-through, female-to-female serial cable, included with the 3Com AirConnect, to the serial port on the computer, and connect the other end to the RS-232 on the back of the access point.

    c. Insert the Administration Utilities CD and select **WLAN Utilities** from the main menu. Then select **Serial Connection**. HyperTerminal starts with a blank window. Press **Enter** to see the AP default settings. After viewing the default settings, press **Esc** to display the main menu.

    d. From the main menu, choose **AP Installation**. You will be prompted to enter the administrative password. The default password is **comcomcom**. This will display the Access Point Installation screen, as shown in Figure 7-16.

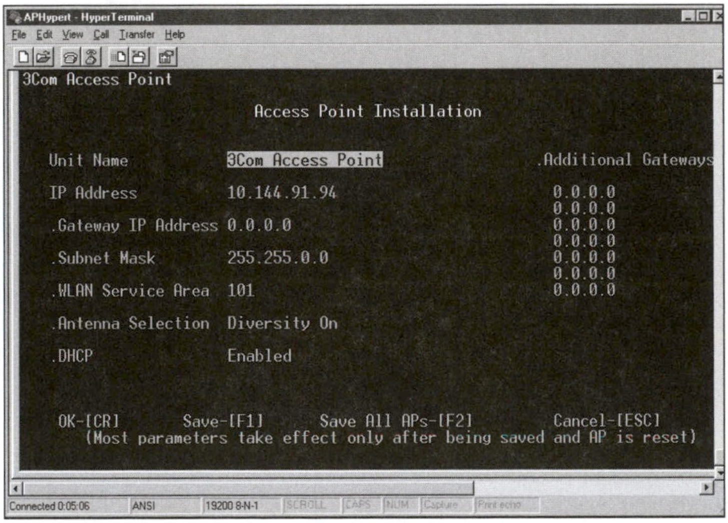

Figure 7-16   Access Point Installation screen

    e. Enter the IP number for this access point.

    f. Enter **Local** as the WLAN Service Area for this access point. Press **F1** and confirm to save the settings and return to the main menu.

    g. From the main menu, choose **Special Functions**. Select **Reset AP** and click **Yes**. The access point reboots and the main menu appears.

    h. Close the terminal-emulation program.

5. View the connections that you have now established.

   a. Double-click **Network Neighborhood** to see all of the stations on the network. Double-click the icon of the other station and display the drive and files. Copy a small file between the two computers.

   b. Double-click the **3Com** icon in the Windows system tray on the lower-right portion of the screen. This will open the 3Com Launcher. Double-click the **AirConnect Monitor** icon to view the signal strength.

   c. While one station remains fixed, roam with the other station. At what point does the transmission begin to dip into the fair and then poor range? What are the reasons for this? Write a short paper on your observations.

6. Create an infrastructure networked WLAN.

   a. Connect a 9-pin, straight-through, female-to-female serial cable, included with the 3Com AirConnect, to the serial port on the computer. Then connect the other end to the RS-232 port on the back of the access point.

   b. Connect an RJ-45 connector that inserts into the back of the access point. The other end of the cable should be connected to the Ethernet network's hub.

   c. If the network to which the access point is attached is using a DHCP server, then stop here.

   d. If the network is not using DHCP, insert the Administration Utilities CD and select **WLAN Utilities** from the main menu. Then select **Serial Connection**. HyperTerminal starts with a blank window. Press **Enter** to see the AP default settings.

   e. From the main menu, choose **AP Installation**. You will be prompted to enter the administrative password. The default password is **comcomcom**. This will display the Access Point Installation screen.

   f. Enter the default gateway and the subnet mask for this access point. Ask your network administrator for this information. Do not change the IP number.

   g. Enter **Network** as the WLAN Service Area for this access point. Press **F1** and confirm to save the settings and return to the main menu.

   h. From the main menu, choose **Special Functions**. Select **Reset AP**. The access point reboots and the main menu appears.

   i. Close the terminal-emulation program.

CASE PROJECTS

Northridge Consulting Group

Northridge Consulting Group (NCG) again wants you to assist the firm with a WLAN project. The local public school board is interested in installing a WLAN in the technology wing of the new high school. Students could check out WLAN laptops for use in their classes or bring a system from home. Teachers could also be given laptops for use in their classrooms. Because many teachers switch rooms during the school day, the WLAN would allow faculty to move freely between rooms without having to connect and disconnect cables.

Although the school board is excited about the new technology, the high school's faculty has several concerns about WLANs. The teachers have compiled a series of questions, and NCG has asked for your help in answering the questions:

1. What are the advantages of the 3Com AirConnect product? What are its disadvantages? For a WLAN of 50 users and two access points, what is the per-user cost?

2. Which type of WLAN will be best—stand-alone infrastructure or networked infrastructure?

3. What if the school wants to expand the lab from 50 stations to 100? What are the implications? What is the additional cost?

4. How long will it take to set up the WLAN?

5. What are the typical problems that could arise with students using a WLAN?

NCG has asked you to write a one-page executive summary of WLANs and then a second page that addresses the school's concerns.

OPTIONAL TEAM CASE PROJECT

The high school's Information Systems department has developed a counterproposal for a 3Com WLAN. The department recommends that students be given Personal Digital Assistants (PDAs) instead of laptops. PDAs would be much cheaper to purchase and easier to carry. Also, one of the faculty has read about the Bluetooth technology and believes that it will be the primary means of wireless networking in the next five years.

NCG needs your input. Create a team of three to four consultants. Each consultant should select a different aspect of the school board proposal and the Information Systems department's counterproposal. The consultants should research that area and develop a recommendation.

CONFIGURING THE CISCO AIRONET AND 3COM AIRCONNECT

After reading this chapter and completing the exercises, you will be able to:

♦ Explain how to access the AP

♦ Describe how to implement security features on the WLAN

♦ Tell how to conduct a site survey

♦ List the necessary steps to enable power management

Remember the last time that you completed a major project? It could have been writing the final sentence on a 10-page report, or driving the last nail into the newly built deck, or lugging that final box inside the new apartment. The feeling of accomplishment and joy produced a warm glow inside as you sat back and exclaimed, "I'm done!" Yet that feeling probably didn't last very long. That's because you soon realized that you still needed to proofread that report, or start painting the new deck, or unpack all of those boxes.

The same is true of a WLAN. Installing the WLAN and watching it operate is very satisfying. However, your work has only begun. Now it's time to configure the WLAN so that it functions properly in its environment. In this chapter, we look at some of the tasks involved in the configuration of the Cisco and 3Com WLAN products. All of these tasks are unique to a WLAN setting.

ACCESSING THE ACCESS POINT

Configuring the WLAN involves making changes to the access point. Cisco and 3Com provide a variety of ways to access the access point.

Accessing the Cisco AP

There are three options for accessing a Cisco AP. The AP can be accessed through:

- Terminal emulator software over a direct serial connection
- Telnet
- A browser such as Microsoft Internet Explorer or Netscape Navigator

To use a direct serial connection with terminal emulator software, connect one end of a 9-pin, straight-through, male-to-female serial cable to the serial port on a computer, and the other end to the RS-232 port on the back of the access point. Once the cable is installed, a terminal-emulation program, such as HyperTerminal, is used to communicate with the access point (see Chapter 6 for more detailed information). The Express Setup screen then appears in the emulator window, as shown in Figure 8-1. If the Express Setup menu does not appear, press = (equal) to display the home page. Then press S and then press E, and then press Enter.

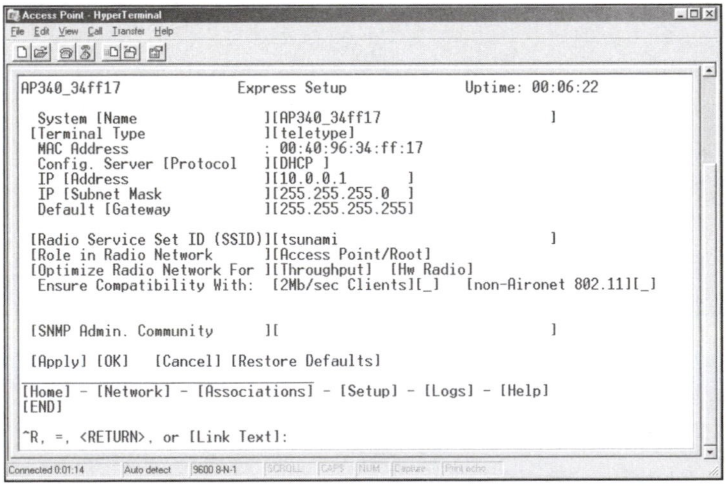

Figure 8-1   Cisco emulator-based Express Setup screen

The second option uses Telnet. **Telnet** is an application protocol within TCP/IP that supports terminal emulation. Telnet enables a user to connect to another computer or device so that the device responds as though it were connected to a terminal. Whereas the direct serial connection requires the computer configuring the access point to be immediately adjacent to the AP (at least within the length of the cable), using Telnet allows configuration of the access point from almost anywhere. To access the AP using Telnet, it is necessary to use a computer that is running TCP/IP and is connected to a wired or wireless network. Go to a command prompt on the computer and enter

```
telnet xxx.xxx.xxx.xxx
```

where *xxx.xxx.xxx.xxx* is the IP number of the AP. This is illustrated in Figure 8-2. The AP displays the Express Setup page in the same format as the direct serial connection using a terminal emulator.

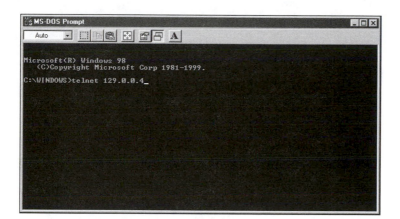

Figure 8-2   Entering the Telnet command

 The computer using Telnet can be on a wired network or a wireless LAN.

The final method to access the Cisco Aironet AP is by using a browser. Open an Internet browser such as Microsoft Internet Explorer or Netscape Navigator. Point to the access point by entering its IP number on the browser's address line and pressing Enter. The browser-based Summary Status page appears, as shown in Figure 8-3. The browser-based screen is easiest to navigate and use to make changes to the access point, and is the preferred method.

 A wireless station can be used to access the Cisco Aironet AP with a browser.

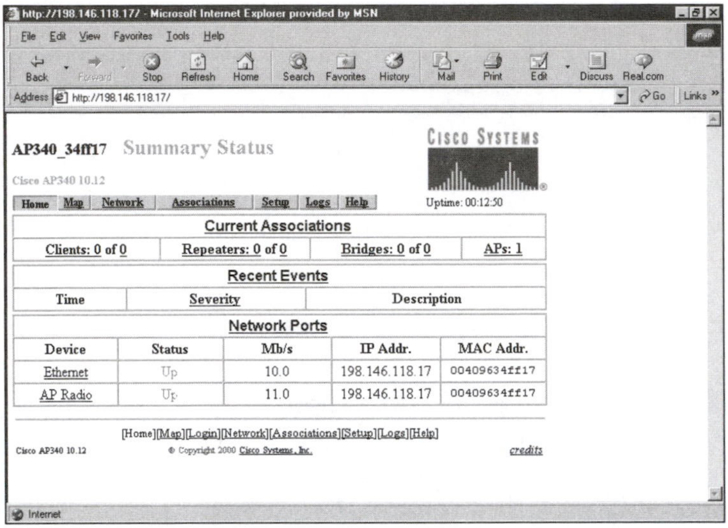

Figure 8-3   Cisco browser-based screen

Accessing the 3Com AP

The 3Com AirConnect has four options for accessing the access point. The AP can be accessed through:

- Terminal emulator software over a direct serial connection
- Telnet
- A dial-up modem connection
- A browser such as Microsoft Internet Explorer or Netscape Navigator

As with the Cisco Aironet, to use a direct serial connection, you connect a 9-pin, straight-through, female-to-female serial cable to the serial port on a computer and the RS-232 port on the back of the access point. Once the cable is installed, a terminal-emulation program on the computer is used to communicate with the access point. The 3Com Administration Utilities CD includes a script that will automatically start and correctly configure HyperTerminal for communicating with the access point through the serial interface. To run the script, insert the CD and select WLAN Utilities from the Main Menu, then select Serial Connection. HyperTerminal starts with a blank window. Press Enter to see the default settings and press Esc to display the Main Menu. The emulator-based screen appears in the window, as shown in Figure 8-4.

> **Tip** The serial cable is only used when accessing the AP with terminal-emulation software. It should not be connected for any other method of AP access.

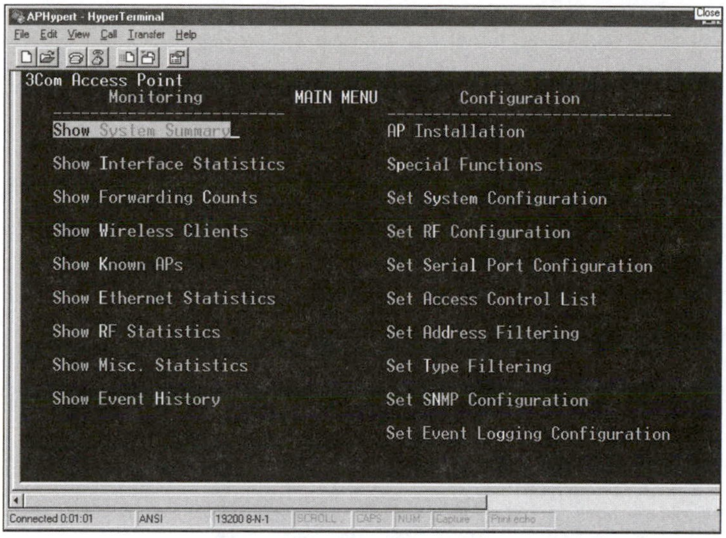

```
APHypert - HyperTerminal                                                    Close
File  Edit  View  Call  Transfer  Help
  ☐ ☞ | ☺ ☎ | ☐ ☞ | ☜
3Com Access Point
          Monitoring              MAIN MENU           Configuration
  --------------------------------------------------------------------------
  Show System Summary_                    AP Installation

  Show Interface Statistics               Special Functions

  Show Forwarding Counts                  Set System Configuration

  Show Wireless Clients                   Set RF Configuration

  Show Known APs                          Set Serial Port Configuration

  Show Ethernet Statistics                Set Access Control List

  Show RF Statistics                      Set Address Filtering

  Show Misc. Statistics                   Set Type Filtering

  Show Event History                      Set SNMP Configuration

                                          Set Event Logging Configuration



Connected 0:01:01   ANSI       19200 8-N-1   SCROLL  CAPS  NUM  Capture  Print echo
```

Figure 8-4   3Com emulator-based screen

The second option uses Telnet. To access the AP using Telnet, it is necessary to use a computer that is running TCP/IP and is connected to either a wired or wireless network. Go to a command prompt and enter

> `telnet xxx.xxx.xxx.xxx`

where *xxx.xxx.xxx.xxx* is the IP number of the AP. When prompted, enter the AP system password (the default is *comcomcom*). Press Esc and the AP displays the Main Menu in the same format as the direct serial connection using a terminal emulator. To end the session, press Ctrl+D.

The third option allows a user to "dial up" the access point using a modem. This option also allows for remote configuration of the AP, as illustrated in Figure 8-5. A dial-up connection requires a null-modem serial cable between an external modem and the AP. A remote computer must also have a modem (internal or external) and a communication program, such as HyperTerminal.

Figure 8-5   Dial-up AP access

The 3Com AP supports modems that use the generic Hayes Smartmodem command set.

You first must configure the AP to use a modem. Connect to the AP either by using a direct serial connection with a terminal emulator or by using Telnet. Select Set Serial Port Configuration from the Main Menu to display the Serial Port Configuration screen, as shown in Figure 8-6. The settings that must be used for a modem connected to an AP are summarized in Table 8-1. Confirm that the settings are the same as in Table 8-1 (press the spacebar or arrow keys to change settings), tab to the Save-[F1] function at the bottom of the screen, then press Enter to save the settings.

```
APHypert - HyperTerminal
File  Edit  View  Call  Transfer  Help

3Com Access Point

                  Serial Port Configuration

       Port Use          UI            Answer Wait Time      60

       Connect Mode      Answer        Inactivity Timeout     5

       Modem Connected  No             PPP Timeout            3

       Dialout Mode      Auto          PPP Terminates        10

       Modem Speaker     On

       Dialout Number   1234567




           OK-[CR]            Save-[F1]            Cancel-[ESC]
      (Use the space bar or left/right cursor keys to change)

Connected 0:17:49    ANSI    19200 8-N-1    SCROLL  CAPS  NUM  Capture  Print echo
```

Figure 8-6   3Com serial port configuration

Table 8-1   3Com AP Serial Port Configuration for a Modem Connection

Modem Parameters	Required Settings
Port Use	PPP
Connect Mode	Answer
Modem Connected	Yes
Answer Wait Time	60 (seconds)
Modem Speaker	On
Inactivity Timeout	5 (minutes)

You also must configure the modem on the remote computer using a communication program. The settings that must be used for the remote modem are summarized in Table 8-2.

Table 8-2 Remote Computer Communication Settings

Modem Parameters	Required Settings
Emulation	ANSI
Bits Per Second	19200
Data Bits	8
Parity	None
Stop Bits	1
Flow Control	None

From the remote computer, a user is now able to dial up the AP. Once the connection has been established, press Esc to refresh the display. The AP displays the Main Menu in the same format as the direct serial connection using a terminal emulator. To end the session, select Special Functions from the Main Menu, then select Modem Hangup.

The final method to access the 3Com AirConnect AP is by using a browser. Open an Internet browser such as Microsoft Internet Explorer or Netscape Navigator. Point to the access point by entering its IP number on the browser's address line, then press Enter. The browser-based AirConnect page appears, as shown in Figure 8-7. Clicking a word or phrase in the left pane expands the tree and makes it easy to navigate through the pages. The browser-based screen is the easiest and preferred method of making changes to the access point.

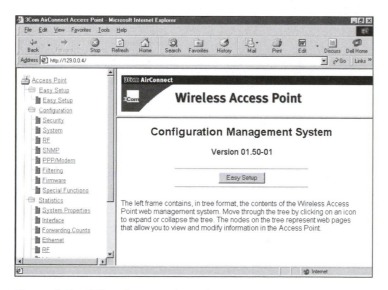

Figure 8-7 3Com browser-based screen

3Com recommends that you use a current version of your Web browser. That is, you should use Microsoft Internet Explorer 4.0 or greater or Netscape 5.0 or greater. You should also enable JavaScript for either browser.

3Com also recommends that you turn off the browser caching function for the browser to display the configuration changes correctly on the Web pages. This ensures that the displayed page is the latest version. To turn off caching for Netscape, select Preferences from the Edit menu, then expand Advanced, then click Cache when the Preferences dialog box opens. Click the Every time option under the *Document in cache is compared to document on network* item. For Internet Explorer, select Tools, then click Internet Options (in earlier versions of Internet Explorer, Internet Options may be found under the View menu). Click Temporary Internet Files and then Settings. Select Every visit to the page under the *Check for newer versions of stored pages* item.

IMPLEMENTING SECURITY

One of the first—and most important—steps to take when configuring a WLAN is to install security features properly. These include settings for the station as well as for the access point.

Protecting the Access Point

You must protect the access point in two ways. First, you should protect the AP itself from theft or tampering. Because the access point generally is mounted in an open area, it is important to ensure its physical security. You should mount an AP high on a wall or on the ceiling to discourage unauthorized tampering. Another option is to place the access point in a secure area such as a wiring closet. If you install an access point in a closet, you many need to mount an optional range extender antenna on the access point.

The second type of protection needed for an AP is to prevent unauthorized users from viewing or changing sensitive settings. Both Cisco and 3Com have extensive security features for protecting the AP.

Protecting the Cisco AP

Cisco provides several options for protecting the access point by using the Security Setup feature. Open a browser and enter the IP number of the access point to display the Summary Status screen. Click Setup from the Summary Status page, then click Security under the Services heading. This displays the Security Setup page, as shown in Figure 8-8.

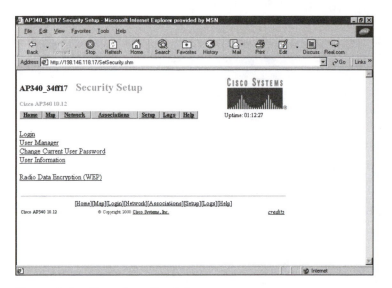

Figure 8-8   Cisco Security Setup

Each user who will be accessing the AP should have his or her own user account. To set up an account, click User Information, then click Add New User, which brings up the User Management dialog box shown in Figure 8-9.

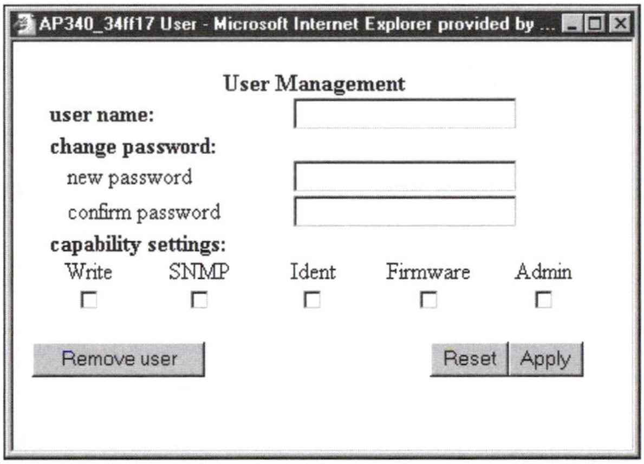

Figure 8-9   Cisco User Management

To set up the account, enter the username and a password in the User Management dialog box. You can also specify user's capabilities with regard to the access point in this dialog box. These capabilities include:

- *Write* allows the specified user to change the system settings. When a user is assigned Write capability, the user also automatically receives Admin capability.

- *SNMP* enables the user to perform specific management operations.

SNMP (Simple Network Management Protocol) is discussed in detail in Chapter 9.

- *Ident* allows a user to change the access point's identity settings (MAC address, IP number, and SSID). When a user has Ident capability, that user also automatically receives Write and Admin capabilities.

- *Firmware* permits a user to update the access point's firmware. Firmware capability also automatically provides Write and Admin capabilities.

- *Admin* enables the user to view all sensitive system screens and, with Write capability, to make changes to the system.

Table 8-3 summarizes these user capabilities.

Table 8-3   Cisco User Capabilities

Assigned Capability	Write Access	Ident Access	Firmware Access	Admin Access
Write	X			X
Ident	X	X		X
Firmware	X		X	X
Admin	X			X

You can also remove users in the User Management dialog box.

Click Apply when you finish entering the User Management information. That information is then be recorded on the AP and displayed on the User Information dialog box.

The next step is to turn on the security features. Return to the Security Setup screen by pressing the Back button on the browser, then click User Manager to display the User Manager Setup screen, as shown in Figure 8-10.

From this page, you can turn on the system security features. Click Enabled to turn on system security. Then only those users who were entered under User Management will have access to the AP. Click Disabled to turn off system security. To allow any user to view the AP's basic screens, click yes on the option Allow Read-Only Browsing without Login. Clicking no here restricts access to all of the access point's screens to the users in the user list. Under the Protect Legal Credit Page? option, click yes to restrict access to the Legal Credit page to users in the user list. Click no to allow any user to view the Legal Credit page.

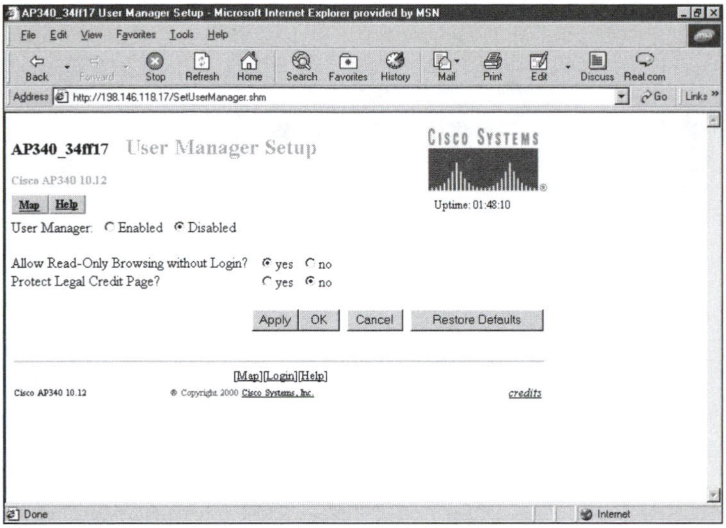

Figure 8-10   Cisco User Manager Setup screen

To enable security, an Administrator user must already have Write, Identity, and Firmware capabilities.

A fundamental rule of security is to turn off any features that will not be used. This narrows the opportunity for unauthorized access. If you are not using Telnet to configure the AP, you should disable it. For Cisco, click Setup from the Summary Status page and then click Console/Telnet under the Services heading to display the Console/Telnet page. Click the Disabled button on the Telnet line, then click the Apply button to disable Telnet.

Telnet logins are enabled by default on both 3Com and Cisco APs.

Protecting the 3Com AP

The 3Com AirConnect does not permit multiple users to have different accounts in order to access the AP. Instead, it allows only a single Administrator account with one system password. To change the system password, open a browser from a computer on the WLAN or on the wired network and enter the IP number of the access point to display the opening screen. On the tree in the left pane, click Access Point, then Configuration, and finally Security. When prompted, enter the username Administrator and the default password *comcomcom*. This displays the Security Setup screen, as shown in Figure 8-11.

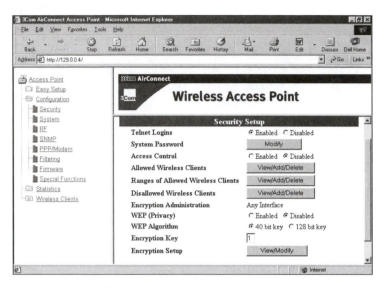

Figure 8-11   3Com Security Setup

Click the Modify button in the System Password line to display the Modify System Password screen. Enter a new password here, then click the Save Settings button.

> 💡 **Tip**   3Com passwords can be up to 13 characters long.

As with the Cisco AP, if you are not using Telnet to configure the AP, you should disable it. Click Access Point, then Configuration, and finally Security to view the Security Setup page. Click the Disabled radio button on the Telnet Logins screen to prevent unauthorized access. Click the Save Settings button at the bottom of the page to retain the settings.

Restricting Station Access

Limiting the ability of stations to associate with the WLAN is another important means of securing the network.

Viewing Current Access

To view the stations that are currently associated with an access point using Cisco Aironet, open a browser and enter the IP number of the access point to display the Summary Status screen. Click the Associations button. The page that appears displays information about stations that the access point knows about, indicates whether they are associated or authenticated, and specifies the name of the AP to which the station is associated.

To view the stations that are associated with an access point using AirConnect, open a browser and enter the IP number of the access point. On the tree in the left pane, click Access Point, then Wireless Clients, and finally Known Wireless Clients. The page that appears displays information about stations that the access point knows about.

Prohibiting Active Scanning Responses

A WLAN station must go through a process of communicating with the access point before the station can become accepted as part of the network. This process is known as association. Association is accomplished by scanning. Active scanning involves the station first sending out a special frame and then waiting for an answer from the access point with the needed information for the station to associate with the WLAN. One of those pieces of information needed is the Service Set Identifier (SSID) number, which is a unique identifier that has been assigned to an access point.

Active scanning, however, can allow any station to associate with the network just by "asking." The AP, when it receives a request, broadcasts back the SSID and any other information needed to associate. Both Cisco and 3Com provide mechanisms to prevent unwanted stations from associating. They do so by prohibiting the AP from responding to active scanning requests. Only those stations that have been previously given the SSID can associate with the WLAN.

To prohibit active scanning in a Cisco WLAN, click the Setup button on the Summary Status page to display the Setup page. Under the Network Ports heading, locate the AP Radio line, then click the Hardware link. This displays the AP Radio Hardware page, as shown in Figure 8-12. This page displays the Service Set Identifier (SSID).

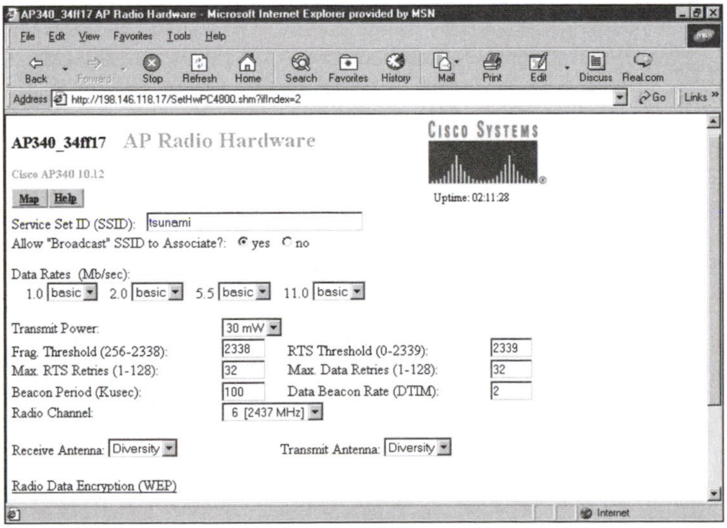

Figure 8-12   Cisco AP Radio Hardware

The option Allow "Broadcast" SSID to Associate? enables you to choose whether devices that do not specify the AP's SSID but instead are using active scanning can associate with this access point. Click no to prohibit devices that do not specify an SSID from associating with this access point.

 With Cisco, the default setting is yes, which allows devices that do not specify an SSID to associate with the access point.

To disable association of stations using active scanning for a 3Com AirConnect AP, click Configuration and then RF in the tree to display the RF Setup screen, as shown in Figure 8-13. For the Accept Broadcast Wireless LAN Service Area, click the Disabled radio button to prevent the AP from accepting stations that are using active scanning and do not know the SSID.

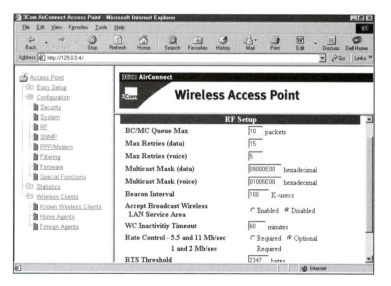

Figure 8-13 3Com RF Setup

 With 3Com, the default setting is Disabled, which does not allow devices that do not specify an SSID to associate with the access point.

Creating an Access Control List

One method of authenticating users is to create a list of approved users. A list of pre-approved MAC addresses can be entered into the Access Control List (ACL) table in the access point. Only those stations on the ACL will be provided admittance. The 3Com AirConnect provides an option to create and manage an ACL.

Cisco Aironet versions 10.12 and below do not support ACLs.

To create a list of stations that can access the AP, on the tree in the left pane click Access Point, then Configuration, and finally Security. This displays the Security Setup screen. Click the Enabled radio button on the Access Control line. Then click View/Add/Delete next to Allowed Wireless Clients. This displays the Allowed Wireless Clients screen, as shown in Figure 8-14.

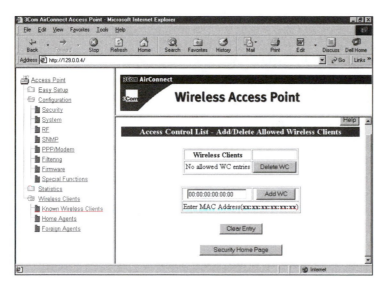

Figure 8-14   3Com Allowed Wireless Clients screen

Enter the MAC address of a wireless station that is permitted to associate with the AP and click Add Wireless Client. Repeat this step for all the wireless stations that are permitted to associate with the AP. Click Security Home Page when finished.

 Click Clear Entry if you decide not to allow the wireless client to associate with the AP.

The AirConnect also allows you to create an ACL of stations that should *not* be permitted access. On the Security Setup screen, click View/Add/Delete next to Disallowed Wireless Clients. This displays the Disallowed Wireless Clients screen, as shown in Figure 8-15. Enter the MAC address of each wireless station that *cannot* associate with the AP. Click Security Home Page when finished.

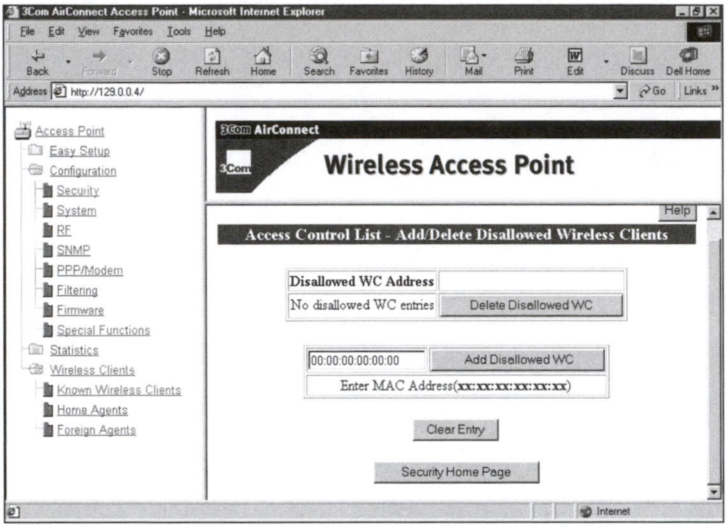

Figure 8-15   3Com Disallowed Wireless Clients screen

> You can also enter a range of MAC addresses for allowed stations. On the Security
> Setup screen, click View/Add/Delete next to Ranges of Allowed Wireless Clients.
> **Tip**   Enter the MAC address of the allowed wireless station that begins the range, then
> the MAC address of the station that ends the range.

Installing WEP Encryption

The 802.11 standard provides an optional Wired Equivalent Privacy (WEP) specification for data encryption between wireless devices to increase privacy and prevent eavesdropping. The WEP standard specifies data encryption using a 40-bit shared key. The standard also allows proprietary privacy extensions by WLAN vendors.

Both 3Com and Cisco offer their own 128-bit encryption mechanism. The access point and each station can have as many as four shared keys. Each key must be manually entered and must correspond to the same key position in each of the other devices.

3Com WEP

To enable WEP on a 3Com product, on the tree in the left pane click Access Point, then Configuration, then Security. This displays the Security Setup screen. Select Enabled for WEP (Privacy) to turn on encryption. Click the 128 bit key radio button next to WEP Algorithm, and then click Save Settings. Click the View/Modify button next to Encryption Setup to display the 128 Bit Shared Key Encryption Setup screen, as shown in Figure 8-16.

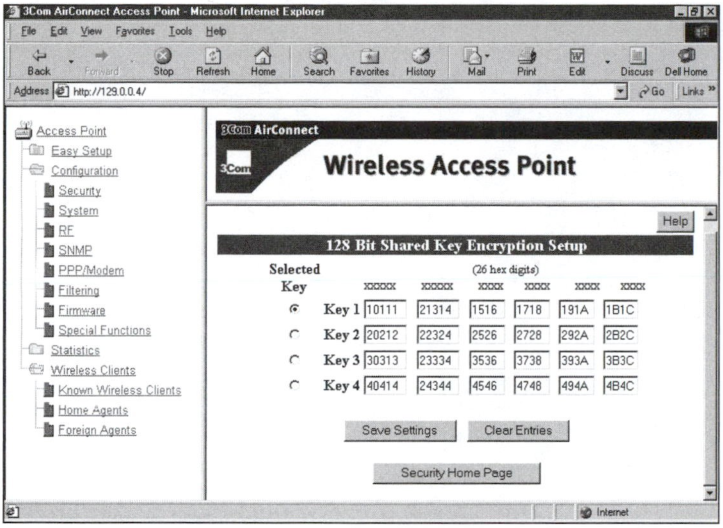

Figure 8-16   3Com 128 Bit Shared Key Encryption Setup

Due to export restrictions, only the 40-bit encryption key is available outside the United States.

Select the key to create by clicking the radio button next to Key 1, Key 2, Key 3, or Key 4. Enter five **hexadecimal** characters in the first two fields and four hexadecimal characters in the remaining four fields (hexadecimal is the base 16 number system). A hexadecimal character is any numeric character 0 through 9 and any letter character A through F (either uppercase or lowercase). Click the Save Settings button when you are finished.

The final step is to reset the AP. Click Configuration, then Special Functions. Select the Reset AP check box. Click the Perform Function button to reset the AP.

You also must enter the WEP key into each station. On the wireless station, right-click Network Neighborhood, then click Properties to display the Network dialog box. Highlight the AirConnect PC Card, then click the Properties button. Click the AirConnect tab, then the Advanced button. Select the Encryption tab, as shown in Figure 8-17. Note that these steps may differ slightly for Windows 2000.

Figure 8-17   Encryption setup on the station

Change the current Encryption setting from the default No Encryption to 128-bit Encryption. Select the key that will be used by clicking the radio button next to that key. Enter the key identically to how it was entered into the AP. Click OK to save changes and close all the windows. Reboot the station. When encryption is enabled, the 3Com launcher shows a lock on the data stream, as shown in Figure 8-18.

Figure 8-18   3Com Launcher with encryption enabled

Cisco WEP

To enable WEP on the Cisco Aironet 340 series of products, the user setting the WEP parameters must have an account with Write, Ident, and Admin capabilities. The system security features must also be turned on, forcing the user to log in. After the user has logged in, he or she must follow these steps:

1. Open a browser and enter the IP number of the access point to display the Summary Status screen.

2. Click **Setup** from the Summary Status page, then click **Security** under the Services heading. This displays the Security Setup page. Click **Radio Data Encryption (WEP)**. The AP Radio Data Encryption page appears, as shown in Figure 8-19.

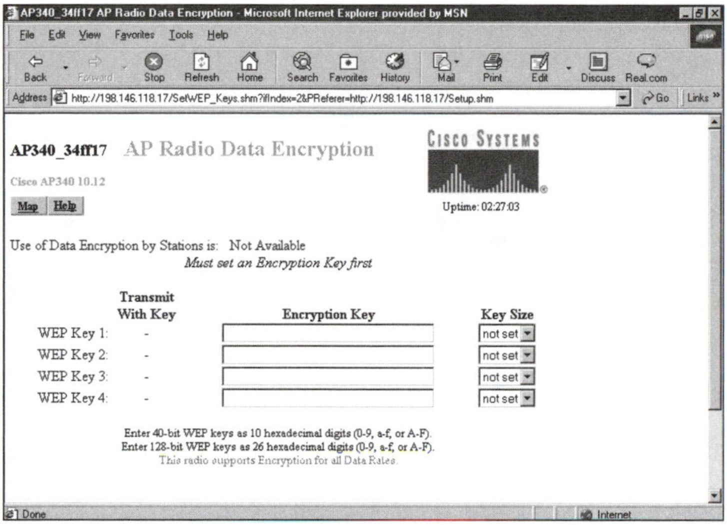

Figure 8-19   Cisco AP Radio Data Encryption

3. Enter a WEP key in one of the WEP key entry fields. Type 10 hexadecimal characters for a 40-bit WEP key or 26 hexadecimal characters for a 128-bit WEP key. Select the WEP level for the key, 40 or 128, from the pull-down menu beside the entry field. Click the radio button to the left of the key that is to be used. Click the **Apply** button.

> You can create as many as four WEP keys. However, only one key at a time can be made active. To activate a key, click the radio button to the left of the key that is to be used.

4. The screen will refresh and the WEP key will no longer appear. In the "Use of Data Encryption by Stations is" line, a pull-down menu is now available. Select **Full Encryption**. Click the **Apply** button.

> The choice Optional allows stations to communicate with the AP either with or without WEP data encryption.

5. The user must also enable WEP on each station. Start the Client Encryption Manager (CEM) program on the station. When prompted for a password, enter **Cisco** (make sure to capitalize the first letter only, as this password is case-sensitive). The CEM window appears, as shown in Figure 8-20.

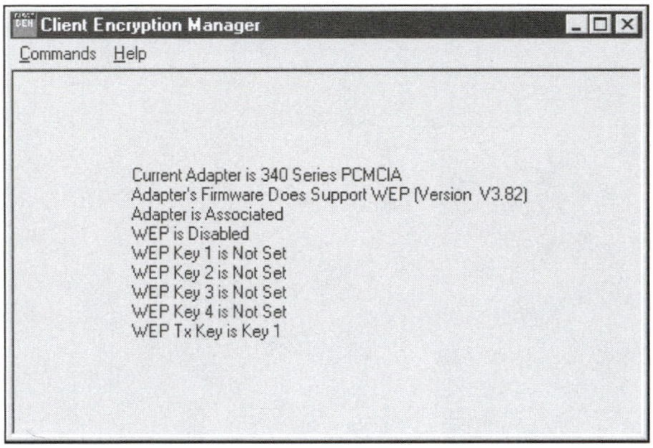

Client Encryption Manager

Commands Help

Current Adapter is 340 Series PCMCIA
Adapter's Firmware Does Support WEP (Version V3.82)
Adapter is Associated
WEP is Disabled
WEP Key 1 is Not Set
WEP Key 2 is Not Set
WEP Key 3 is Not Set
WEP Key 4 is Not Set
WEP Tx Key is Key 1

Figure 8-20   Cisco CEM

As of this writing, the Cisco Aironet PC Card Client Adapter documentation incorrectly lists the CEM password as *Aironet*.

6. To enter a WEP Key, choose **Enter WEP Key** from the Commands pull-down menu on the main screen. The Enter WEP Key(s) screen appears, as shown in Figure 8-21.

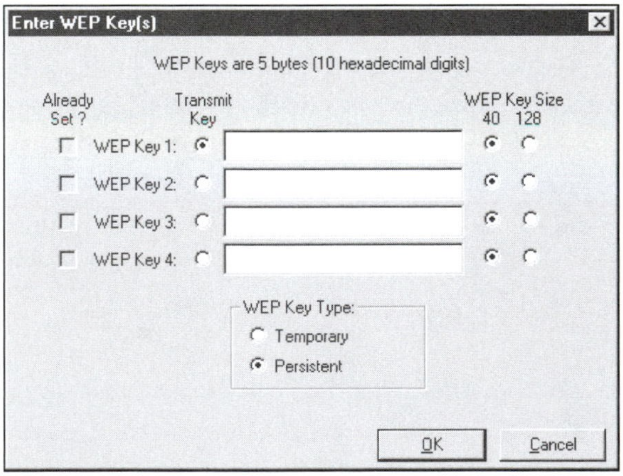

Enter WEP Key(s)

WEP Keys are 5 bytes (10 hexadecimal digits)

Already Set ?	Transmit Key		WEP Key Size 40 128
☐ WEP Key 1: ⦿			⦿ ○
☐ WEP Key 2: ○			⦿ ○
☐ WEP Key 3: ○			⦿ ○
☐ WEP Key 4: ○			⦿ ○

WEP Key Type:
○ Temporary
⦿ Persistent

OK   Cancel

Figure 8-21   Cisco Enter WEP Key(s) screen

7. Click the *Transmit Key* radio button next to the WEP key that is to be used. Also, click the radio button for the correct key size (40 or 128). Enter the WEP key identically to the one entered in the AP.

8. There are two types of WEP keys, temporary and persistent. A temporary WEP key is in effect only as long as this station is turned on. Once the station is rebooted, the key must be reentered. A persistent WEP key causes the computer to retain the key even after the station is rebooted. Click **Persistent**. Click **OK**. Click **OK** to the WEP Key Write Complete message.

9. The final group of settings is set through the Aironet Client Utility (ACU). Click **Start**, point to **Programs**, point to **Cisco Systems, Inc.**, then click **Aironet Client Utility** to start the ACU program.

10. Click the **Commands** menu, then **Edit Properties**. Click the **RF Network** tab to display the RF Network screen, as shown in Figure 8-22. Click the **Enable WEP** check box. Click **OK**.

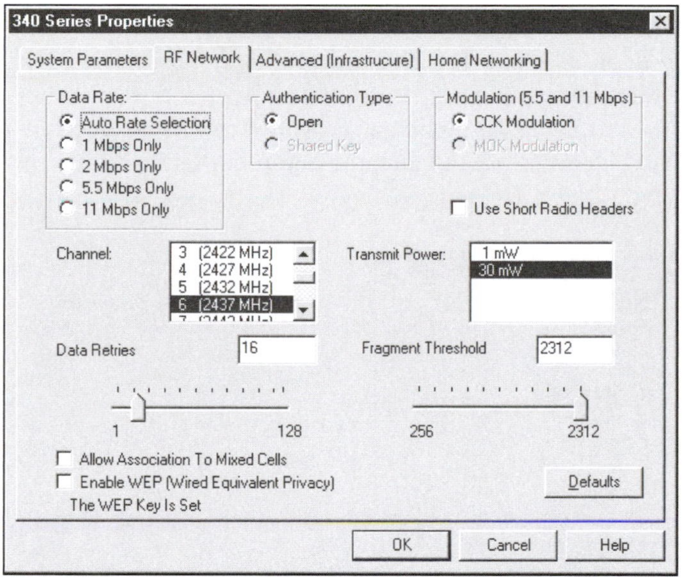

Figure 8-22 RF Network tab

11. Reboot the system to enable WEP encryption.

CONDUCTING A SITE SURVEY

A site survey is used to help determine the best location for the access point and to determine the boundaries of the WLAN cell. Where to place an AP can be a difficult decision. The geographic center of a proposed WLAN cell may not always be the best location.

A number of factors can impact radio wave transmission, such as physical obstacles (walls and doors) as well as devices that may emit their own waves (microwave ovens) that can interfere with a WLAN. All of these affect the placement of the AP. A site survey is an important tool that helps locate the best place to install the AP.

However, site surveys are not just used when a WLAN is first installed. Wireless stations can roam within the entire area of the cell and may encounter interference from a variety of obstacles or devices in that area. It's very likely that several weeks after the WLAN is installed a user may roam into an area of the cell that no one has ever roamed into before, encountering previously unknown interference. Site surveys conducted on a regular basis can help identify problem areas and determine what adjustments are needed.

Site surveys are run from the local station and not on the access point.

Cisco Site Surveys

The Cisco Site Survey utility is a very fundamental tool that is part of the Aironet Client Utility (ACU). Click Start, point to Programs, point to Cisco Systems, Inc., then click Aironet Client Utility to start the ACU program. Click the Commands menu and then Site Survey to display the Site Survey window. Click the Setup button to display the settings, as shown in Figure 8-23.

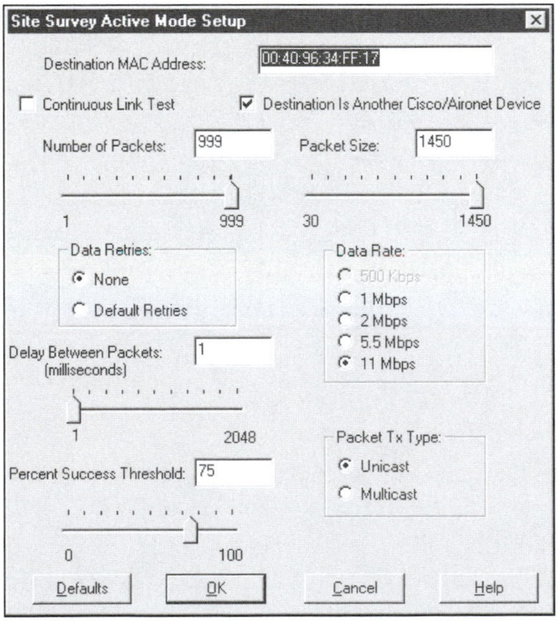

Figure 8-23   Cisco Site Survey Active Mode Setup

Some of the settings include:

- *Destination MAC Address* specifies the AP that will be involved in the test. The default is the MAC address of the access point with which the client adapter is currently associated.

- *Continuous Link Test* causes the Active Mode test to run repeatedly until the user clicks the Stop button on the Site Survey page.

- *Destination Is Another Cisco/Aironet Device* specifies that the access point named in the Destination MAC Address field is a Cisco Aironet 340 Series access point.

- *Number of Packets* sets the quantity of packets that will be sent during the test.

- *Packet Size* sets the size of the packets that will be sent during the test. The Packet Size setting should be a size that typically would be found during normal use of the WLAN.

- *Data Retries* sets the number of times a transmission will be repeated if the destination device does not return an acknowledgment (ACK) frame.

- *Data Rate* sets the bit rate at which packets will be transmitted.

- *Delay Between Packets* specifies the delay in milliseconds between successive transmissions.

- *Packet Tx Type* sets the packet type that will be used during the test. A **unicast** transmission means that a frame is sent from one sender to a single receiver. A **multicast** transmission means that a frame is sent from one sender to multiple receivers with a single "transmit" operation. If you select the Unicast option, the station will expect an ACK from the destination and will continue to retry until the station receives one. The Multicast option does not perform packet retries.

- *Percent Success Threshold* allows the user to establish a baseline for what is considered satisfactory performance. Percentages that are greater than or equal to this baseline will be displayed as green bars, whereas percentages below this value will show up as yellow bars on the Percent Successful histogram.

When the Cisco Site Survey program is running, the screen in Figure 8-24 appears. A user should roam through the entire service area with the station, noting areas in which signal strength and quality fall below the threshold level. A more thorough evaluation may then be needed to determine whether the AP should be moved or if sources of interference such as microwave ovens can be relocated.

Passive mode or passive scanning involves a station listening to each available channel for a set period of time for a beacon frame transmitted from all available access points. Active mode or active scanning involves the station first sending out a special frame on each available channel and then waiting for an answer from all available access points.

```
┌─────────────────────────────────────────────────────┐
│ Site Survey - PC4800 - Passive Mode              [X] │
│                                                       │
│       Signal Strength          Beacons Received       │
│     ┌───────────────────┐    ┌───────────────────┐   │
│     │       100%         │    │       100%         │   │
│     └───────────────────┘    └───────────────────┘   │
│     ┌───────────────────┐    ┌───────────────────┐   │
│     │||||||||||||||||||||│    │||||||||||||||||||||│   │
│     └───────────────────┘    └───────────────────┘   │
│                              ┌───────────────────┐   │
│     Link Speed    11 Mbps    │||||||||||||||||||||│   │
│                              └───────────────────┘   │
│       Overall Link Quality        Excellent           │
│     Associated Access Point    No Name Specified      │
│     Access Point IP Address       0.0.0.0             │
│       Channel (Frequency)      6   (2437 MHz)         │
│                                                       │
│       Percent Complete    ┌───────────────────────┐  │
│                           │        100%            │  │
│                           └───────────────────────┘  │
│       Percent Successful  ┌───────────────────────┐  │
│                           │                  ||||||│  │
│                           └───────────────────────┘  │
│       Lost To Target              0                   │
│       Lost To Source              0                   │
│                                                       │
│  ┌──────┐ ┌──────┐ ┌──────┐ ┌────────┐ ┌──────┐     │
│  │ Setup│ │ Start│ │  OK  │ │ Cancel │ │ Help │     │
│  └──────┘ └──────┘ └──────┘ └────────┘ └──────┘     │
└─────────────────────────────────────────────────────┘
```

Figure 8-24   Cisco Site Survey

3Com Site Surveys

The 3Com site survey provides several options that the Cisco site survey does not. To install the 3Com site survey software, insert the Administrator CD-ROM and start the 3Com AirConnect WLAN utilities program. Click WLAN Utilities, then Install Site Survey Software. Follow the instructions to complete the installation. When the software is installed, click Start, point to Programs, point to 3Com AirConnect, then click Site Survey to display a blank AirConnect Site Survey screen, as illustrated in Figure 8-25.

 If the station has previously been used for a site survey, a Welcome screen will appear first. Close this dialog box.

Click the View menu to see the status of the current WLAN. Clicking the Adapter Info option displays the information (driver version, adapter type, etc.) about the currently installed wireless NIC. The Known APs selection shows the access points that are in range of the wireless station and information about those APs. The Noise Meter selection displays a graph of the relative signal strength indicator values, as displayed in Figure 8-26. The Signal Quality selection displays the percentage of missed signals, transmission retries, and errors logged during its ping test.

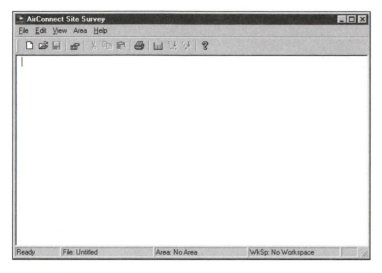

Figure 8-25   3Com Site Survey

> The Signal Quality information is useful in determining whether the AP loca-
> tions are effective for providing radio coverage to the coverage area.

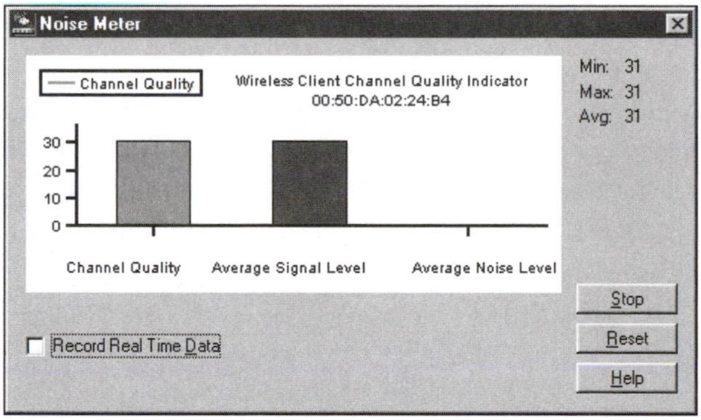

Figure 8-26   3Com Noise Meter

Before running a site survey, you should change several of the default settings. Click the Edit menu and select Default Settings to display the Site Survey Settings dialog box, as shown in Figure 8-27. Click the Setup tab. The IP number must be that of the access point with which the station is associated. Change the ICMP Host Addr to the IP number of the AP. Next click the Meter Settings tab. This allows you to set the baseline for the signal quality bars for the

8

Round Trip, Missed Beacon, and Transmit Retry fields. The indicators on the Site Survey Test screen show green if the average of the previous tests is below the lower threshold, red if the average is above the upper threshold, and yellow if the test results are between these threshold values.

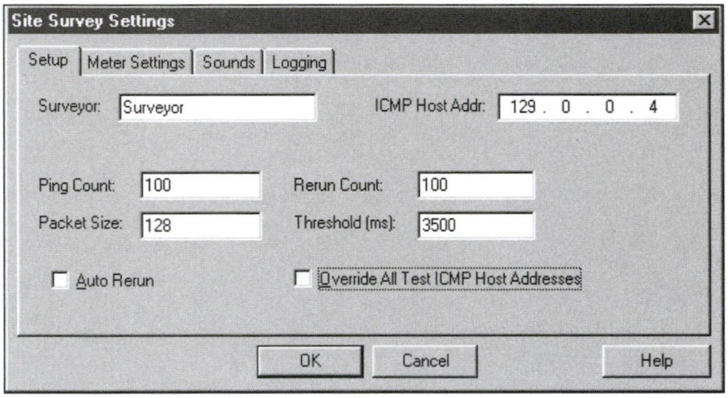

Figure 8-27 3Com default site survey settings

If you receive the error message "Destination Host Unreachable," the IP number has not been set. If, after setting the ICMP Host Addr, you receive the same error message, return to the Default Settings page and select the check box Override All Test ICMP Host Addresses.

By default, an audible tone sounds every time that a ping test timeout is reached, a wireless station roams between APs, a threshold is met or exceeded, or a suite of ping tests has been transmitted. You can turn off the tones by clicking the Sounds tab on the Site Survey Settings dialog box.

To run a site survey test, click the File menu, then New Site Survey. Enter the Date, Site Name, the name of the Surveyor, and any descriptive notes in the Site Survey Settings dialog box. When the Site Survey Area dialog box appears, enter an Area Name and a Test Name. The Save As dialog box then appears. The test results are saved in a text file that can be imported into a word processing document. Enter the filename to save the test results.

The Site Survey Test dialog box then reappears. Click Start Test to begin the site test. Figure 8-28 illustrates the results of such a test. A user should roam through the entire service area with the station, noting areas in which signal strength and quality fall below the threshold level. A more thorough evaluation may then be needed to determine whether the AP should be moved or if obstacles such as microwave ovens can be relocated. Click Stop Test when the test is finished.

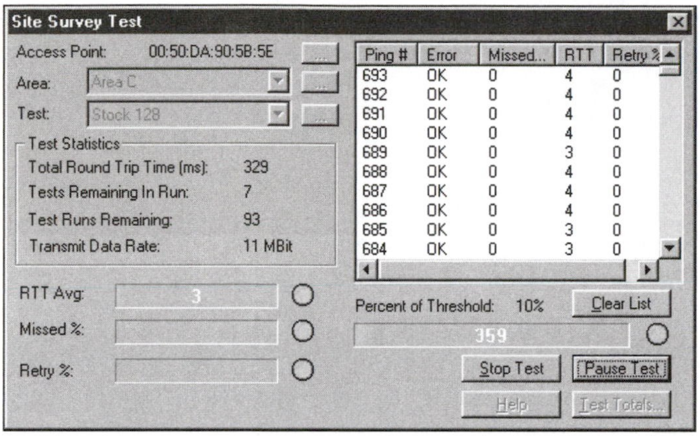

Figure 8-28   3Com Site Survey Test dialog box

8

ENABLING POWER MANAGEMENT

Most stations in a WLAN are portable laptop computers, which often depend on batteries as their primary power source. To conserve battery power, laptops go into sleep mode after a period of time. In sleep mode, the computer temporarily powers down some hardware functions, such as the hard drive or display screen. However, the laptop must continue to be able to receive network transmissions, even in sleep mode. Power management allows the mobile station to be off as much as possible to conserve battery life but not miss out on data transmissions. Power management is transparent to all protocols and applications so that it will not interfere with the normal network functions.

Cisco Power Management

To enable power management on a Cisco station, click Start, point to Programs, point to Cisco Systems, Inc., then click Aironet Client Utility to start the ACU program. Click the Commands menu, then select Edit Properties. Click the System Parameters tab, as shown in Figure 8-29.

The three options for Cisco power management are:

- *Constant Awake Mode (CAM)* is the default mode that keeps the radio always powered on.

- *Maximum Power Save Mode (Max PSP)* allows the client adapter to conserve the most power while still maintaining a connection. When the station goes into sleep mode, the access point is informed. As the access point receives transmissions for that station, the AP temporarily stores those frames. At set intervals, the access point sends to all stations a beacon frame indicating which stations have buffered frames waiting at the access point. At that same set time, all stations that have been sleeping switch from sleep mode into an active listening mode. If a station has buffered frames waiting for it, that station can send a request to the access point to have those frames forwarded to it and then go back to sleep.

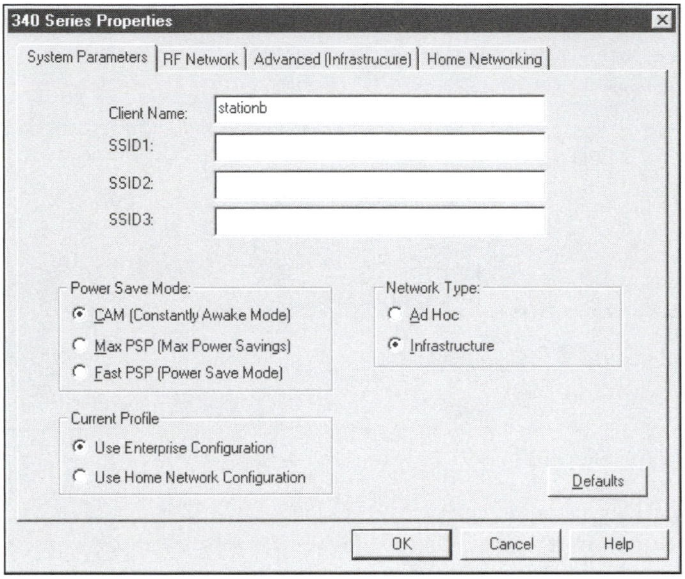

Figure 8-29   Cisco System Parameters tab

- *Fast Power Save Mode (Fast PSP)* switches the radio on and off depending on network traffic. When a station is retrieving a large number of frames, Fast PSP switches the radio to CAM to retrieve all the frames. Once all the frames are retrieved, the radio switches to power save mode.

3Com Power Management

The 3Com power management feature is similar to the Cisco feature. The 3Com wireless NIC adapters support two power management modes:

- *Continuous Active Mode* ensures that the radio always remains on.

- *Power Save Polling* conserves power by suspending the adapter's communication with an associated access point. The access point saves data for transmission to the station. When the station awakens to check for data, it switches back into Continuous Active Mode until it is again ready to suspend communications.

To enable 3Com power management, click the 3Com icon in the Windows system tray on the lower-right portion of the screen. This opens the 3Com Launcher. Click the Settings icon and click the Power Mode tab to display the Power Mode screen, as shown in Figure 8-30.

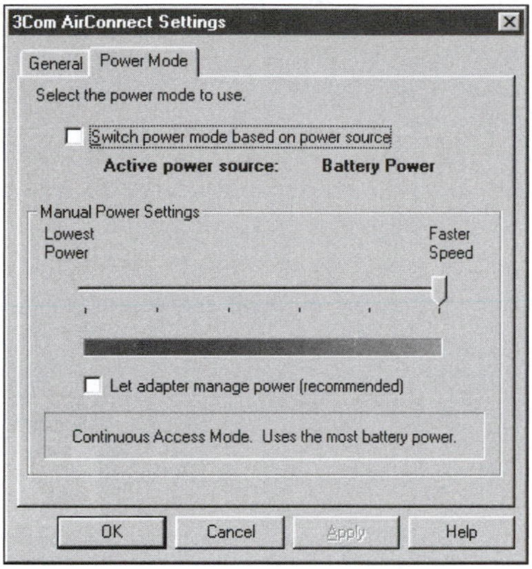

3Com AirConnect Settings   ☒

General | Power Mode |

Select the power mode to use.

☐ Switch power mode based on power source

Active power source: Battery Power

Manual Power Settings
Lowest   Faster
Power   Speed

☐ Let adapter manage power (recommended)

Continuous Access Mode. Uses the most battery power.

[OK]   [Cancel]   [Apply]   [Help]

Figure 8-30   3Com Power Mode tab

Selecting the check box *Switch power mode based on power source* causes the power mode to be switched based on whether the station is using AC or battery power. When this option is selected, the station uses continuous polling mode with an AC power source and power save polling when a battery is powering the station. The Power Save Polling slider also permits the user to balance network performance against power consumption. When the slider is set to the lowest power, the adapter checks network traffic less frequently, reducing power consumption. When the slider is set to highest performance, the adapter tries to maintain constant contact with the network, increasing network performance but consuming more power. Selecting the check box *Let adapter manage power* allows the system to use the best setting available at any given time.

The interval at which the AP is polled is based on whether the system has received data recently. If no data is being received, the polling interval becomes less frequent over time, gradually decreasing power consumption.

CHAPTER SUMMARY

❑ Cisco and 3Com provide a variety of ways to access the access point. Both Cisco and 3Com offer access to the AP through (1) direct serial connection using terminal emulator software, (2) Telnet, an application protocol within TCP/IP that enables a user to connect to another computer or device so that the device responds as though it were connected to a terminal, and (3) a browser. The 3Com AirConnect has one additional option for accessing the access point: "dial-up" access via a modem. For accessing either Cisco or 3Com access points, the browser-based screen is the easiest option and is the preferred method.

❑ One of the most important steps to take when configuring a WLAN is to install appropriate security features. You must protect the access point in two ways: from theft or tampering and from unauthorized users viewing or changing sensitive settings. Both Cisco and 3Com have extensive security features for protecting the AP. Cisco grants a user account to each user who will be accessing the AP. The 3Com AirConnect does not permit multiple users to have accounts in order to access the AP. Instead, there is a single Administrator account with one system password. Limiting the ability of a station to associate with the WLAN is another important means of securing the network. You can accomplish this by prohibiting the AP from responding to active scanning requests. Another method of authenticating users is to create a list of approved users. You can enter a list of preapproved MAC addresses into the Access Control List (ACL) table in the access point. The AP will then admit only those stations listed in the ACL. The 802.11 standard provides an optional Wired Equivalent Privacy (WEP) specification for data encryption between wireless devices to increase privacy and prevent eavesdropping. The WEP standard specifies data encryption using a 40-bit shared key. The standard also allows proprietary privacy extensions by the WLAN vendors. Both 3Com and Cisco offer proprietary 128-bit encryption mechanisms.

❑ A site survey is used to help determine the best location for the access point and to determine the boundaries of the WLAN cell. When running the 3Com or Cisco site survey software, a user should roam through the entire service area with the station, noting areas in which signal strength and quality fall below the threshold level. A more thorough evaluation may then be needed to determine whether the AP should be moved or whether obstacles can be relocated.

❑ Most stations in a WLAN are portable laptop computers, which often depend on batteries as their primary power source. 3Com and Cisco provide power management options to allow stations to conserve battery power by going into sleep mode, yet continue to be able to receive network transmissions. The two main options for power management for both 3Com and Cisco are Constant Awake Mode (CAM), which keeps the radio always powered on, and an alternate mode that conserves power by suspending the adapter's communication with an associated access point. The access point saves data for transmission to the station.

Key Terms

hexadecimal — The base 16 numbering system.

multicast — A transmission mode that sends a frame from one sender to multiple receivers with a single transmit operation.

Telnet — An application protocol that is part of the TCP/IP suite that provides support for terminal emulation.

unicast — A transmission mode that sends a frame from one sender to a single receiver.

REVIEW QUESTIONS

1. Each of the following is a means by which a Cisco user can access the AP except _____.
   a. direct serial connection using terminal-emulator software
   b. modem
   c. browser
   d. Telnet

2. _____ is an application protocol within TCP/IP that provides support for terminal emulation.
   a. Telnet
   b. Ping
   c. ARP
   d. Reverse ARP

3. To use a browser to access an AP, point to the access point by entering the _____ on the browser's address line.
   a. station's MAC address
   b. AP's MAC address
   c. AP's IP number
   d. WLAN SSID number

4. A(n) _____ can be used to access the access the Cisco Aironet AP using a browser.
   a. wireless station
   b. AP
   c. 3Com AP
   d. Telnet AP

5. The default 3Com administrator password is _____.
   a. comcomcom
   b. 3com
   c. 3COM
   d. AirConnect

6. To end a Telnet session, press Ctrl+D. True or false?

7. The computer using Telnet can be on a wired network or a wireless LAN. True or false?

8. A dial-up connection requires a null-modem serial cable between an internal modem and the AP. True or false?

9. 3Com recommends that the browser caching function be turned off for the browser to display the configuration changes correctly on the Web pages. True or false?

8

10. Security features involve only the station but not the access point. True or false?

11. If an access point is installed in a closet, an optional _____ may need to be mounted on the access point.

12. With the _____ product, each user who will be accessing the AP should be given his or her own user account.

13. The _____ Cisco capabilities allow the specified user to change the system settings.

14. When the Cisco Ident capability is given to a user, that user also automatically receives Write and _____ capabilities.

15. If Telnet will not be used to configure the AP, it should be _____.

16. Explain how to view the stations that are currently associated with an access point using Cisco Aironet.

17. Explain how to view the stations that are currently associated with an access point using 3Com AirConnect.

18. Explain active scanning and how it can be prevented.

19. What is an Access Control List? Which product supports it?

20. Tell how to create a WEP key.

HANDS-ON PROJECTS

1. Access the access point of the Cisco Aironet (by either a direct serial connection using terminal-emulator software, Telnet, or a browser) or the 3Com AirConnect (by either a direct serial connection using terminal-emulator software, Telnet, a browser, or a modem). Record each step as you perform it. What problems did you encounter? Write a one-page step-by-step instruction sheet about how to connect to the access point.

2. Protect the access point from unauthorized users. If you are using the Cisco Aironet 340 series, follow these steps:

   a. Open a browser and enter the IP number of the access point to display the Summary Status screen. Click **Setup** from the Summary Status page and then click **Security** under the Services heading.

   b. Click **User Information**, then **Add New User**. Create two user accounts: The first should be an account with your name with Write and Ident capabilities, and the second should be Administrator with all capabilities.

   c. Click **Apply** when finished entering the User Management information.

   d. Turn on security by returning to the Security Setup screen by pressing the **Back** button on the browser. Then click **User Manager** to display the User Manager Setup screen. Click **Enabled** to turn on the system security, and click **OK**.

   e. Click **Login**. Log in both your personal account and the new Administrator account.

If you are using 3Com AirConnect, follow these steps:

a. Open a browser and enter the IP number of the access point to display the opening screen. On the tree in the left pane, click **Access Point**, then **Configuration**, then finally **Security**. When prompted, enter the username **Administrator** and the default password **comcomcom**. This displays the Security Setup screen.

b. Click the **Modify** button in the System Password line to display the Modify System Password screen. Enter a new system password. 3Com passwords can be up to 13 characters long. Click the **Save Settings b**utton.

3. View the stations that are currently associated with an access point. If you are using Cisco Aironet, open a browser and enter the IP number of the access point to display the Summary Status screen. Click the **Associations** button. The page that appears displays information about stations that the access point knows about, whether they are associated or authenticated, and the name of the AP to which the station is associated. If you are using 3Com AirConnect, open a browser and enter the IP number of the access point. On the tree in the left pane, click **Access Point**, then **Wireless Clients**, then finally **Known Wireless Clients**. The page that appears displays information about stations that the access point knows about.

4. Prohibit the AP from responding to active scanning requests. If you are using a Cisco WLAN, follow these steps:

a. Log in as the administrator.

b. Click the **Setup** button on the home page to display the Setup page. Under the Network Ports heading, locate the AP Radio line, then click **Hardware** to display the AP Radio Hardware page.

c. Record the Service Set ID (SSID) displayed on this page.

d. Click **no** under the option Allow "Broadcast" SSID to Associate? Then click **Apply**.

If you are using a 3Com AirConnect, follow these steps:

a. Log in as the administrator.

b. Click **Configuration**, then **RF** in the tree to display the RF Setup screen.

c. For the Accept Broadcast Wireless LAN Service Area, click the **Disabled** radio button to prevent the AP from accepting stations that are using active scanning and do not know the SSID.

5. Use 3Com's AirConnect to create and manage an ACL. Follow these steps:

a. Log in as the administrator.

b. On the tree in the left pane, click **Access Point**, then **Configuration**, then **Security** to display the Security Setup screen.

c. Click the **Enabled** radio button on the Access Control line.

d. Click **View/Add/Delete** next to Allowed Wireless Clients. This displays the Allowed Wireless Clients screen.

e. Enter the MAC address of a wireless station that is permitted to associate with the AP. Click **Add WC**.

f. Click **Security Home Page** when finished.

8

6. Enable WEP privacy. If you are using a 3Com product, follow these steps:

   a. Log in as administrator.

   b. On the tree in the left pane, click **Access Point**, then **Configuration**, then **Security**. This displays the Security Setup screen. Select **Enabled** for **WEP (Privacy)** to turn on encryption.

   c. Click the **128 bit key** radio button next to WEP Algorithm and click the **Save Settings** button. Click the **View/Modify** button next to Encryption Setup to display the 128 Bit Setup screen.

   d. Select **Key 1** by clicking the radio button next to Key 1. Enter the following characters as the key: **1234567890123456789a12345b**.

   e. Click the **Save Settings** button when finished.

   f. Reset the AP by clicking **Configuration**, if necessary, then **Special Function**. Select the check box **Reset AP**. Click the **Perform Function** button to reset the AP.

   g. On the wireless station, right-click **Network Neighborhood**, then click **Properties** to display the Network dialog box.

   h. Highlight **AirConnect PC Card**, then click the **Properties** button. Click the **AirConnect** tab, then the **Advanced** button. Click the **Encryption** tab.

   i. Change the current Encryption setting from the default No Encryption to **128-bit Encryption**. Select the key that will be used by clicking the radio button next to that key. Enter the key identically to how it was entered into the AP.

   j. Click **OK** to save changes and close all the windows. Reboot the station.

   If you are using the Cisco Aironet 340, follow these steps:

   a. Log in as the administrator.

   b. Click **Setup** from the Summary Status page, then click **Security** under the Services heading to see the Security Setup page.

   c. Click **Radio Data Encryption (WEP)** to view the AP Radio Data Encryption page.

   d. Enter this WEP key in the Key 1 field: **987654321f987654321e98765c**.

   e. Select the WEP level for the key, **128**, from the pull-down menu beside the entry field. Click the radio button to the left of **Key 1**. Click the **Apply** button.

   f. Select **Full Encryption** from the *Use of Data Encryption by Stations is* field. Click the **Apply** button.

   g. Enable WEP on each location station. Start the program Client Encryption Manager (CEM) on the station. When prompted for a password, enter **Cisco** (remember to capitalize the password, as passwords are case-sensitive). Click **OK**.

   h. At the CEM window, choose **Enter WEP Key** from the Commands pull-down menu on the main screen.

   i. At the Enter WEP Key(s) screen, click the radio button **Transmit Key** next to the WEP Key 1. Also, click the radio button for the correct key size of **128**. Enter the WEP key identically to the one entered in the AP.

    j. Click **Persistent**, then click **OK**, and close all windows.

    k. Click **Start**, point to **Programs**, point to **Cisco Systems, Inc.**, then click **Aironet Client Utility** to start the ACU program.

    l. Click the **Commands** menu, then **Edit Properties**. Click the **RF Network** tab to display the RF Network screen.

    m. Click the box **Enable WEP**. Click **OK**.

    n. Reboot the system.

7. Conduct a site survey. If you are using Cisco products, follow these steps:

    a. Click **Start**, point to **Programs**, point to **Cisco Systems, Inc.**, then click **Aironet Client Utility** to start the ACU program.

    b. Click the **Commands** menu, then **Site Survey** to display the Site Survey window. Click the **Setup** button to display the settings. Click **OK**.

    c. Roam through the entire service area with the station, noting areas where signal strength and quality fall below the threshold level. Write a one-page paper on your observations and suggestions about improving the range of the cell.

If you are using 3Com products, follow these steps:

    a. Install the site survey software from the Administrator CD-ROM on a WLAN Station.

    b. Click **Start**, point to **Programs**, point to **3Com AirConnect**, then click **Site Survey** to display the 3Com Site Survey program. If the welcome screen appears, close it.

    c. Click the **Edit** menu, then **Default Settings** to display the Site Survey Settings window.

    d. Click the **Setup** tab. The IP number must be that of the access point with which the station is associated. Change the ICMP Host Addr to the IP number of the AP. Click **OK**.

    e. To run a site survey test, click the **File** menu, then **New Site Survey**. Enter the date, site name, the name of the surveyor, and any descriptive notes in the Site Survey dialog box. When the Site Survey Area dialog box appears, enter an area name and a test name. The Save As dialog box then appears. Enter the filename to save the test results.

    f. The Site Survey Test dialog box appears. Click **Start Test** to begin the site test.

    g. Roam through the entire service area with the station, noting areas where signal strength and quality fall below the threshold level. Write a one-page paper on your observations and suggestions for improving the range of the cell.

8. Enable power management on a laptop computer that is part of a WLAN. If you are using the Cisco product, follow these steps:

    a. Click **Start**, point to **Programs**, point to **Cisco Systems, Inc.**, then click **Aironet Client Utility** to start the ACU program. Click the **Commands** menu, then **Edit Properties**.

8

b. Click the **System Parameters** tab to display the 340 Series Parameters dialog box.

c. Click **Fast PSP**, then click **OK**.

If you are using 3Com products, follow these steps:

a. Click the **3Com** icon in the Windows system tray on the lower-right portion of the screen to open the 3Com Launcher.

b. Click the **Settings** icon, then click the **Power Mode** tab to display the Power Mode screen.

c. Click the box **Let adapter manage power**.

d. Click **OK**.

CASE PROJECT

Northridge Consulting Group

Northridge Consulting Group (NCG) again wants you to assist it with a WLAN project. The Gibbons Sports Medicine Group is interested in installing a WLAN in its offices for both physicians and the office staff. After attending seminars from vendors, the managers have narrowed their choices down to Cisco Aironet 340 or 3Com AirConnect. Because you have knowledge of both products, NCG has asked you to write a paper comparing the two products. Write a one-page executive summary paper for the Gibbons Sports Medicine Group that answers these questions:

1. What are the advantages of the 3Com AirConnect product? What are the advantages of the Cisco Aironet?

2. Which product provides the best security features? What are they?

3. Based on your observations, which product has more features? Which product is easier to use?

OPTIONAL TEAM CASE PROJECT

The Gibbons Sports Medicine Group wants four members of the office staff to be trained in enabling WEP on the WLAN. However, the company wants its employees to have a clear understanding of what is taking place, not just how to do it. These employees should understand the need for encryption, the difference between shared and private keys, and hexadecimal notation.

NCG needs your input. Create a team of three to four consultants. Each consultant should select a different aspect of WEP encryption. Research that area and create a PowerPoint slide presentation on WEP encryption for the office members.

MANAGING THE CISCO AIRONET AND 3COM AIRCONNECT

After reading this chapter and completing the exercises, you will be able to:

♦ Tell how to monitor the status of a WLAN

♦ List the steps for upgrading WLAN firmware

♦ Explain how to modify the access point's radio settings

Changing the oil in your car, replacing furnace filters, and cleaning leaves out of the gutters around the house are routine maintenance tasks. Although these jobs may not be very exciting and are sometimes downright inconvenient, they are necessary to prevent problems and keep things rolling smoothly. Neglecting routine maintenance can result in a breakdown by the side of the road, premature failure of a heating system, or a leaky roof.

Routine maintenance is also important for WLANs. Once the network is installed and properly configured, your work is not done. You need to monitor and maintain a WLAN on a regular basis to keep it running smoothly. This chapter looks at procedures for WLAN management.

MONITORING THE NETWORK

Monitoring the status of the network is a critical part of managing a network. Because the network often reveals symptoms of problems before there is a major crisis, keeping a watchful eye on the status of the network can help identify these early symptoms and prevent more serious problems.

Monitoring the status of the network is also important when initially configuring or making changes to the WLAN. Configuring or changing WLAN settings involves entering or modifying parameters for access points, wireless NICs, or the WLAN as a whole. A mistake in any of these settings could bring the network to a screeching halt. Before you attempt to make changes in the configuration of a WLAN, however, a good first step is to view the WLAN's current network connections and status. In this way, you can verify that the network is functioning properly after making changes.

Both Cisco and 3Com offer standard network monitoring tools, as well as proprietary utilities for observing the current network status. Some of the Cisco and 3Com utilities run from the station itself, whereas other utilities run from the access point.

Standard Network Monitoring Tools

SNMP and RMON are standard network monitoring tools that are used on wired networks. Both 3Com and Cisco incorporate these standard tools into their arsenal of network monitoring utilities.

SNMP

One of the most common software tools used for monitoring a network, wired or wireless, is the **Simple Network Management Protocol (SNMP)**. SNMP is a protocol that allows computers and network equipment to gather data about network performance. SNMP is part of the TCP/IP protocol suite.

Another protocol for gathering network statistics is the Common Management Interface Protocol (CMIP), which is part of the Open Systems Interconnection (OSI) model. However, CMIP requires a greater amount of resources to operate. For example, the RAM requirement for CMIP is 1.5 MB, whereas SNMP needs only 64 KB.

To use SNMP, you load **software agents** onto each network device that SNMP will manage. Each agent monitors network traffic and stores that information in its **management information base (MIB)**. In addition, a computer with the SNMP management software, known as the **SNMP management station**, must also be on the network, as shown in Figure 9-1.

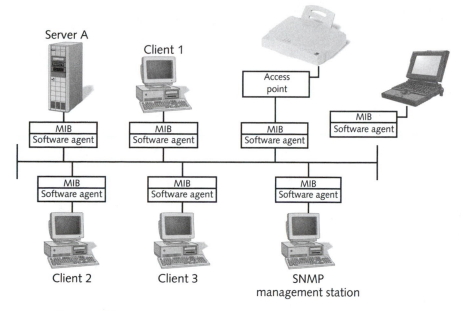

Figure 9-1   SNMP

The SNMP management station communicates with the software agents on each network device and collects the data stored in the MIBs. The station then combines all of the data and produces statistics about the network. This data includes transmission or connectivity errors, the number of bytes or data packets sent, and information on IP activity and addressing.

You can set an SNMP alarm using the network statistics. Whenever the network exceeds a predefined limit, it triggers an alert message, called an **SNMP trap**, which is sent to the management station. The management station then queries all stations for details of that specific event, including when and where the event took place and the current status of that network node.

The original version of SNMP had serious security deficiencies. The second version, called **SNMPv2**, addresses these concerns. It provides encryption as well as faster data transmission and the ability to retrieve more information at one time.

Both 3Com and Cisco support SNMP. To view the Cisco Aironet 340 SNMP page, open a browser and enter the IP number of the access point to display the Summary Status screen. Click Setup from the Summary Status page, then click SNMP under the Services heading. This displays the SNMP Setup page, as shown in Figure 9-2.

To view the 3Com AirConnect SNMP page, open a browser and enter the IP number of the access point to display the opening screen. On the tree in the left pane, click Access Point, then Configuration, then finally SNMP. When prompted, enter the username Administrator and the password *comcomcom*. This displays the SNMP screen, as shown in Figure 9-3.

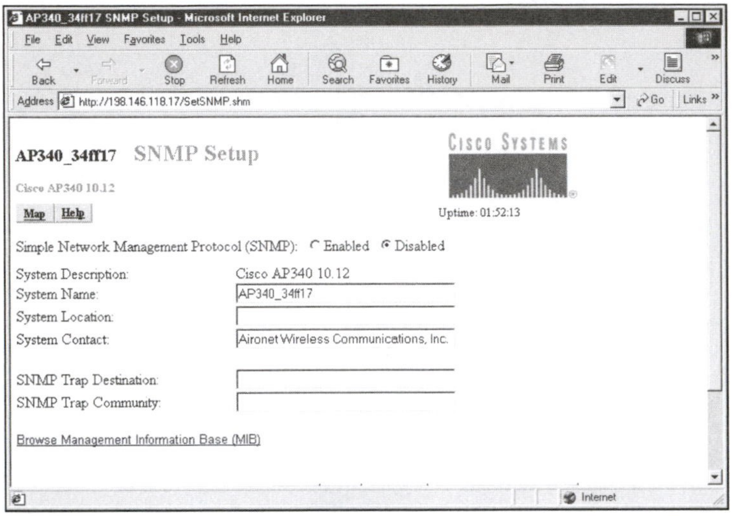

Figure 9-2 Cisco SNMP page

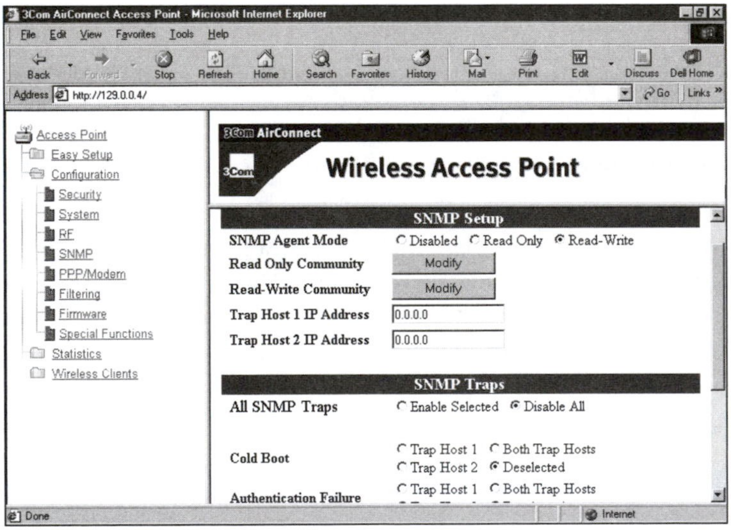

Figure 9-3 3Com SNMP page

Note: The topics of setting up software agents and installing SNMP management stations are beyond the scope of this book.

RMON

Remote Network Monitoring (RMON) is an SNMP-based tool that is used to monitor LANs that are connected through a wide area network (WAN). A WAN provides communication over a larger geographical area than a LAN. RMON allows a remote network node to gather network data at almost any point on a LAN or a WAN. RMON uses SNMP but also incorporates a special database for remote monitoring that includes different groups of statistics.

 Some access points support only a limited number of RMON statistical groups due to a lack of memory.

With a WLAN, you can monitor the access point using RMON. The statistics gathered can contain data measured for both the wired LAN and the wireless LAN interfaces. RMON can also compare these statistical samples to previously configured thresholds. If the monitored variable crosses a threshold, RMON can generate an event alarm.

 Although neither Cisco nor 3Com currently supports RMON, it is found in WLAN packages from several other vendors.

Station Utilities

Station utilities are utility programs that are run from the local station on the WLAN. The station utilities for Cisco and 3Com provide a wealth of information about the station itself as well as about the WLAN.

3Com Station Utilities

3Com AirConnect provides several station utilities to monitor the status of the network. The Signal Strength utility tracks signal strength in real time and displays a graph showing the historical trend of signal strength, as shown in Figure 9-4.

To run the Signal Strength utility, start the 3Com Launcher, then click the Connection Monitor icon. Click the Signal tab to display the graph.

Another 3Com station utility is Link Performance. This program runs a test between the wireless station and another IP device on the network. A ping signal is sent to the receiving station, which then responds. You can use ping to test the internal TCP/IP configuration as well as the connectivity between devices on the WLAN. When you run the ping test to another wireless device, the round-trip ping time can give you an idea of the upper limit for connection speed.

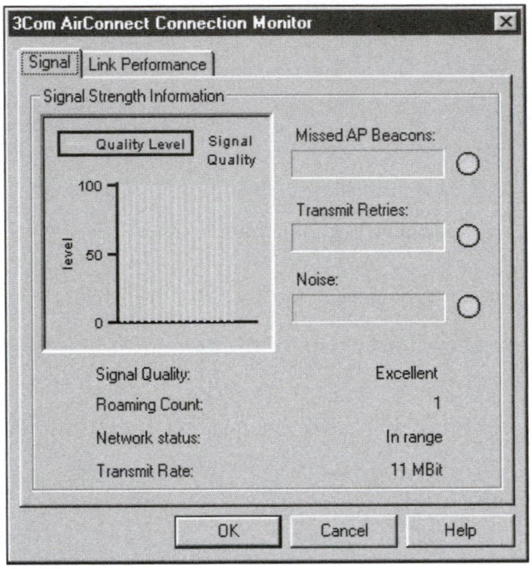

Figure 9-4   3Com Connection Monitor

Instructions for using ping from a command prompt are given in Chapter 6.

To run the Link Performance utility, start the 3Com Launcher, then click the Connection Monitor icon. Click the Link Performance tab. On the Link Performance page, in the Host Address line enter the IP number of the wireless device that is to receive a signal. Click Start Test to begin sending the signals. A graph appears indicating the round-trip ping time of each ping and displaying timing statistics, as shown in Figure 9-5.

The final 3Com station utility is actually a series of utilities that provides a range of information. These are included under the Adapter Information feature of the 3Com Launcher. Clicking the Adapter Information icon displays the feature's opening screen, as shown in Figure 9-6. This screen displays information about the status of the wireless NIC, the hardware, and the network.

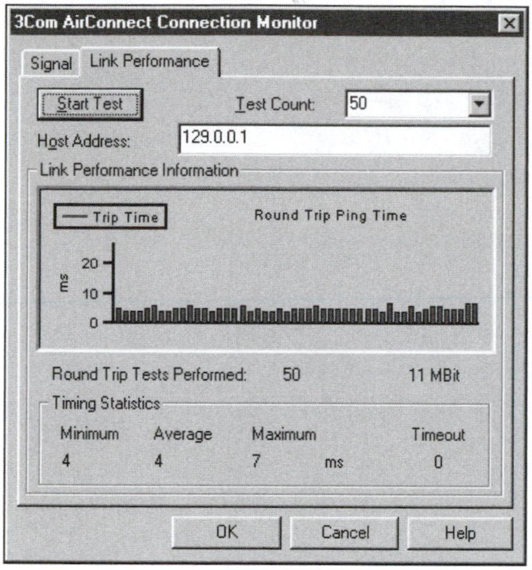

Figure 9-5   Link Performance test

> The Test Count field of the Link Performance tab lets you select the number of
> pings to perform, from one test to continuous testing.

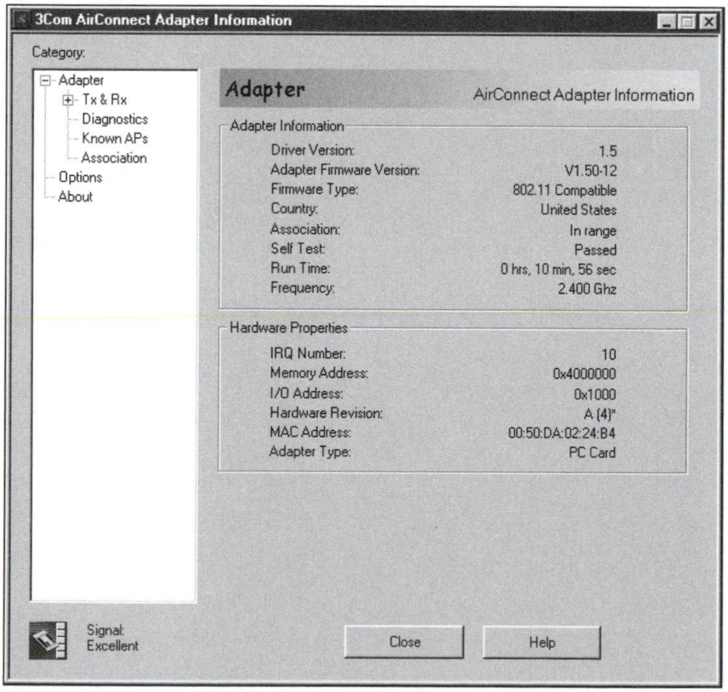

Figure 9-6   3Com AirConnect Adapter Information screen

Clicking a selection in the Category tree in the left panel displays additional data screens. These screens include the following:

- *Tx & Rx* displays statistics of data transmitted and received. The screen can display these statistics as text, as shown in Figure 9-7, or as a graph, as shown in Figure 9-8.

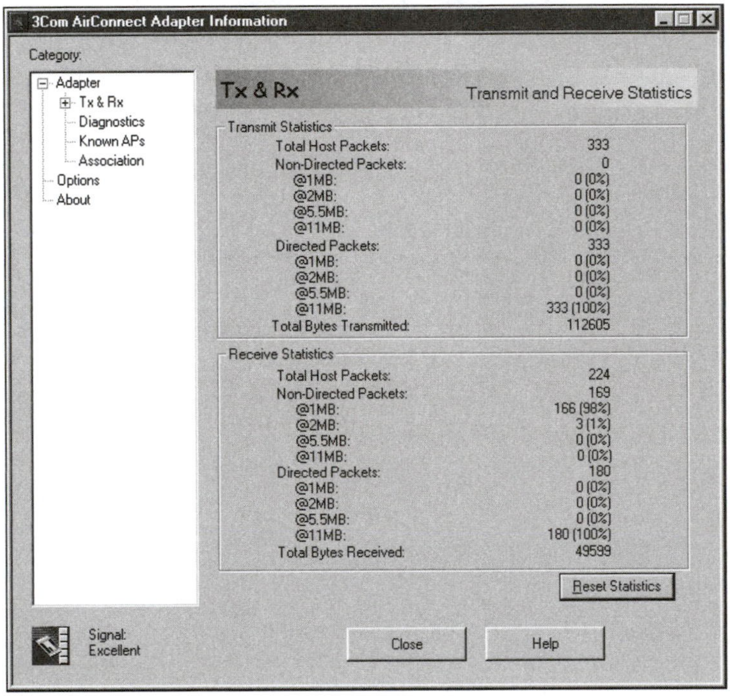

Figure 9-7   3Com Transmit and Receive (Tx & Rx) text data

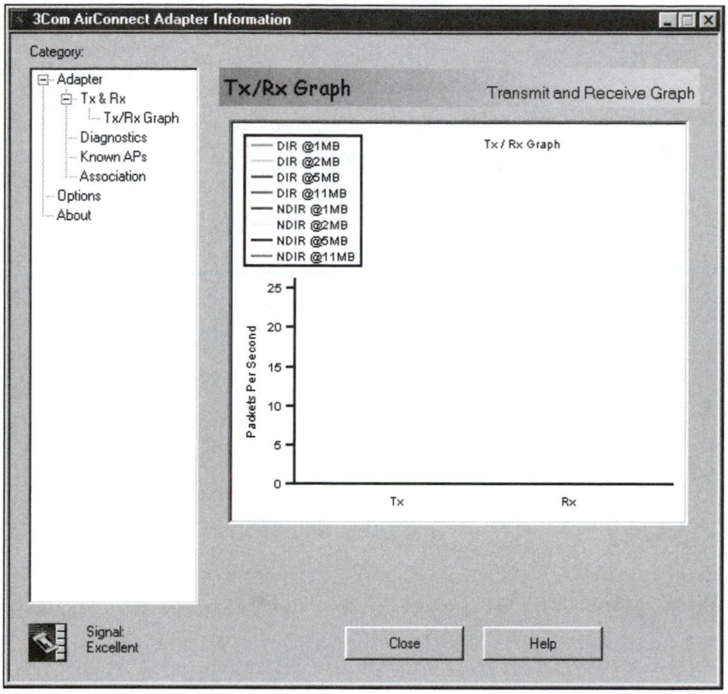

Figure 9-8 3Com Transmit and Receive (Tx & Rx) graph

> **Caution**
> The Tx & Rx graph does not retain the statistics over time. When a frame is sent or received, the graph displays this information for approximately one second before erasing it.

- *Diagnostics* enables the user to perform a test on the wireless NIC. The Self Test option instructs the NIC to perform a test upon itself. The message "Self Test Passed" appears if the NIC functions correctly. The Reset Adapter option turns off the wireless NIC adapter for a few seconds, then turns it back on.

- *Known APs* displays how many access points the adapter can discover from its current location, as shown in Figure 9-9. The known APs screen identifies each access point by the following information:

  - *Access Point Address* lists the MAC addresses of each available AP.

  - *Channel* shows the direct-sequence channel used by each AP.

  - *Type/Status* presents the access point association status and roaming information.

- *Noise* provides noise level statistics and signal strength information that you can use when determining the access point with which to associate.

- *Signal* identifies the strength of the signal transmitted by each access point.

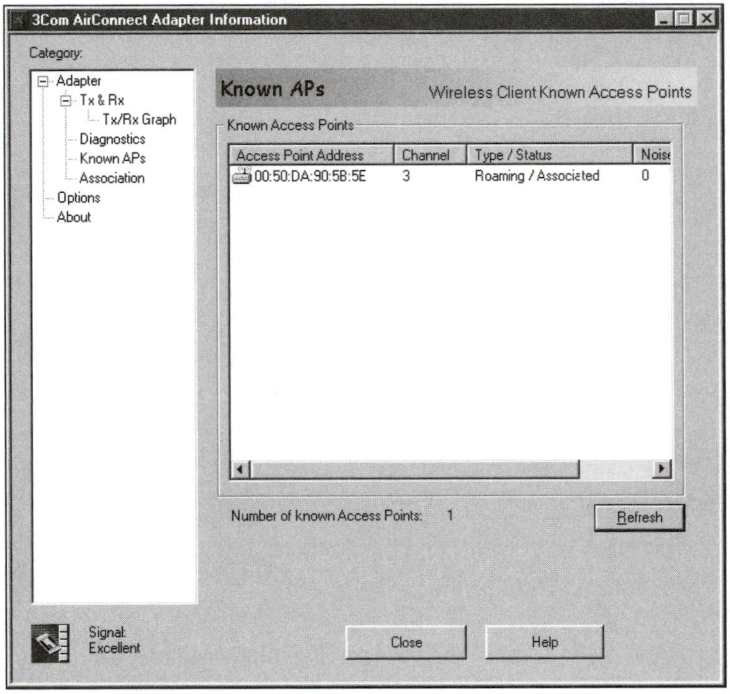

Figure 9-9 3Com Known APs

- *Association*, shown in Figure 9-10, provides information regarding the WLAN area of service in three categories. The Association Statistics section displays the number of known access points along with their BSSIDs. The Roaming Reasons section of the page displays information such as whether a radio transmission was received from an AP, the signal quality and relative signal strength, and access point load balancing. The load balancing statistic indicates whether an access point has terminated its association with the station because the AP cannot maintain its current load of associated mobile devices. The Miscellaneous Statistics section of the page displays the number of received beacons, the percentage of missed beacons, and the number of transmitted errors compared to the total number of transmitted beacons. A signal quality icon appears in the lower-left corner of the page.

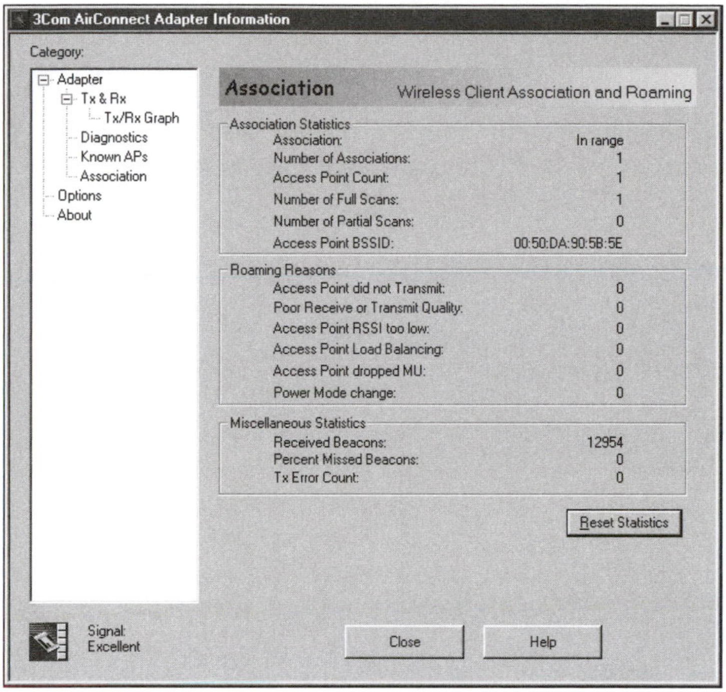

Figure 9-10   3Com Association statistics

The statistics obtained from these programs can help you locate and eliminate WLAN problems. For example, if stations are having difficulty maintaining a connection with the AP, it could be a result of interference (noise) from other devices. A high noise level may indicate that one or more non-network devices are emitting radio signals in the same frequency band. The source of the noise may be closest to the device that has the highest noise level. The solution is to try to eliminate or move the source of the noise. A low signal level, on the other hand, indicates that the station and the AP may be too far apart or that there may be obstructions between them. Removing obstructions, moving the devices closer together, or using an optional range extender antenna may solve the problem.

Cisco Station Utilities

The Cisco Aironet 340 Series also includes several utilities that can be run from the local station. These utilities provide information about the current status of the WLAN as well as information about the station.

Previous chapters have already introduced two of these programs, Statistics and the Link Status Meter. To see information about the number of frames that are being sent and received, click Start, point to Programs, point to Cisco Systems, Inc., then click Aironet Client Utility to start the ACU program. Click the Commands menu, then click Statistics to display the 340 Series Statistics window. The Link Status Meter (LSM) displays the relative signal strengths of the stations. Click Start, point to Programs, point to Cisco Systems, Inc., then click Link Status Meter to display the signal strengths.

The Status program displays current status information for the station and the wireless NIC. Click Start, point to Programs, point to Cisco Systems, Inc., then click Aironet Client Utility to start the ACU program. Click the Commands menu, then Status to display the 340 Series Status window, as shown in Figure 9-11.

340 Series Status		
Device	=	340 Series PCMCIA
Manufacturer	=	Cisco Systems, Inc.
Firmware Version	=	V3.82
Boot Block Version	=	V1.41
NDIS Driver Version	=	V6.10
Using Short Radio Headers	=	No
WEP (Wired Equivalent Privacy)	=	Not Enabled
Authentication Type	=	Open
Antenna Selection	=	Rx->Diversity Tx->Diversity
Channel Set	=	North America
Client Name	=	Station B
MAC Address (Factory)	=	00:40:96:32:28:65
Current Link Speed	=	11 Mbps
Data Rate	=	Auto Rate Selection
Current Power Level	=	30 mW
Available Power Levels	=	1, 30 mW
Channel (Frequency)	=	6 (2437 MHz)
Status	=	Associated
SSID	=	tsunami
Network Type	=	Infrastructure
Power Save Mode	=	CAM
Associated Access Point Name	=	AP340_34ff17
Associated Access Point IP Address	=	198.146.118.17
Associated Access Point MAC	=	00:40:96:34:FF:17
Up Time (hh:mm:ss)	=	00:19:05

Current Signal Strength   100%

Current Beacons Received   100%

Overall Link Quality   **Excellent**

Help   OK

Figure 9-11   Cisco Status window

The Screen Update Timer controls how often the Statistics and Status screens are updated. The screen can be updated in one-second increments, from once per second to once every 60 seconds. The default is once every five seconds. To change the value, click Options, then Preferences in the ACU program screen.

The Linktest utility is used to evaluate the performance of the radio frequency (RF) link at different points in the service area. You can also use the results of the link test to determine the required number and placement of access points, and to eliminate "dead spots," where low RF signal levels can result in the loss of the connection between the wireless NIC and the access point. Click Start, point to Programs, point to Cisco Systems, Inc., then click Aironet Client Utility to start the ACU program. Click the Commands menu, then Linktest to display the 340 Linktest screen. Enter the IP number of the access point that is to be used in the test. The Number of Packets parameter specifies the number of packets that the link test will attempt to send. The Packet Size parameter specifies the size of the data packet to be sent to the Aironet access point.

After entering the parameters, click the Start button at the bottom of the dialog box to start Linktest. While running, Linktest periodically displays and updates the statistics. The display shows the number of packets of the specified size that were successfully transmitted and received, as shown in Figure 9-12. To stop Linktest, click Stop, OK, or Cancel at the bottom of the dialog box.

9

Linktest	☒

IP Address of Access Point: `198.146.118.17`

Number of Packets: `100`   Packet Size: `64`

```
 ┬ ┬ ┬ ┬ ┬ ┬ ┬ ┬ ┬ ┬          ┬ ┬ ┬ ┬ ┬ ┬ ┬ ┬ ┬ ┬
 1                  1000    64                    2048
```

☐ Continuous Linktest (Ignore Number of Packets)

Receive Statistics	Current	Cumulative Total
Packets Received OK	= 2	103

Transmit Statistics		
Packets Transmitted OK	= 2	110

Status   = Associated
Associated Access Point Name   = AP340_34ff17
Associated Access Point MAC   = 00:40:96:34:FF:17

Current Signal Strength   **100%**
Current Beacons Received   **100%**
Overall Link Quality   **Excellent**

Stop	Defaults	Help	OK	Cancel

Figure 9-12   Cisco Linktest utility

Tip The Continuous Linktest option causes Linktest to run continuously until you select Stop, OK, or Cancel. The program ignores the Number of Packets parameter if you select Continuous Linktest.

Once Linktest has sent the number of packets specified in the Number of Packets parameter, the Stop button at the bottom of the dialog box changes back into a Start button.

The Overall Link Quality rating near the bottom of the Linktest screen evaluates the ability of the wireless LAN adapter to communicate successfully with an access point. The ratings are Excellent, Good, Fair, and Poor. The rating derives from a combination of the current signal strength and the current signal quality. Table 9-1 shows how the program determines the ratings.

Table 9-1   Overall Link Quality

Current Signal Strength	Current Signal Quality	Rating
Greater than 75%	Greater than 75%	Excellent
Greater than 40% but less than 75%	Greater than 40% but less than 75%	Good
Greater than 20% but less than 40%	Greater than 20% but less than 40%	Fair
Less than 20%	Less than 20%	Poor

Access Point Utilities

The access point utilities for Cisco and 3Com also make available data and statistics that you can use to monitor the status of the WLAN.

3Com Access Point Utilities

The AirConnect AP keeps statistics of its transactions during operation. These statistics include traffic, transmission success, and the existence of other radio network devices. To view these statistics, open a browser and enter the IP number of the access point to display the opening screen. On the tree in the left pane, click Access Point, then Statistics. You can view eight different categories of AP statistics. Some of the most informative include the following:

- *Interface Statistics* monitors packets sent to the AP, and provides information on packet-forwarding statistics and performance information in packets per second (PPS) and bytes per second (BPS). The Interface Statistics screen is illustrated in Figure 9-13.

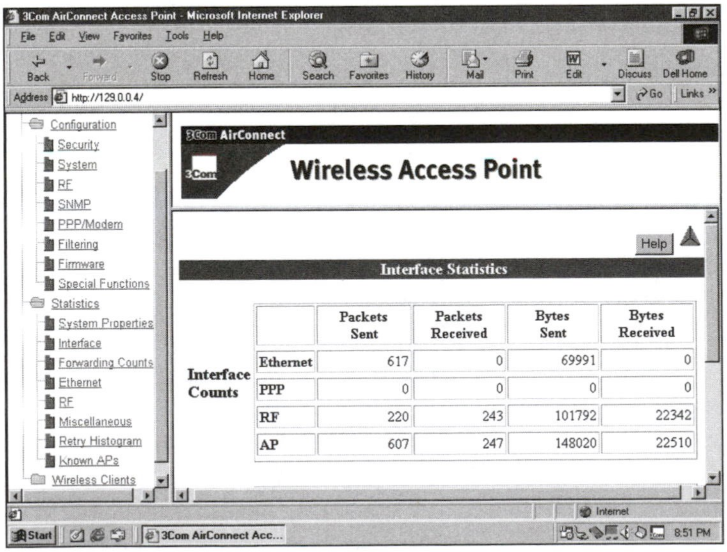

Figure 9-13   3Com Interface Statistics

You can update the Interface Statistics information by using the Refresh option. Click Start Refresh at the bottom of the page to update the values approximately once every two seconds. Click Stop Refresh to end the dynamic updates.

- *RF Statistics* lists radio performance statistics, including packet and communication information, as illustrated in Figure 9-14.

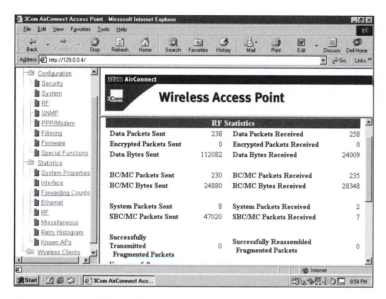

Figure 9-14 3Com RF Statistics

- *Known Access Points* provides valuable data regarding the access points, as shown in Figure 9-15. Some of the statistics include:
  - *Chnl* provides the channel number used by the access point.
  - *WCs* lists the number of wireless clients associated with this access point.
  - *Away* reveals whether the access point is functioning as part of the network. If the AP's last known transmission took place over 12 seconds ago, it is indicated as Away.

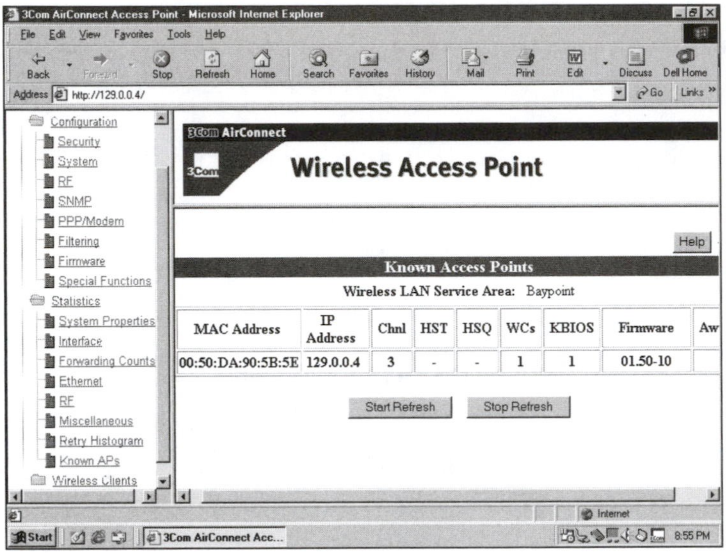

Figure 9-15 showing the 3Com AirConnect Access Point browser window with Known Access Points table:

MAC Address	IP Address	Chnl	HST	HSQ	WCs	KBIOS	Firmware	Aw
00:50:DA:90:5B:5E	129.0.0.4	3	-	-	1	1	01.50-10	

Wireless LAN Service Area: Baypoint

Figure 9-15   3Com Known Access Points

The statistics gathered from the AP utilities can also be helpful in identifying problems that may not be readily apparent. For example, the number of messages lost typically should be less than 1 percent of the number of messages sent. If this number increases to 5 percent, there may be communication problems.

In addition, data from AP utilities as well as station utilities can be combined to identify problems. For example, when noise data is combined with quality of the radio communications data, it can reveal the source of network communications problems. If the noise is low and the number of messages lost is high, the problem is likely due to poor communication quality. If the noise level is adequate or good but there are a large number of messages lost or received after a retry, the problem may indicate one of the following:

- The network is very busy because many stations are trying to access the medium at the same time.

- A microwave oven may be in close vicinity (within 9 feet or 3 meters) of the station or access point and is causing short bursts of interference. This noise might not be displayed by the noise level indicator, but could still be forcing the clients to retransmit frames.

- Another client is suffering from poor communications quality and is sending many retransmissions.

- Many frame collisions are occurring due to a hidden node problem.

> **Tip**: If it appears that there are transmission problems, it is a good idea to run the data throughput efficiency test from multiple stations to determine whether the problem involves only one station or is being experienced by all stations.

If all clients suffer from poor data throughput efficiency despite a low noise value, the traffic load could be caused by one of the following:

- Many wireless clients are trying to communicate simultaneously.

- Clients are deferring data transmissions to avoid frame collisions.

- Clients are retransmitting frames repeatedly because the initial transmissions failed due to frame collisions.

If one or more clients are transmitting simultaneously with the access point in an infrastructure network, the solution may be to lower the RTS threshold on the access point (this solution is covered later in this chapter). Other solutions may be to move the access points closer together to distribute the load, or to add additional access points to the network.

Cisco Access Point Utilities

The Cisco Aironet 340 Series access point can provide a broad array of information regarding the access point and the WLAN. Open a browser and enter the IP number of the access point to display the Summary Status screen, as shown in Figure 9-16.

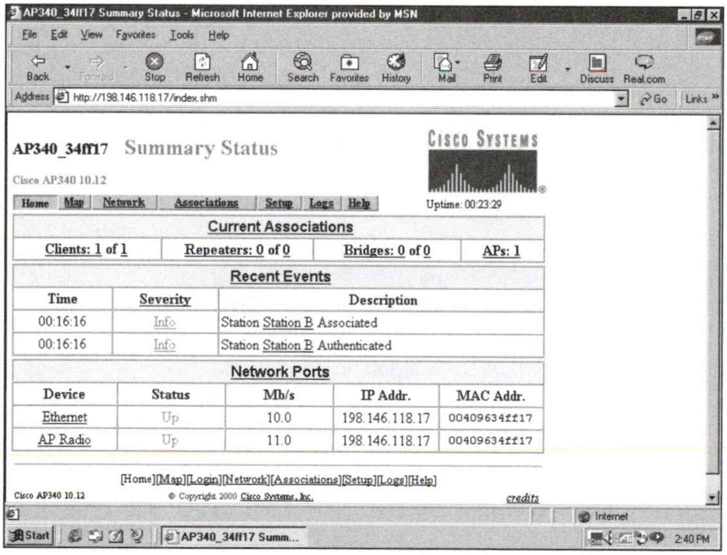

9

Figure 9-16   Cisco Summary Status

The following options are most frequently used and are associated with the buttons across the top of the screen:

- *Home* displays the Summary Status page.

- *Map* displays another page with links to network ports and setup pages.

- *Network* displays statistics regarding both the Ethernet network and the access point, as shown in Figure 9-17.

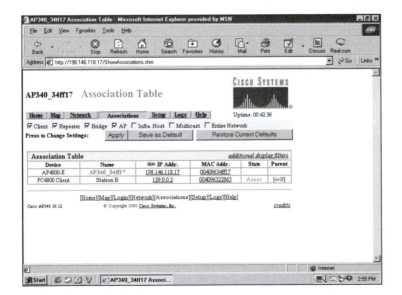

Figure 9-17   Cisco Network Ports

■ *Associations* displays information about stations that the access point knows about. The State column indicates whether the station is associated with an AP (Assoc), is unauthenticated with any AP (Unauth), or is authenticated but not associated with an AP (Auth). The Parent column shows the name of the station with which the station is associated. The name Self indicates that the station is associated with the current AP. The Association Table page is shown in Figure 9-18.

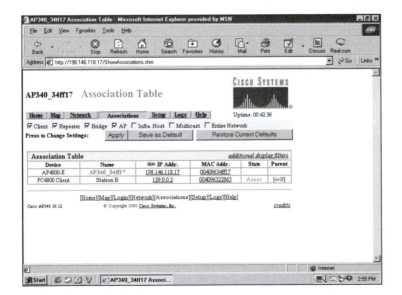

Figure 9-18   Cisco Association Table

UPGRADING THE **WLAN**

Cisco and 3Com, along with all other WLAN vendors, continue to improve and modify their products. The best way for users to keep their systems current with the latest changes is to download changes to the APs or wireless NICs.

Firmware (also called **flash memory**) is software that is embedded in a silicon chip. Firmware is semipermanent: It is not erased when the device is turned off, but it can be modified. Both 3Com and Cisco post firmware upgrades on their Internet sites for access points as well as wireless NICs. This firmware can be downloaded and used to update both the access point and wireless NICs.

Updating AP Firmware

The access points from Cisco and 3Com use a browser-based management system. The AP settings are contained on Web pages stored in the access points that are accessed with a browser such as Microsoft Explorer or Netscape Navigator. Unlike Web pages found on the Internet, the AP Web pages are not stored on a file server and cannot be changed by modifying the HTML code. AP Web pages are stored on the access point as firmware. To upgrade AP Web pages, you must install firmware upgrades.

Updating Cisco AP Firmware

Cisco APs have three categories of firmware: system firmware, Web page firmware, and radio firmware. To view the current versions of these categories of firmware, click the Setup button on the Summary Status home page. Select Cisco Services under the Services heading, then from the Cisco Services Setup page click Distribute Firmware to Other Cisco Devices. This displays the Distribute Firmware page, as shown in Figure 9-19.

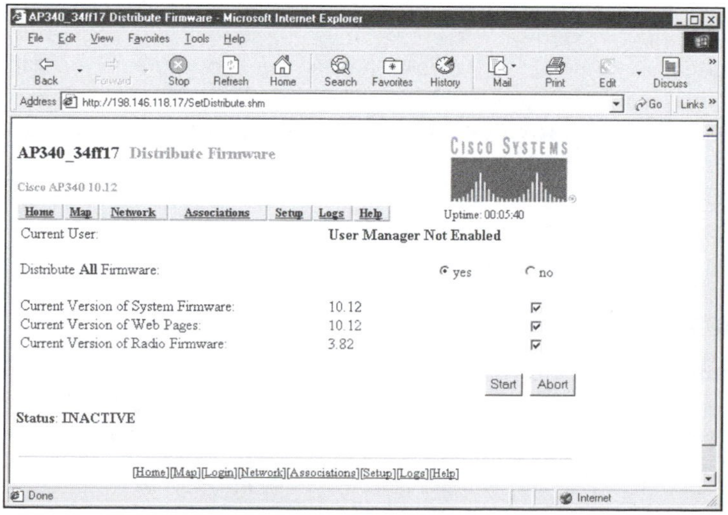

Figure 9-19   Cisco Distribute Firmware screen

To upgrade the firmware of the Cisco AP, browse to the Cisco Internet site and download the latest firmware for the access point. Run the program and follow the instructions on the screen.

After you upgrade a single AP to the latest firmware, you can then easily distribute this firmware to all other access points on the WLAN. The upgraded AP (Distribution AP) sends the update to all other APs (Receiving APs) on the network. You must configure each Receiving AP as follows:

- The Receiving AP must be able to hear the IP multicast issued by the Distribution AP. Some network devices such as routers can block multicast messages. You must temporarily turn off this blocking feature at the router.

- The Receiving AP must be set to allow access through a Web browser. If this feature is not enabled, you can turn it on from the Web Server Setup page. From the Summary Status home page, click the Setup button. Click Web Server on the Cisco Services Setup page. This displays the Web Server Setup page. Click Yes for the Allow Non-Console Browsing option.

- If the Receiving AP has the User Manager feature enabled, the AP's User List must contain a user with the same username, password, and capabilities as the user who is logged into the Distribution AP.

To upgrade all the APs, go to the Distribute Firmware page, then click the yes radio button to distribute all the firmware (System firmware, Web Page firmware, and Radio firmware) to each Receiving AP. If only certain firmware is to be distributed, click the no radio button, then place a check mark next to the category of firmware that should be sent. Click the Start button to begin the process.

 Each AP will automatically reboot after the firmware has been distributed.

 You can also place firmware upgrades on a file server and distribute them to each AP. You can do so through the Update All Firmware From File Server page. From the Summary Status home page, click the Setup button. Select Cisco Services under the Services heading, then from the Cisco Services Setup page, click From File Server under the Fully Update Firmware heading. This displays the Update Firmware from File Server feature. Click the Update From Server button to update the AP's firmware from the file server.

Updating 3Com AP Firmware

To upgrade the firmware on a 3Com AP, you must use a computer connected to the same Ethernet segment as the access point. This computer must be using **Trivial File Transfer Protocol (TFTP)**. Much like FTP, TFTP is used to transport data files. However, TFTP transmits files slightly differently than FTP and is not as robust. The latest firmware files for the access point can be downloaded from the 3Com Internet site.

Note There are two major differences between TFTP and FTP. TFTP does not guarantee the connection between the devices as FTP does. Also, TFTP does not require a username or password to be used.

 Caution TFTP is not generally part of the TCP/IP package. You might need to secure TFTP software from a third party.

 Tip The computer serving TFTP can be a 3Com AirConnect station.

To update the 3Com AP firmware, open a browser and enter the IP number of the access point to display the opening screen. On the tree in the left pane, click Access Point, then Configuration, then finally Firmware. When prompted, enter the username Administrator and the password *comcomcom*. This displays the Firmware Download screen, as shown in Figure 9–20.

Figure 9-20   3Com Firmware Download screen

Enter the IP number of the TFTP server. To update only the current AP, select Firmware, HTML File, or both under *TFTP update THIS Access Point's*. To update all APs, select Firmware, HTML File, or both under *TFTP update ALL Access Points'*. Click Perform Function to start the process.

Updating the Wireless NIC Firmware

In addition to enabling you to upgrade the AP firmware, both Cisco and 3Com allow for updating of the wireless NIC firmware on the local station.

Updating Cisco Wireless NIC Firmware

To upgrade the wireless NIC firmware for the Cisco Aironet 340 on a local station, browse to the Cisco Internet site and download the latest firmware for the wireless NIC. Go to that local station and click Start, point to Programs, point to Cisco Systems, Inc., then click Aironet Client Utility to start the ACU program. Click Commands, then Load New Firmware. This displays a Windows Open dialog box. Enter the appropriate path for the firmware image file, then click Open. This loads the selected image in the wireless NIC firmware.

Updating 3Com Wireless NIC Firmware

To upgrade the wireless NIC firmware for the 3Com AirConnect on a local station, browse to the 3Com Internet site and download the latest firmware for the wireless NIC. Go to that local station and click Start, point to Programs, point to 3Com AirConnect, then click AirConnect Firmware Upgrade Utility. Figure 9-21 shows the 3Com AirConnect Firmware Upgrade dialog box that appears.

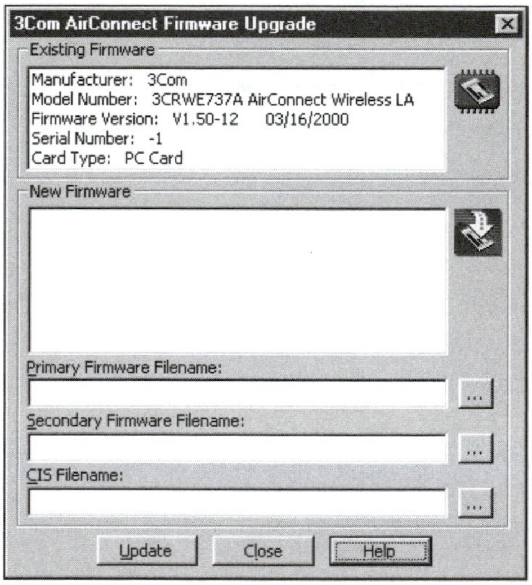

Figure 9-21   3Com Firmware Upgrade utility

To upgrade the firmware, enter the following settings:

- *Primary Firmware Filename* — Enter the path and filename of the new firmware binary file to load on the adapter.

- *Secondary Firmware Filename* — This setting allows you to specify another new firmware binary file to load on the adapter. This file will be used in the firmware upgrade only if its version is equal to or greater than the version of the primary firmware filename.

- *CIS Filename* — A **Card Information Structure (CIS)** file contains information about the PC Card installed, such as its speed, its size, and the system resources required. The CIS filename is optional.

After entering the information, click Update.

For either 3Com or Cisco wireless NICs, you may need to upgrade driver software on the station if there is a software problem or if new features have become available for the NIC. This software should be available on the vendor's Internet site.

MODIFYING THE AP RADIO SETTINGS

The radio settings of the access point are automatically set with default values when the AP is installed. However, occasionally you may need to "tweak" these settings. For example, if a station has difficulty roaming into a certain area of a cell because of obstacles or interference, minor adjustments to the AP radio settings may improve the transmission.

Exercise care when adjusting these parameters. An incorrect change can bring the entire WLAN to a halt. The recommended approach is to adjust one setting, then review the performance of the network. If the network performance is poor or nonexistent, you need to change that setting back to its original state.

Cisco AP Radio Settings

To view the Cisco Aironet 340 AP radio settings, click the Setup button on the Summary Status page. Under the heading of Network Ports, locate the AP Radio line. Click the Hardware link to display the AP Radio Hardware page, as shown in Figure 9-22.

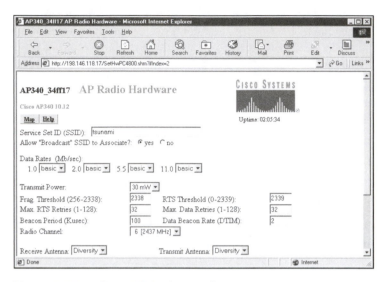

Figure 9-22   Cisco AP Radio Hardware page

Chapter 8 discussed some of this page's settings. The settings that have not already been covered that may be easily adjusted for performance or enhancements are as follows:

- *Service Set ID (SSID)* enables you to insert a non-ASCII character in the SSID by typing a backslash (\ ), a lowercase *x*, and then characters to represent the non-ASCII character. For example, \xbd inserts the symbol ½.

- *Data Rates (Mb/sec)* specifies the range of data transmission rates in megabits per second. The Cisco WLAN always attempts to transmit at the highest rate selected. If obstacles or outside interference occur, the system automatically drops down to the highest rate that allows successful data transmission. For each of four rates, the pull-down menu gives three options:

  - *basic* is the default rate. This option allows transmission at this rate for all packets, both unicast and multicast. Setting a lower basic rate may slow performance but increase the range of transmission.

  - *yes* allows transmission at this rate for unicast packets only.

  - *no* disallows transmission at this rate.

 At least one data rate must be set to Basic.

- *Transmit Power* sets the power level of the radio transmission. Four options are available: 1 **milliwatt (mW)** or one-millionth of a watt, 5 mW, 15 mW, and 30 mW. These settings are government-regulated and conform to standards for the country of operation. To reduce interference or conserve power, you can change the level to a lower setting.

- *Frag. Threshold (256-2338)* specifies the size into which packets will be fragmented or sent as several pieces instead of as one block. Changing to a lower setting in areas where communication is poor or where there is strong radio interference may improve communications.

- *RTS Threshold (0-2339)* may be used when collisions occur due to a hidden node. A station transmits a Request to Send (RTS) frame that contains a duration field defining the length of time needed for transmission. The access point then alerts all stations that the medium is now being reserved and that they should suspend any transmissions. Because the RTS protocol imposes significant additional over-head, short data packets may still be transmitted without RTS. This limit is known as the RTS threshold. Only packets that are longer than the RTS threshold are transmitted using RTS. A low RTS threshold setting can help communications in areas where many clients are associating with the AP or in areas where the clients are far apart.

- *Max. RTS Retries (1-128)* specifies the maximum number of times that the AP will issue an RTS before stopping the attempt to send the packet from the radio port.

3Com AP Radio Settings

To view the 3Com AirConnect radio settings, open a browser and enter the IP number of the access point to display the opening screen. On the tree in the left pane, click Access Point, then Configuration, then finally RF. When prompted, enter the username Administrator and the password. This displays the RF Setup screen, as shown in Figure 9-23.

Figure 9-23   3Com RF Setup screen

Some of these settings have been discussed in Chapter 8. The settings that have not already been covered that may be easily adjusted are as follows:

- *BC/MC Queue Max* specifies the number of frames that the AP will temporarily hold of broadcast or multicast messages sent to a station. The actual frame size corresponds to the maximum size of Ethernet packets. The default setting is 10 frames.

- *WC Inactivity Timeout* specifies the number of minutes that the AP allows for wireless client (WC) inactivity. An AirConnect AP recognizes wireless client activity through data packet transmission and reception as well as through scanning.

3Com AirConnect wireless stations conduct active scanning. Because stations from other vendors can perform passive scanning, an AirConnect AP would not recognize these scans and could classify the stations as inactive. Be careful when mixing AirConnect and other vendors' products in the same WLAN.

- *Rate Control* sets the transmission rates at 11 Mbps and 5.5 Mbps. If you select Required, then the AP will communicate at those higher rates; selecting Optional means that the access point can transmit at those rates.

Do not make any changes to the RTS Threshold setting. 3Com does not currently support RTS/CTS.

CHAPTER SUMMARY

◻ Monitoring the status of the network is a critical part of managing a network. A network often reveals symptoms of network problems before there is a major crisis, and monitoring the network can reveal these preliminary symptoms. Monitoring the status of the network is also an important tool that you can use when initially configuring or making changes to the WLAN. Cisco and 3Com provide several utilities for observing the current network status. Some of these utilities run from the station, whereas others run from the access point.

◻ Both products offer standard network monitoring tools. Simple Network Management Protocol (SNMP) is a protocol that allows computers and network equipment to gather data about network performance. Remote Network Monitoring (RMON) is an SNMP-based tool that is used to monitor LANs that are connected through a wide area network (WAN). At this writing, neither the Cisco or the 3Com product supports RMON.

◻ Station utilities are programs that run from the local station on the WLAN. The station utilities for Cisco and 3Com provide a wealth of information about the station itself as well as about the WLAN.

◻ The access point utilities for Cisco and 3Com also make available data and statistics that can be used to monitor the status of the WLAN.

❑ The access points use a browser-based management system. AP settings are contained on Web pages stored in the access points. You can access these Web pages with a browser and store them on the access point as firmware. Firmware (also called flash memory) is software that is embedded in a silicon chip. 3Com and Cisco post firmware upgrades on their Internet sites for access points as well as wireless NICs. You can download this firmware and use it to update both the access point and wireless NICs.

❑ The radio settings of the access point are automatically set with default values when the AP is installed. However, you may need to change these settings to improve network performance.

KEY TERMS

Card Information Structure (CIS) — A file that contains information about the PC Card installed, such as its speed, its size, and the system resources required.

Common Management Interface Protocol (CMIP) — A protocol, based on the OSI model, that gathers network statistics.

firmware — Semipermanent software that is embedded in a silicon chip; also called flash memory.

flash memory — Semipermanent software that is embedded in a silicon chip; also called firmware.

management information base (MIB) — The repository where SNMP software agents store their data.

milliwatt (mW) — One-millionth of a watt.

Remote Network Monitoring (RMON) — An SNMP-based tool used to monitor LANs that are connected through a wide area network.

Simple Network Management Protocol (SNMP) — A protocol that is part of TCP/IP that allows computers and network equipment to gather data about network performance.

SNMP management station — A computer on a network using SNMP that controls the management software.

SNMP trap — An alert message sent to an SNMP management station whenever a network exceeds a predefined limit.

SNMPv2 — The second version of SNMP that provides encryption, faster data transmission, and the ability to retrieve more information.

software agents — Special SNMP software that is loaded onto each network device that monitors network traffic.

Trivial File Transfer Protocol (TFTP) — A program used to transport data files that does not guarantee the connection between the devices and does not require a username or password.

9

REVIEW QUESTIONS

1. _____ is a protocol that allows computers and network equipment to gather data about network performance and is part of the TCP/IP protocol suite.

   a. SNMP

   b. CIP

   c. RNOM

   d. WATCH

2. A protocol for gathering network statistics that requires more resources than SNMP is _____.

   a. RMON

   b. CMIP

   c. CBASE

   d. TOPS

3. When using SNMP, each agent monitors network traffic and stores that information in its _____.

   a. MIB

   b. Active Directory

   c. Base Repository

   d. CLIST

4. Whenever the network exceeds a predefined limit, it triggers an alert message, called a(n) _____.

   a. SNMP trap

   b. trigger

   c. active alert

   d. OSI warning

5. Each of the following is an improved feature of SNMPv2 except _____.

   a. better security

   b. encryption

   c. faster data transmission

   d. the ability to retrieve less information at one time

6. Both 3Com and Cisco support SNMP. True or false?

7. Both Cisco and 3Com currently support RMON. True or false?

8. 3Com's Signal Strength utility displays a graph of signal strength but not in real time. True or false?

9. The 3Com station utility Link Performance runs a Telnet test between the wireless station and another IP device on the network. True or false?

10. The Test Count field of the 3Com Link Performance test lets you select the number of pings to perform, from one test to continuous testing. True or false?

11. 3Com's _____ screen displays statistics of data transmitted and received as either text or a graph.

12. The _____ option of Cisco's Linktest utility causes the link test to run continuously.

13. If signal strength exceeds 75 percent and signal quality is also above 75 percent, then the signal strength rating is _____.

14. 3Com's Interface Statistics provides information on packet-forwarding and performance in both packets per second and _____ per second.

15. Typically the number of messages lost should be less than _____ percent of the number of messages sent.

16. Tell how data from both AP utilities as well as station utilities can be combined to identify problems.

17. If all clients suffer from poor data throughput efficiency despite a good noise value, what could be the cause?

18. What is firmware and how can you use it when upgrading a WLAN?

19. What is needed to upgrade a 3Com access point?

20. Why do you need to be careful when changing AP radio settings?

9

Hands-on Projects

1. Research SNMP, CMIP, and RMON. How do they function? What are their similarities? What are their differences? What statistics do they provide? How is SNMPv2 being used today? Write a one-page paper on your findings.

2. Use station utilities to view the status of the WLAN network and station. If you are using 3Com AirConnect, follow these steps:

   a. Run the Signal Strength program to display a graph of signal quality strength. Start the 3Com Launcher. Click the **Connection Monitor** icon, then click the **Signal** tab to display the Signal Strength Information graph.

   b. Run the 3Com Link Performance test between the wireless station and the AP. Start the 3Com Launcher, then click the **Connection Monitor** icon to display the graph. Click the **Link Performance** tab to display the dialog box.

   c. Enter the IP number of the AP in the Host Address line. Click **Start Test** to begin sending the signals.

   If you are using Cisco Aironet 340, follow these steps:

   a. Run the Statistics program to see information about the number of frames that are being sent and received. Click **Start**, point to **Programs**, point to **Cisco Systems, Inc.**, then click **Aironet Client Utility** to start the ACU program.

b. Click the **Commands** menu, then **Statistics** to display the 340 Series Statistics window.

c. Next, run the Link Status Meter (LSM) program to display the relative signal strengths of the stations. Click **Start**, point to **Programs**, point to **Cisco Systems, Inc.**, then click **Link Status Meter** to display the signal strengths. What observations can you make about the signal strength?

d. Now move the laptop computer to another location and run the programs again. What conclusions can you draw from the data?

3. Use station utilities to view the status of the WLAN network and station. If you are using 3Com AirConnect, follow these steps:

a. Click the **Adapter Information** icon under the 3Com Launcher to display the opening screen.

b. Double-click **Adapter** in the left pane.

c. Double-click **Tx & Rx**.

d. Click **Tx/Rx Graph** to display the graph.

e. Click **Known Aps**. Record the following information about each access point:

 ❑ Access Point Address

 ❑ Channel

 ❑ Type/Status

 ❑ Noise

 ❑ Signal

f. Click **Association** in the left pane.

g. Answer these questions:

 i. What is the number of known access points? What are their BSSIDs?

 ii. What is the signal quality and relative signal strength?

 iii. What is the number of received beacons? What is the percentage of missed beacons and transmitted errors out of the total number of transmitted beacons?

 iv. What is the signal quality?

If you are using Cisco Aironet 340, follow these steps to run the Linktest utility to evaluate the performance of the radio frequency (RF) link at different points in the service area:

a. Click **Start**, point to **Programs**, point to **Cisco Systems, Inc.**, then click **Aironet Client Utility** to start the ACU program.

b. Click the **Commands** menu, then click **Linktest** to display the 340 Linktest screen.

c. Enter the IP number of the access point that is to be used in the test.

    d. Click the **Start** button at the bottom of the dialog box to start Linktest. While running, Linktest displays and updates statistics periodically. The display shows the number of packets of the specified size that are successfully transmitted and received.

    e. Stop Linktest by clicking **Stop** at the bottom of the dialog box, then record the statistics.

    f. The Overall Link Quality indicates the ability of the wireless LAN adapter to communicate successfully with an access point. The ratings are Excellent, Good, Fair, and Poor. If the current rating is not Excellent, move the laptop computer to another location until the rating shows Excellent. What made the rating change?

4. The AP can provide information about the overall WLAN network. If you are using 3Com AirConnect, follow these steps:

    a. Open a browser and enter the IP number of the access point to display the opening screen. On the tree in the left pane, click **Access Point**, then **Statistics**.

    b. Click **Interface**. Record the performance information in packets per second (PPS) and bytes per second (BPS).

    c. Click **RF**. What types of radio performance statistics are helpful?

    d. Click **Known APs**. Record information about the channel number used by the access point, the wireless clients associated with this access point, and whether the access point is functioning as part of the network.

If you are using the Cisco Aironet 340 Series, follow these steps:

    a. Open a browser and enter the IP number of the access point to display the Summary Status screen.

    b. Click the **Network** button. A screen appears that shows statistics regarding both the Ethernet network and the access point. What can you tell about the performance of the network?

    c. Click the browser's **Back** button.

    d. Click the **Associations** button. The Associations page displays information about stations that the access point knows about. Record information about the stations, including whether a station is associated, unauthenticated, or authenticated but not associated with an AP, and the AP with which the station is associated.

5. Research the topic of firmware (also called flash memory). How does firmware work? What are its greatest advantages and disadvantages? In what other devices besides APs and wireless NICs do you find firmware? How does firmware erase the old code and replace it with new instructions on the chip? Write a one-page paper on your findings.

6. View the AP radio settings. *Do not change any of these settings without permission.* If you are using Cisco Aironet, follow these steps:

    a. Click the **Setup** button on the Summary Status page.

9

b. Under the heading of Network Ports, locate the AP Radio line. Click the **Hardware** link to display the AP Radio Hardware.

c. Record the settings for Data Rates, Transmit Power, Frag. Threshold, RTS Threshold, and Max. RTS Retries. How do these settings compare to the default values?

If you are using the 3Com AirConnect, follow these steps:

a. On the tree in the left pane, click **Access Point**, then **Configuration**, then finally **RF**.

b. When prompted, enter the username **Administrator** and the password. This displays the RF Setup screen.

c. Record the settings for BC/MC Queue Max and WC Inactivity Timeout. How do these settings compare to the default values?

CASE PROJECT

Northridge Consulting Group

Northridge Consulting Group (NCG) again wants you to assist with a WLAN project. The Moonlight Internet Café is now providing laptop computers to customers who want to purchase coffee and surf the Internet from their table. However, after installing a WLAN several months ago, the café has received complaints from the customers that the system is slow. Moonlight is not sure where the bottleneck may be located. The cafe wants to perform a system check on the data throughput of the WLAN, but is unsure which statistics would be most helpful in identifying problems.

1. Select either the Cisco Aironet or 3Com AirConnect product and list the different station and AP utilities that Moonlight could use. Include a brief description of how to launch the utility programs.

2. Under each program, indicate which statistics may be most helpful in identifying a data throughput bottleneck.

OPTIONAL TEAM CASE PROJECT

Because Moonlight has no centralized Information Technology staff, different managers have been known to "tweak" the AP radio settings to improve performance. This tweaking often results in the entire network crashing.

NCG needs your help. Create a team of three to four consultants. Each consultant should select one or two AP radio settings from either the Cisco or 3Com product. Research the settings and determine what impact changes in the settings will have. Create a PowerPoint slide presentation illustrating your findings.

10

NETWORK SETTINGS AND TROUBLESHOOTING THE CISCO AIRONET 340 AND 3COM AIRCONNECT

> **After reading this chapter and completing the exercises, you will be able to:**
>
> ♦ Describe the 3Com and Cisco wired Ethernet settings that are used in a WLAN
>
> ♦ List some of the warnings associated with the Aironet and AirConnect systems
>
> ♦ Explain troubleshooting tips for WLANs
>
> ♦ Respond to FAQs associated with Cisco and 3Com WLAN operation

Think back to the last time that you undertook a project that you had never done before, like building a wooden deck, installing a CD-RW drive in your computer, or installing brakes on a car. Have you ever tackled such a new project and had absolutely *nothing* go wrong? Almost any major project involves several "glitches" and some trial and error.

When these "gotchas" spring up in installing or operating a WLAN, finding the cause of the problem and solving it can sometimes be a challenge. This chapter adds to your problem-solving arsenal by giving you an overview of common problems with WLANs, lists of potential problem areas to be aware of for the Cisco and 3Com products, as well as answers to frequently asked questions about WLAN setup and operation. First, however, we'll discuss the network settings for connecting a WLAN to a wired network.

NETWORK CONNECTIONS

Of the two primary modes of WLAN operation outlined by the IEEE 802.11 standard (peer-to-peer and infrastructure), only infrastructure mode allows for connection of a wireless network to a wired network. You usually connect a WLAN to a wired network through the RJ-45 connection on APs that allows them to connect to an Ethernet hub, thus providing wireless stations access to network resources. Occasionally you may need to adjust the settings for connecting to the Ethernet network to improve performance or provide additional capabilities to the station.

Cisco also offers APs that have Digital Subscriber Line (DSL), cable modem, or standard 56 Kbps modem connections.

Cisco Network Connection Settings

The Cisco Aironet 340 provides several settings that can be modified for the connection to the Ethernet network. In addition, you can adjust settings to other network resources.

Ethernet Parameters

The Cisco Ethernet Identification page provides basic information regarding the configuration of the Ethernet port on the Cisco AP. To view this page, open a browser and enter the IP number of the access point to display the Summary Status screen. Click Setup from the Summary Status page, then click Identification on the Ethernet row under the Network Ports heading. This displays the Ethernet Identification page, as shown in Figure 10-1.

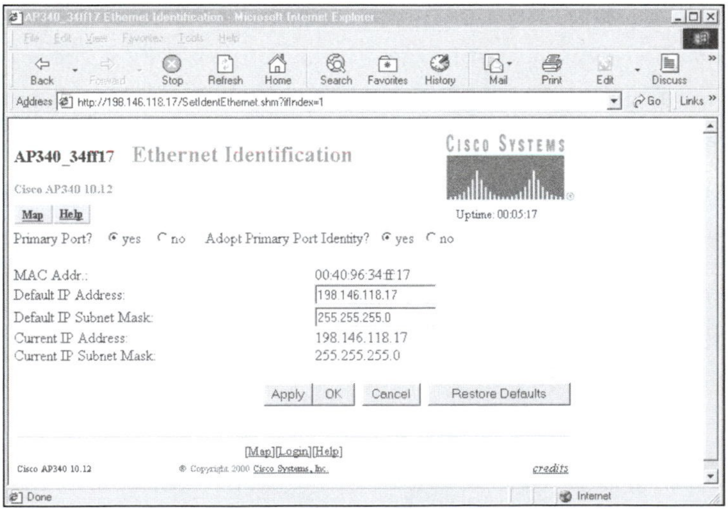

Figure 10-1   Cisco Ethernet Identification

Two sets of yes/no options allow you to designate this port as the primary port of the access point and select whether this port adopts the identity of the primary port. The primary port of the AP is almost always the Ethernet network port. The only time that you would identify another port as the primary port is when using a special advanced bridge on the wired network. A **bridge** is a network hardware device that knows the segment on which the destination computer is located and sends frames only to that segment. Administration of some advanced bridges requires distinguishing between Ethernet and radio ports.

Selecting "no" for either the Primary Port or Adopt Primary Port Identity options may block all network traffic to the AP.

Changes to the Ethernet Identification page require Administrator privileges with Identity and Write capabilities.

The Adopt Primary Port Identity option indicates whether this port adopts the MAC and IP number settings of the AP. These settings are used for identification purposes of the Ethernet network. You should set this radio button to "yes." The MAC Addr field displays the default MAC address for the AP assigned by the manufacturer. You cannot change this setting. The Default IP Address and Default IP Subnet Mask fields are used only when DHCP is enabled for the network. If DHCP is not enabled, these fields are the same as the Current IP Address and Current IP Subnet Mask. If DHCP is enabled, these fields provide an IP number and subnet mask for the AP if no DHCP server responds to the AP. This provides a backup that prevents the AP from sitting "dead" if it receives nothing from the DHCP server.

10

Changing a default address on the AP can cause the AP to lose its network connection or force a reboot of the AP.

The Current IP Address and Current IP Subnet Mask fields display the IP number currently assigned to or used by the station. These fields contain the same addresses as the Default IP Address and Default IP Subnet Mask if DHCP is not enabled. If DHCP is enabled and it responds to the access point's DHCP request, this field displays the IP number and subnet mask addresses that have been dynamically assigned to the station for the duration of its lease on the network. The field's value may not match the default IP address. These settings are summarized in Table 10-1.

Table 10-1   Ethernet Identification

DHCP Condition	Default IP Address	Default Subnet Mask	Current IP Address	Current IP Subnet Mask
DHCP not used	Not used; displays the same value as the current IP address	Not used; displays the same value as the current subnet mask	Manually set on the AP	Manually set on the AP
DHCP enabled and responding	Not used; displays the same value as the current IP address	Not used; displays the same value as the current subnet mask	Automatically assigned by the DHCP server	Automatically assigned by the DHCP server
DHCP enabled but not responding	Used by the AP as the current IP address	Used by the AP as the current subnet mask	Displays the same value as the default IP address	Displays the same value as the default subnet mask address

The Cisco Ethernet Hardware page allows you to modify the connection to the Ethernet network. To view this page, open a browser and enter the IP number of the access point to display the Summary Status screen. Click Setup from the Summary Status page, then click Hardware on the Ethernet row under the Network Ports heading. This displays the Ethernet Hardware page, as shown in Figure 10-2.

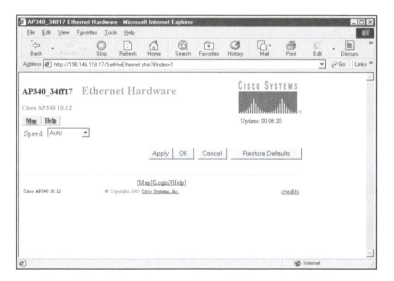

Figure 10-2   Cisco Ethernet Hardware

The drop-down Speed menu lists three options for the type of connector and the connection speed used by the Ethernet port. The option selected must match the actual connector type and speed used to link the port with the wired network. The three options are as follows:

- *Auto*, the default setting that instructs the system to select the correct connection speed

- *10 BaseT*, for connecting to a wired Ethernet network with a 10 Mbps transmission speed over twisted-pair wire

- *100 BaseT*, for connecting to a wired Ethernet network with a 100 Mbps transmission speed over twisted-pair wire

 Changes to the Ethernet Hardware page require Administrator privileges with Write capabilities.

The Cisco Ethernet Advanced page allows changes to an AP connected to the Ethernet network. To view this page, open a browser and enter the IP number of the access point to display the Summary Status screen. Click Setup from the Summary Status page, then click Advanced on the Ethernet row under the Network Ports heading. This displays the Ethernet Advanced page, as shown in Figure 10-3.

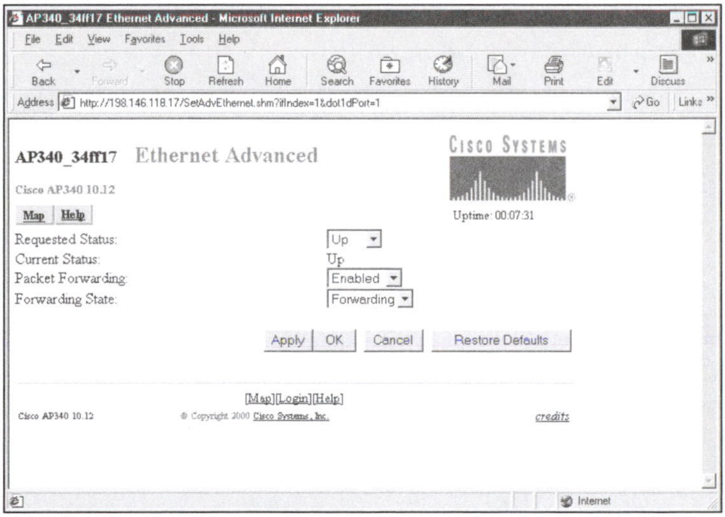

10

Figure 10-3 Cisco Ethernet Advanced

 Changes to the Ethernet Advanced page require Administrator privileges with Write capabilities.

Changing the settings on the Ethernet Advanced page can remove a station from the network or block all Ethernet network traffic.

The Ethernet Advanced page is used to change the operational status of an AP temporarily. It can be a helpful tool when troubleshooting network problems. The Requested Status field allows you to change the operating condition of the Ethernet port. The two options are Up and Down. Selecting Down can block network traffic. The Current Status field displays the current status (Up or Down) of the Ethernet port. This field can also display Error, which means that the port is operating but is in an error condition.

The Packet Forwarding field displays and allows you to set the forwarding capability of the Ethernet port on the access point. The two options are Enabled or Disabled. If you change the setting to Disabled, the AP will be effectively disconnected from the wired network, which means that although the AP will accept wired network data, the AP will not move the data between the Ethernet port and the radio port.

The Forwarding State field displays and allows the user to change how frames (packets) are being forwarded. The following are the seven possible conditions:

- *Unknown* — The state cannot be determined.

- *Disabled* — Forwarding capabilities are disabled.

- *Blocking* — The Ethernet port is blocking transmission. This is the state when no stations are associated with the AP.

- *Listening* — This setting applies only to wireless bridges and not to APs.

- *Learning* — This setting applies only to wireless bridges and not to APs.

- *Forwarding* — The port is operating and forwarding packets. This is the default setting.

- *Broken* — This condition indicates some type of Ethernet failure.

 The Ethernet Port page enables you to view detailed statistics about the number of frames (packets) that the AP is receiving and transmitting. You can access the Ethernet Port page by clicking Ethernet under the Network Ports heading on the Summary Status page.

Other Cisco Network Settings

You can adjust several other network settings on a Cisco Aironet WLAN. The first is linking the AP to a DNS server. A DNS server is a server that contains a database of Internet domain names (such as *www.course.com*) and their corresponding IP numbers (like *198.146.117.7*). The DNS server uses the Domain Name System (or Service), one of the core services of the TCP/IP protocol, to allow users to enter domain names rather than IP numbers to identify domains.

You can configure Cisco Aironet 340 AP to work with the network's DNS server (or servers) on the Name Server Setup page. To view this page, open a browser and enter the IP number of the access point to display the Summary Status screen. Click Setup from the Summary Status page, then click Name Server under the Services heading. This displays the Name Server Setup page, as shown in Figure 10-4.

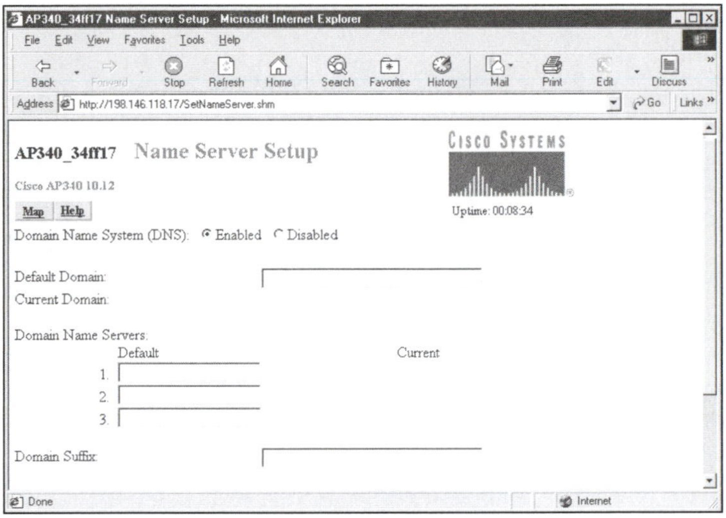

![Screenshot of AP340_34ff17 Name Server Setup page in Microsoft Internet Explorer. Address: http://198.146.118.17/SetNameServer.shm. Shows AP340_34ff17 Name Server Setup, Cisco AP340 10.12, Map and Help buttons. Domain Name System (DNS): Enabled selected, Disabled. Default Domain and Current Domain fields. Domain Name Servers with Default and Current columns numbered 1, 2, 3. Domain Suffix field. Cisco Systems logo, Uptime: 00:08:34.]

Figure 10-4   Cisco Name Server Setup

To make changes to the Name Server Setup page, you must have Administrator privileges with Write capabilities.

If the wired network is using DNS, the Enabled button should be set under Domain Name System (DNS). This allows the AP to work with the service. In the Default Domain field, you enter the name of the network's IP domain, such as course.com. In the Current Domain field, you enter the domain that is serving the AP.

The Current Domain field's value should differ from the Default Domain field's value only if the AP is set to use DHCP as the Configuration Server Protocol and the No option was selected for the *Use previous Configuration Server settings when no server responds?* prompt on the Boot Server Setup page.

Under the Domain Name Servers — Default heading, you can enter the IP addresses of up to three DNS servers. The DNS servers that are currently used by the AP are listed under the Domain Name Servers — Current heading. In the Domain Suffix field, you should enter the last portion of the domain name of the current network domain. For example, in the domain course.com there may be a computer with the name www.course.com and another computer named ftp.course.com. Each of these computers has a unique "first" name (*www* and *ftp*) but they share the same "last" or domain name (course.com). In this instance, you should enter the domain suffix *.course.com* in the Domain Suffix field.

Caution

The leading period is required in the Domain Suffix field. The correct entry would be *.course.com.*

In addition to configuring the Cisco AP to link to the DNS server, you can also make a link between the AP and the network routing system. Recall from Chapter 4 that a router examines the network number portion of the IP number and forwards it to its destination. You can configure the Aironet 340 access point to communicate with the existing network routing system. The Routing Setup page enables you to do so. To view this page, open a browser and enter the IP number of the access point to display the Summary Status screen. Click Setup from the Summary Status page, then click Routing under the Services heading. This displays the Routing Setup page, as shown in Figure 10-5.

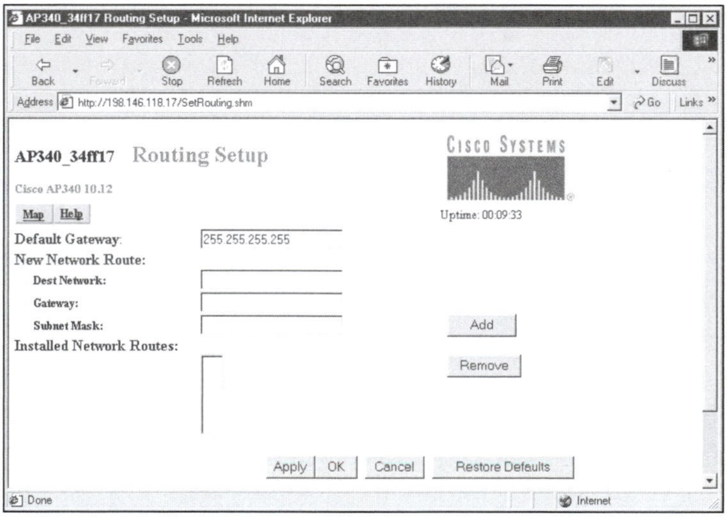
AP340_34ff17 Routing Setup - Microsoft Internet Explorer
File Edit View Favorites Tools Help
Back Forward Stop Refresh Home Search Favorites History Mail Print Edit Discuss
Address http://198.146.118.17/SetRouting.shm
Go Links
AP340_34ff17 Routing Setup
Cisco AP340 10.12
Cisco Systems
Uptime: 00:09:33
Map Help
Default Gateway:
255.255.255.255
New Network Route:
Dest Network:
Gateway:
Subnet Mask:
Add
Installed Network Routes:
Remove
Apply OK Cancel Restore Defaults
Done
Internet

Figure 10-5 Cisco Routing Setup

Tip

To make changes to the Routing Setup Identification page, you must have Administrator privileges with Identity capabilities.

Enter the default gateway's IP number in the Default Gateway field. The entry 255.255.255.255 indicates that no gateway exists. For each new network route, you must make three entries under New Network Route:

- *Dest Network* is the IP number of the destination network.

- *Gateway* is the IP number of the gateway used to reach that destination network.

- *Subnet Mask* is the subnet mask that is associated with the destination network.

Click the Add button to place the New Network Route into the Installed Network Routes field. Then click the Apply button. To remove a route, highlight that route from the Installed Network Route field, then click Remove. Click the Apply button to complete the process.

 You can also configure the Cisco AP to synchronize its time with the network's time, if a network time server is running. The field that enables you to configure this setting is on the Time Server Setup page.

Making changes to Cisco network settings pages requires different Administrator capabilities. These capabilities are summarized in Table 10-2.

Table 10-2 Administrator Capabilities Required to Change Network Pages

10

Cisco Network Page	Write Capabilities	Identity Capabilities
Ethernet Identification	Yes	Yes
Ethernet Hardware	Yes	No
Ethernet Advanced	Yes	No
Name Server Setup	Yes	No
Routing Setup Identification	No	Yes

3Com Network Settings

The 3Com AirConnect AP likewise has network settings that can be adjusted for the WLAN.

3Com Ethernet Parameters

One Ethernet setting that can be adjusted on the 3Com AirConnect is the Ethernet Timeout setting. This setting disables any radio transmissions from the access point if it detects no activity on the Ethernet line. To view the 3Com Ethernet Timeout setting, open a browser and enter the IP number of the access point to display the opening screen. On the tree in the left pane, click Access Point, then click Configuration, then finally click System. When prompted, enter the username *Administrator* and the password. This displays the System Setup page, as shown in Figure 10-6.

Figure 10-6   3Com System Setup

To enable the Ethernet Timeout function, click the drop–down arrow box and select Enabled. In the seconds field, enter a value between 30 and 255. Reset the AP for the new values to take effect. In the tree in the left pane, under Configuration, click Special Functions. Place a check box in the Reset AP field. Click the Perform Function button to reset the AP.

If there is no Ethernet activity from the wired network after the time indicated in the sec- onds field, the access point disassociates all wireless stations. In addition, it will prevent wire- less stations from further associations with the AP until Ethernet activity is detected.

If the Ethernet Timeout setting is disabled when the Ethernet connection is broken, the access point disassociates all wireless stations and disables the radio interface until the Ethernet connection is restored.

Another Ethernet setting that can be made on the 3Com AirConnect is filtering. **Filtering** allows you to control the types of network traffic that pass from the wired Ethernet network to the WLAN stations. You can filter traffic by configuring the AP so that it acts as a type of firewall. The access point can either forward the frames that it receives from the Ethernet wired network to the wireless stations on the WLAN or block frames from entering the WLAN. This is illustrated in Figure 10-7.

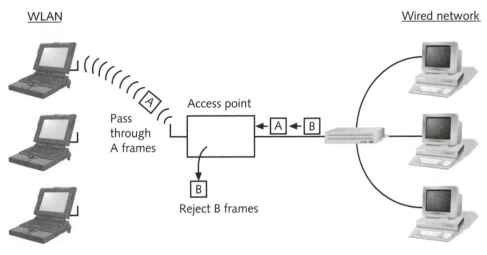

WLAN   Wired network

Pass through A frames

Access point

Reject B frames

Figure 10-7   Filtering

Filtering is disabled by default.

Filtering takes place at different levels. Some devices filter at a high level and can block an application from being requested. For example, such a device might discard a frame requesting execution of a payroll program. Other devices filter at an intermediate level, and thus might reject a request for a specific IP port, for example. At the lowest level, a filter can block a received frame based on the type of frame. The 3Com AirConnect AP performs filtering at the lowest level by blocking based on the type of frame.

Not all network authorities agree that low-level filtering should be used. Some argue that a filter set up to trap data based on the type of frame could also block a frame type that the person who set up the filter didn't even know existed.

The AirConnect AP filters frames based on the type of protocol of the frame. TCP is one type of protocol. Another type is **Internetwork Packet Exchange (IPX)**. IPX is based on a protocol developed by Xerox in the late 1970s and is the default protocol of older Novell NetWare LANs. Another protocol is the **User Datagram Protocol (UDP)**, which is sometimes used instead of TCP.

IPX was the default protocol used by Novell NetWare servers through version 4.11. Beginning with NetWare version 5.0, servers could use either the IPX or TCP/IP protocol, but TCP/IP became the default protocol.

The 3Com AP can only filter frames coming into the WLAN from the wired Ethernet network; it does not filter outgoing frames from the WLAN to the wired network.

There are also different types of Ethernet frame formats. One type of frame format, called the 802.3 frame format, is based on IEEE standards. Another frame format is the Ethernet II frame, which varies slightly from the IEEE 802.3 frame in order to make network transmissions more efficient. A third type of frame is known as the SubNetwork Access Protocol (SNAP). SNAP is used to provide a way to quickly adapt protocols that are not fully compliant with IEEE standards.

Each frame has a four-character hexadecimal number that indicates the type of protocol and frame format. An AP can be configured to reject frames that contain a specific hexadecimal number but accept frames that do not have this number. Those hexadecimal numbers and their frame types are listed in Table 10-3.

Table 10-3   Frame Format/Protocol Hexadecimal Numbers

Frame Format	Protocol	Hexadecimal Number
SNAP	IPX	00E0
802.3	IPX	00FF
Ethernet II	IPX	8137 and 8138
Ethernet II	TCP	0800
Ethernet II	UDP	0806

To filter frames on the 3Com AP, open a browser and enter the IP number of the access point to display the opening screen. On the tree in the left pane, click Access Point, then Configuration, then Filtering. When prompted, enter the username *Administrator* and the password. This displays the Filtering Setup page, as shown in Figure 10-8.

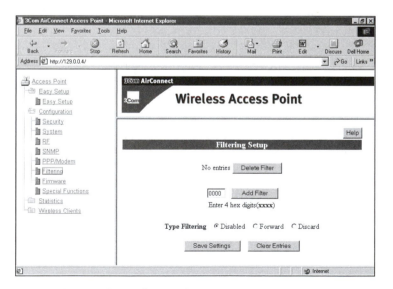

Figure 10-8   3Com Filtering Setup

To configure the AP to pass along specific types of frames (called **forwarding**), click Forward as the Type Filtering option. Enter the four hexadecimal digits associated with the network protocol and frame type that is to be forwarded. Click Add Filter. You may repeat these steps for additional types of protocols to forward.

To configure the AP to discard specific types of frames, click Discard as the Type Filtering option. Enter the four hexadecimal digits associated with the frame type/network protocol that is to be discarded, then click Add Filter. Again, you may repeat these steps for additional types of protocols to discard.

If you want to remove a frame type that you have placed on the forwarding or discarding filter lists, to prevent packets from being forwarded or discarded, you can delete that type of packet from the list. Highlight the hexadecimal number representing the frame type that you want to delete, then click Delete Filter. Although forwarding or discarding will still be turned on, that type of frame will no longer be examined. To turn off all filtering so that all frames pass through the AP, select Disabled as the Type Filtering option. Click Save Settings to save any changes made on the Filtering Setup page.

3Com Mobile IP

Mobile IP enables a host to be identified by a single IP address even while it moves from one network to another. Computers are given a home address, which is a static IP number, on their home network. The computer also has a home agent, which is a forwarding mechanism that keeps track of where the mobile computer is located. When the computer roams to a foreign network, a foreign agent assigns the mobile computer a new temporary IP number known as the care-of address.

You must configure Mobile IP at the 3Com AP as well as at the wireless station. To set the parameters of the access point, open a browser and enter the IP number of the access point to display the opening screen. On the tree in the left pane, click Access Point, then Configuration, then System. When prompted, enter the username *Administrator* and the password. This displays the System Setup page, as shown in Figure 10-9. Click the Enabled option for Mobile IP.

To enable Mobile IP on the local station, right-click Network Neighborhood, then select Properties. Click 3Com AirConnect Wireless LAN PC Card. Click Properties to display the AirConnect WLAN Easy Setup dialog box. Click the Advanced button to display the 3Com AirConnect WLAN Advanced Properties dialog box, click the Mobile IP tab, then select the Enable Mobile IP check box. This displays the settings for Mobile IP, as shown in Figure 10-10.

10

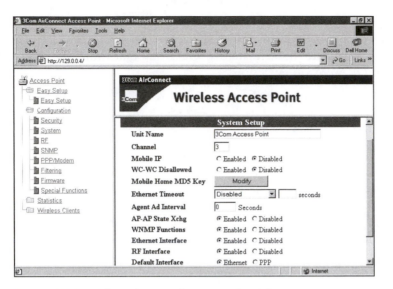

Figure 10-9   3Com System Setup on the AP

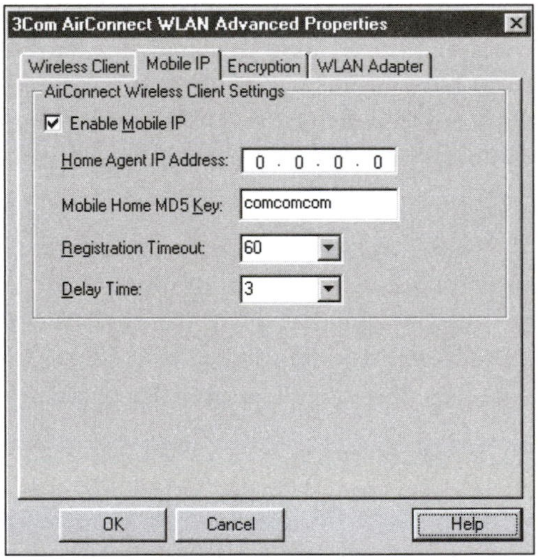

Figure 10-10   3Com Mobile IP setup on the station

You need to set four fields:

- *Home Agent IP Address* lets you register the station with the home AP through a foreign subnet AP (the foreign agent) and tell the foreign AP where the home AP is located.

- *Mobile Home MD5 Key* is a password that protects the registration packets from being tampered with by others while the packets are being forwarded to the home AP. The value should match the MD5 key on the access point of your home subnet.

- *Registration Timeout* is a value from 5 to 3600 seconds. When a wireless client registers with the home agent through a foreign agent, that registration has an expiration time associated with it. The Registration Timeout value tells the wireless client how often it needs to reregister with the home agent. The default value is 60 seconds. If the wireless client does not reregister in the time allowed, the home agent will remove the wireless client from its list of registered clients when the time expires.

- *Delay Time* is a value from 1 to 10 seconds. This is the amount of time that the wireless client will wait for a response from a home agent when trying to register with the home agent. The wireless client will try to register a maximum of three times.

CAVEATS

A *caveat* is a warning or caution. Just as there are warning signs when driving ("Dangerous Curve Ahead"), there are cautions when working with a WLAN. A caveat, however, does not mean that something is wrong. Just as the sign does not mean that a disaster is looming over the next hill, WLAN caveats do not identify problems with the Cisco Aironet 340 or 3Com AirConnect hardware or software, but provide advice about potential issues you should be aware of.

10

WLAN Warnings

The following are cautions that apply to all WLANs:

- Exercise care when adjusting any WLAN parameters. An incorrect change could bring down the entire WLAN. Adjust one setting, then review the performance of the network, instead of making several changes all at once. This helps to isolate any incorrect setting and makes it easy to restore the network to its original condition if necessary.

- You should use the browsers Microsoft Internet Explorer version 4.0 and higher and Netscape Navigator version 4.0 and higher when accessing Web pages on the APs. You should also enable JavaScript on your browser.

- Computers running Windows 95 or Windows 98 have limited network connections. If you try to install a wireless NIC adapter when four network devices (such as an Ethernet card, a modem, VPN adapter, or docking station Ethernet card) are already connected to your computer, the new card will not be able to establish a network connection.

- Static electricity can ruin a wireless NIC. Discharge any building static by touching a metal part of a grounded object before removing the client adapter from its antistatic packaging.

3Com Alerts

The following alerts apply specifically to the 3Com wireless LAN product:

- The 3Com AirConnect does not support peer-to-peer (ad hoc) mode.

- An ISA card is not available for the 3Com AirConnect.

- The 3Com AirConnect does not support Linux.

- The name of the Wireless LAN Service Area must match exactly the name assigned to the access point. Characters, capitalization, and spacing must all be identical.

- Profiles can be present in more than one configuration. If a profile is changed or deleted, all configurations using that profile are affected.

- You should use the Mobile Connection Manager (MCM) instead of the Windows Control Panel to modify network settings for the NIC.

- Telnet logins are enabled by default. If you are not using Telnet, you should disable this type of login.

- When the 3Com Site Survey program is running, if you receive the error message "Destination Host Unreachable," the IP number has not been set. If, after setting the ICMP Host Addr, you receive the same error message, return to the Default Settings page and select the Override All Test ICMP Host Addresses check box.

- The 3Com AP can only filter frames coming into the WLAN from the wired Ethernet network; it does not filter outgoing frames from the WLAN to the wired network.

Cisco Alerts

The following alerts apply specifically to the Cisco wireless LAN product:

- The Reset System Factory Defaults Except IP Identity button on AP Web pages returns all AP settings to their factory defaults *except:*
  - The AP's IP number, the subnet mask, the default gateway, and the boot protocol
  - The users in the User Manager list

- The Reset All System Factory Defaults button returns *all* AP settings to their factory defaults *except* the users in the User Manager list.

- If a Cisco Aironet PC card was installed on a computer with the version 6.10 driver, you must remove the card before upgrading the driver to version 6.21 or higher.

- To open Cisco utilities from a command prompt, type the correct pathname and *windgs* to open ACU, type *linkscope* to open LSM, and type *wepkey* to open CEM.

- If the access point is configured to communicate with either WEP-enabled or WEP-disabled stations, you must select the Allow Association To Mixed Cells check box in the ACU utility, even if the station is not using WEP. Failure to do so may prevent the station from establishing connection with the access point.

- Turn the computer on before inserting a PC Card wireless NIC into a laptop that is running Windows ME or Windows 98.

- The Home Radio Network Name is case-sensitive.

- Make sure that the AP is not receiving power (that is, make sure that the AP is not plugged in) when you connect the network cable.

- When you initially configure the AP, the client computer and the access point must be on the same network segment. If the access point receives an IP address from a DHCP server, you may need to configure the client computer's IP number manually.

- Telnet logins are enabled by default. If you are not using Telnet, you should disable this type of login.

- The Cisco default setting allows devices that do not specify an SSID to associate with the AP.

- The Cisco CEM password is *Cisco*.

10

TROUBLESHOOTING

Identifying a problem and then solving it—called *troubleshooting*—is as much an art as it is a science. Troubleshooting a WLAN can be a challenge, because it is a new technology and there are so many things that can go wrong. Even if you meticulously follow instructions and are aware of caveats, sometimes the WLAN just does not work as it should—or at all. These problems can be the result of anything from overlooking a check box on a dialog box to installing the wrong software. However, with a systematic approach (the science) along with some helpful hints (the art), the troubleshooting process can be much easier.

Cisco Troubleshooting

This section poses possible problems with Cisco WLANs and suggests solutions.

I can't get the wireless NIC adapter to go into the laptop.

Examine the client adapter closely. One end is a dual-row, 68-pin client adapter connector. The other end contains an embedded antenna and will protrude from the laptop. Insert the adapter end into the PC Card adapter slot with the logo facing up. Apply just enough pressure to make sure that it is fully seated. Do not force the client adapter into the PC Card slot, because this could damage both the card and the slot. If the card does not go in easily, remove the card and try again.

My computer can't locate the drivers for the wireless NIC adapter.

The drivers for the Cisco Aironet 340 are on the Installation CD-ROM. When the Add New Hardware Wizard dialog box opens, click Next to display another dialog box asking how to locate the new driver. Select Search and click Next. Insert the CD-ROM and select the CD-ROM drive, unselect all the other options, then click Next.

My coworker says that she can't see the hard drive on my station through the WLAN.

The File and Print Sharing option must be selected to allow other WLAN stations to access the files or print capabilities on your station. Right-click Network Neighborhood (for Windows 95 and 98), then click Properties to display the Network dialog box, as shown in Figure 10-11. Click the File and Print Sharing button to display the File and Print Sharing dialog box, as shown in Figure 10-12. Select the check boxes for file sharing, print sharing, or both. If a station appears in Network Neighborhood but no drives or files are displayed, go to that station and double-click My Computer to display the drive that is to be shared. If the drive icon does not have a hand symbol under it, then it is not set up for sharing files. Select the drive by clicking it, then right-click and click Sharing to access the Sharing tab, where you can specify sharing for that drive.

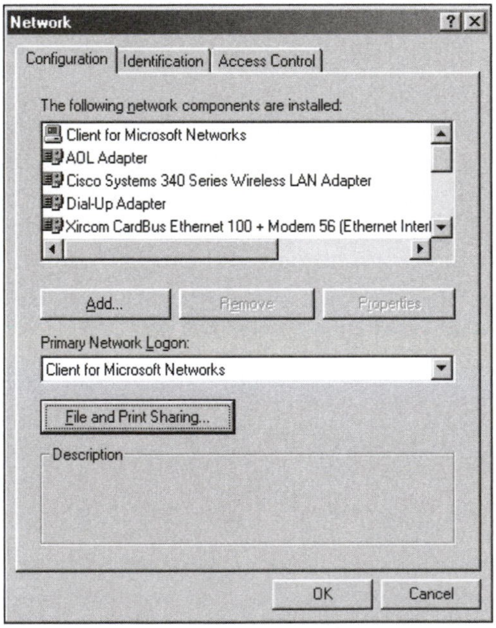

Figure 10-11 Network dialog box

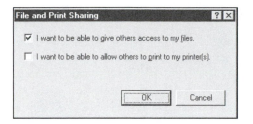

Figure 10-12   File and Print Sharing dialog box

I've set up the ad hoc network but I can't see any other stations.

Check the settings on the ACU utility on the wireless station. Click Start, point to Programs, point to Cisco Systems, Inc., then click Aironet Client Utility to start the ACU program. Click Commands, then Edit Properties. Click the System Parameters tab to display the dialog box shown in Figure 10-13.

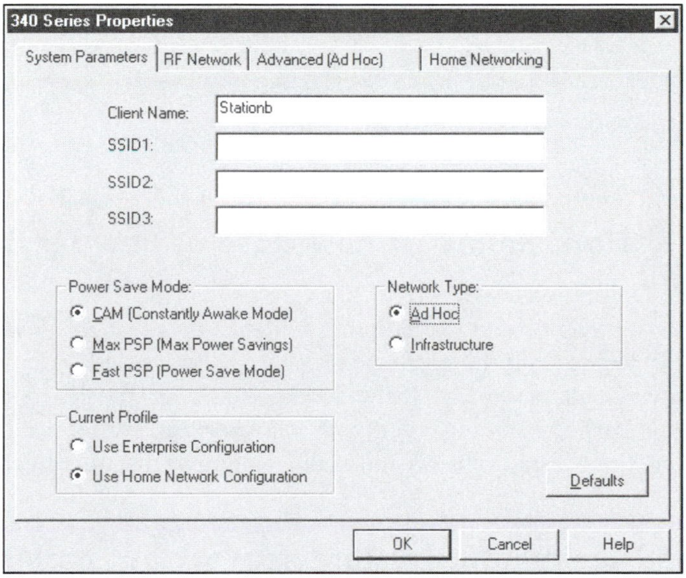

Figure 10-13   Cisco System Parameters tab

The Client Name should be the same as that which was entered in the Network Adapter dialog box. In the Power Save Mode panel, the radio button CAM (Constantly Awake Mode) should be selected. In the Current Profile panel, Use Home Network Configuration should be selected. Network Type should be set to ad hoc. Click the Home Networking tab to display the options for a Home Network, as shown in Figure 10-14. Enter a unique name for the Home Computer Name. The Home Radio Network Name must be the same as that entered on the other computers. The Home Encryption Key must also be the same as that entered on the other computers. Select No Base Station. Click OK when finished.

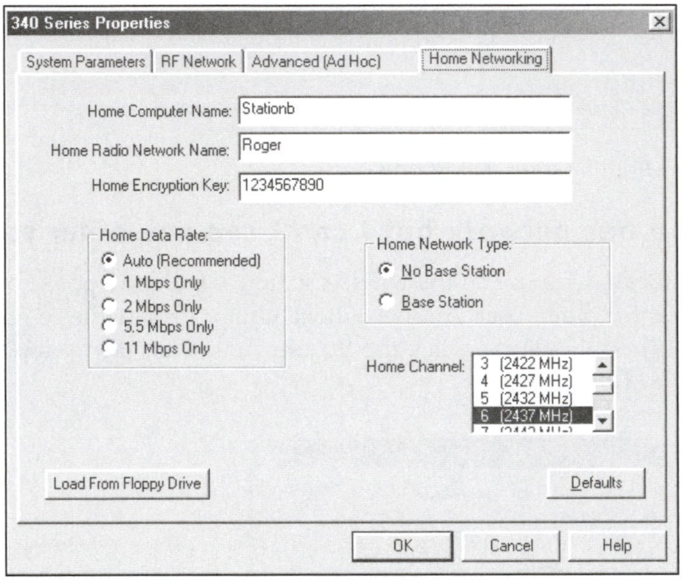

Figure 10-14 Cisco Home Networking tab

The WLAN is very slow, no matter how close or how far the laptop is from the AP.

The antennae on the access point should be pointing straight up or straight down, no matter where access point is mounted. If the access point is on a table or desk, you should turn the antennae so that they point straight up. If the access point will later be mounted on a wall or a pole, you should turn the antennae so that they are vertical, even if the access point is on its side. Mounting the access point on the ceiling requires that the antennae point straight down.

I've set up a stand-alone infrastructure network but nothing happens.

Look at the AP settings and record the default IP number and Radio Service Set ID. Launch the ACU program and go to the System Parameters page. Check the following settings:

- *Client Name* — Must be different from other stations

- *SSID1* — Must be the same as the access point

- *Current Profile* — Select Enterprise configuration

- *Network Type* — Select Infrastructure

When I try to get to the AP from my browser to configure the AP, I get a message back that the browser cannot find that site. I know I'm entering the correct IP number.

Test the connection by using the ping command (see Chapter 6). If the connection fails, make sure that the AP and the computer are on the same network segment. If you are using DHCP, you may need to configure the computer's IP number manually.

3Com Troubleshooting

This section addresses possible problems with 3Com WLANs and suggests solutions.

What do the flashing lights on the AP mean when you first plug it in?

After the AP is turned on, it first performs a memory test. If the test fails, the LEDs all turn off and the AP resets. If the test passes, all three LEDs turn on and then turn off sequentially, in the order shown in Table 10-4, as each of the indicated tests are passed.

Table 10-4   3Com AP LEDs

LED	Tests Performed When Powered On
Power	Bootup and special codes have been downloaded into memory
Wireless LAN Activity	Serial port has been initialized
Wired LAN Activity	LAN adapter is present

10

My station can't communicate with the AP.

Check the AP configuration by Telnet or the Web. Also, check to be sure that there are no duplicate IP numbers by turning off the AP and trying to ping that IP number. Be sure that no other device responds to that ping.

We are experiencing slow and erratic performance on the WLAN. What should I check for?

Check wireless client and communications range by performing a site survey. Look at the antennae, connectors, and cabling of the AP. 3Com says that network traffic should not exceed 37 percent of the entire bandwidth. Also, check that the wired network does not exceed 10 broadcast messages per second.

I can't see the printer that is attached to another station.

You must enable Windows Print and File Sharing to allow other WLAN users to access printers. Right-click Network Neighborhood, then click Properties to display the Network dialog box. Select 3Com AirConnect Wireless LAN PC Card, then click the File and Print Sharing button. Select the check box for print sharing.

I seem to have a weak signal or intermittent connection on my station.

The NIC antenna is attached to the end of the card. For best use of the antenna, keep the area around the antenna clear from materials that could block radio transmission (metal objects, electronic devices, cordless telephones, and so on). Move your computer to find a better signal. Use the Signal Strength display in the AirConnect Status application to determine the best location and orientation for a network connection.

My station won't attach to the network.

Be sure that the Wireless LAN Service Area ID matches that found on the AP. Also, be sure that the adapter Data Rate is configured correctly for the access point.

We have a Novell NetWare server, and the network drive mappings disappear when my Windows 98 laptop goes into sleep mode or the adapter is removed and then reinserted.

Windows 98 will not restore NetWare network drive mappings under these conditions. You must log out and log in again, or restart the computer to restore the connections.

FAQs

FAQs, or frequently asked questions, are commonly used as a support tool. FAQs are lists of questions that are common to most users. Even if your question is not exactly the same as one listed in the FAQ, usually there is information in a similar FAQ on that topic that can be helpful.

Cisco FAQs

Following are questions that come up frequently for Cisco WLANs.

What are the steps for setting up a Cisco ad hoc WLAN?

The general steps for setting up an ad hoc WLAN are as follows:

1. Install a wireless NIC adapter.

2. Load any necessary drivers and utilities.

3. Configure the Windows operating system for the network.

4. Configure the station using the Cisco Aironet Client Utility (ACU).

What are the minimum hardware requirements for a Cisco WLAN?

Any desktop computer that has a PCI slot or a laptop that has a Type II PC Card can accept a wireless NIC and become a station on a Cisco WLAN.

What operating systems does the Cisco WLAN support?

Any of the following operating systems can support a Cisco wireless NIC:

- Windows 2000

- Windows NT (with Service Pack 4 or 5)

- Windows ME

- Windows 98 or 98SE

- Windows 95 B

- Windows CE

- Linux

Should the laptop be on or off when I install the Cisco wireless NIC adapter in a Windows NT system?

When installing a PC Card into a laptop that is running the Windows NT operating system, turn the computer off before inserting the wireless NIC. For all other Windows operating systems, turn the computer on.

How do I assign an IP number and subnet mask to the wireless station?

Right-click Network Neighborhood (for Windows 95 and 98), then click Properties to display the Network dialog box. Click TCP/IP -> Cisco System 340 Series Wireless LAN Adapter from the list of network components installed. Click Properties and then click the IP Address tab. Enter a valid IP number and subnet mask. This is illustrated in Figure 10-15.

10

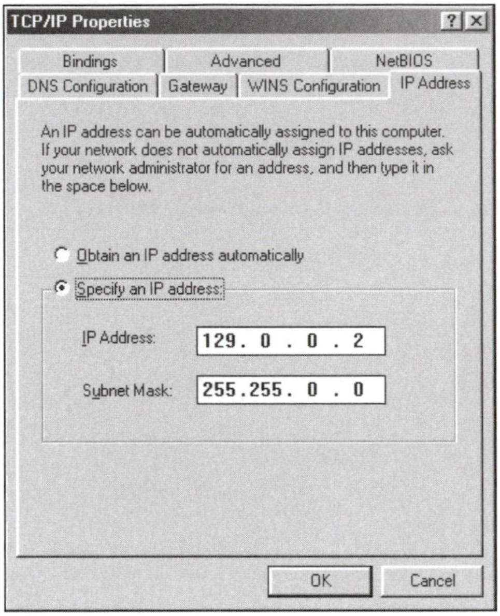

Figure 10-15   Entering the Cisco IP number and subnet mask

How do I know that my WLAN network is functioning correctly?

Double-click Network Neighborhood to see all of the stations on the network. If permission was granted to share files, then double-clicking the icon of a station displays its drives and files. To see information about the number of frames that the WLAN is sending and receiving, start the ACU program, then click the Commands menu and then Statistics to display the 340 Series Statistics window illustrated in Figure 10-16. The Statistics window shows the number of frames and errors that this station has sent and received. To display the relative signal strengths of the stations, click Start, point to Programs, point to Cisco Systems, Inc., then click Link Status Meter to display the signal strengths, as shown in Figure 10-17.

340 Series Statistics   ☒

Receive Statistics   Transmit Statistics
-----------------------------   ------------------------------

Multicast Packets Received	=	3
Broadcast Packets Received	=	120
Unicast Packets Received	=	114
Bytes Received	=	36722
Beacons Received	=	57509
Total Packets Received OK	=	103872
Duplicate Packets Received	=	0
Overrun Errors	=	0
PLCP CRC Errors	=	8
PLCP Format Errors	=	24
PLCP Length Errors	=	0
MAC CRC Errors	=	2
Partial Packets Received	=	0
SSID Mismatches	=	0
AP Mismatches	=	0
Data Rate Mismatches	=	0
Authentication Rejects	=	0
Authentication T/O	=	0
Association Rejects	=	0
Association T/O	=	0
Packets Aged	=	0
Up Time (hh:mm:ss)	=	03:05:40
Total Up Time (hh:mm:ss)	=	03:05:40

Multicast Packets Transmitted	=	3
Broadcast Packets Transmitted	=	213
Unicast Packets Transmitted	=	99
Bytes Transmitted	=	46968
Beacons Transmitted	=	51132
Ack Packets Transmitted	=	114
RTS Packets Transmitted	=	0
CTS Packets Transmitted	=	0
Single Collisions	=	0
Multiple Collisions	=	0
Packets No Deferral	=	0
Packets Deferred Protocol	=	0
Packets Deferred Energy Detect	=	182
Packets Retry Long	=	6
Packets Retry Short	=	0
Packets Max Retries	=	3
Packets Ack Received	=	104
Packets No Ack Received	=	6
Packets CTS Received	=	0
Packets No CTS Received	=	0
Packets Aged	=	1

[Pause]   [Help]   [Reset]   [OK]

Figure 10-16   Cisco Statistics window

10

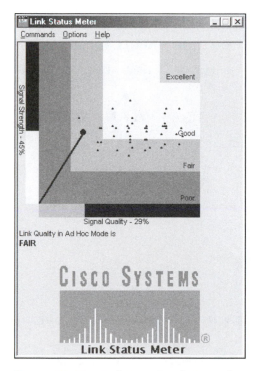

Figure 10-17   Relative signal strength

If I use an AP, does it have to be connected to a wired Ethernet network?

No. An infrastructure stand-alone WLAN has an access point, but that access point is not connected to a wired network. Infrastructure stand-alone WLANs are sometimes used when a basic ad hoc network does not provide functions that are needed. Power-saving features are not available in an ad hoc network, but they are available in an infrastructure stand-alone WLAN. In addition, infrastructure stand-alone WLANs can take advantage of special security features.

3Com FAQs

Following are questions that come up frequently for 3Com WLANs.

What are some of the differences between the 3Com and Cisco WLANs?

Many users indicate that the 3Com AirConnect is easier to set up and manage, whereas the Cisco Aironet 340 has more detailed parameters that can be set. The Cisco WLAN can run in ad hoc mode and also supports RTS, whereas the 3Com AirConnect does not. Cisco also supports Linux and has ISA wireless NIC adapters, whereas 3Com does not. 3Com has Mobile IP and frame filtering available, but Cisco does not have these features.

What are the minimum hardware requirements for a 3Com WLAN?

Any desktop computer that has a PCI slot or a laptop that has a Type II PC Card can accept a wireless NIC and become a station on a 3Com WLAN.

What operating systems does the 3Com WLAN support?

Any of the following operating systems can support a Cisco wireless NIC:

- Windows 2000
- Windows NT (with Service Pack 4 or 5)
- Windows ME
- Windows 98 or 98SE
- Windows 95 B
- Windows CE

Should the laptop be on or off when I install the 3Com wireless NIC adapter?

If a PC Card is being installed in a laptop, you should not insert it into the system until the 3Com setup software prompts you to do so. If the wireless NIC was already installed before you ran the setup utility, remove the card, wait five seconds, then reinsert the card.

What are the steps for setting up a 3Com infrastructure stand-alone WLAN?

The following are the general steps to set up a 3Com infrastructure stand-alone WLAN:

1. Install the wireless NIC adapters, drivers, and utility programs.

2. Configure the wireless stations.

3. Configure Windows file and/or printer sharing.

4. Install the access point.

5. Configure the access point.

How do I install the 3Com utility software?

Insert the AirConnect Installation CD-ROM. Click Start, click Run, then enter *D:\Setup.exe*, where *D:* is the letter of the CD-ROM drive. The 3Com AirConnect WLAN menu appears. Click Installation for Windows, then select Install WLAN Applications. The DynamicAccess Mobile Connection Manager Setup dialog box appears. Click Next and follow the steps to install the WLAN utilities.

What's the best way to configure the local station for the 3Com WLAN?

The 3Com Mobile Connection Manager (MCM) stores the configuration information. These preferred settings are categorized by and stored in MCM profiles and configurations. When the 3Com driver and utility software is first installed, MCM automatically creates a General Access Profile and LAN Profile based on configurations already present on the laptop. Click the 3Com icon in the Windows system tray on the lower-right portion of the screen. The 3Com Launcher opens. Click the MCM icon. To view the profiles that were automatically created when the software was installed, click the File menu, then point to Profiles, then finally click LAN Profiles to bring up the LAN Profiles screen, as shown in Figure 10-18. Select a profile, then click View to see the settings for that profile. Follow the same procedure to see the General Access Profile. If all of the settings of the LAN Profile and General Access Profile are acceptable, you need not do anything more. However, if any of the settings need to be changed, you should create a new configuration with the modified profiles.

10

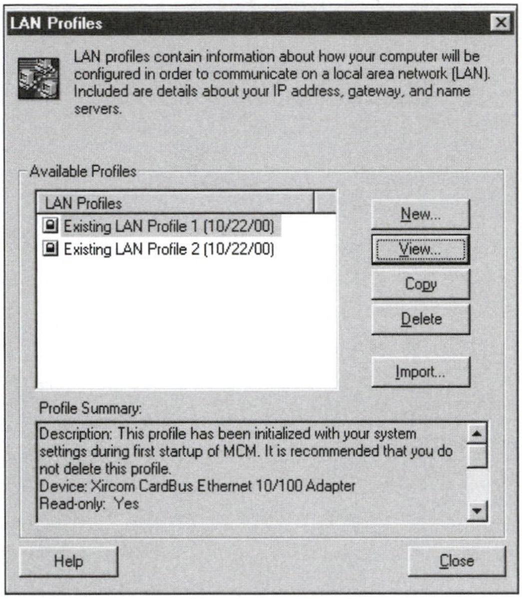

Figure 10-18   3Com LAN Profiles

How do I configure the 3Com AP for the first time?

When setting up an access point, you first must change the settings of the access point. A 9-pin, straight-through, female-to-female serial cable, included with the 3Com AirConnect, is needed to change those settings of the access point. One end of the cable is connected to the serial port on the computer and the other end to the RS-232 port on the back of the access point. Insert the Administration Utilities CD. When the 3Com Access Point main menu appears, select WLAN Utilities, then select Serial Connection. HyperTerminal starts with a blank window. Press Enter to see the default settings, then press Esc to see to the main menu, as shown in Figure 10-19. Choose AP Installation and enter the administrative password (*comcomcom*). This displays the Access Point Installation screen. Enter the IP number and a Wireless LAN Service Area for this access point. Save the settings, then reset the AP for the new settings to take effect.

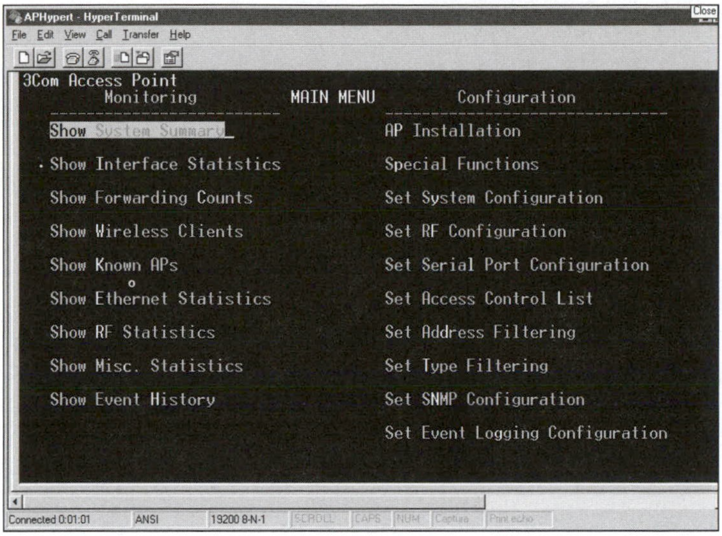

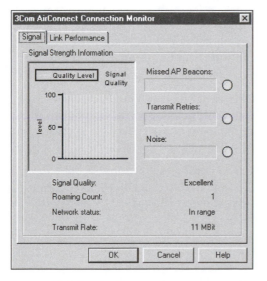

Figure 10-19   3Com AP Main Menu

Is there any way to tell whether the connection to the 3Com AP is actually working?

10

Click the 3Com icon in the Windows system tray in the lower-right portion of the screen. This opens the 3Com Launcher. Click the Connection Monitor icon to view the signal strength, as shown in Figure 10-20.

Figure 10-20   AirConnect Connection Monitor

CHAPTER SUMMARY

❑ Both Cisco and 3Com APs have an RJ-45 connection that allows them to connect to an Ethernet hub to provide wireless stations access to resources on a wired network. You can adjust the settings to Ethernet networks to improve performance and provide additional capabilities to the WLAN. The Cisco Aironet 340 provides several settings that you can modify. You can link a Cisco Aironet AP to a Domain Name Server and also to the network routing system. One of the Ethernet settings that can be adjusted on the 3Com AirConnect is the Ethernet Timeout setting. This setting disables any radio transmissions from the access point if it detects no activity on the Ethernet line. Another Ethernet setting that can be made on the 3Com AirConnect is filtering, which allows you to control the types of network traffic that pass from the wired Ethernet network to the WLAN stations. You can also set Mobile IP using a 3Com AP. Mobile IP enables a host to be identified by a single IP address even while it moves from one network to another.

❑ A *caveat* is a warning or caution; it does not mean that something is wrong. Some of the general WLAN cautions include the need to exercise care when adjusting any WLAN parameters, that you should use Microsoft Internet Explorer version 4.0 and higher and Netscape Navigator version 4.0 and higher when accessing the Web pages on the APs, and that it is important to touch a metal part of a grounded unit first before removing the client adapter from its antistatic packaging. Users also need to be aware of specific caveats—not problems—with the Cisco Aironet 340 or 3Com AirConnect hardware and software. Some of the 3Com caveats are that the name of the Wireless LAN Service Area must match exactly the name assigned to the access point; that if a profile is changed or deleted, all configurations using that profile are affected; and that Telnet logins are enabled by default. Cisco caveats include that if the access point is configured to communicate with either WEP-enabled or WEP-disabled stations, you must select the Allow Association To Mixed Cells check box in the ACU utility, even if the station is not using WEP; that the Home Radio Network Name is case-sensitive; and that the Cisco default setting allows devices that do not specify an SSID to associate with the AP.

❑ Troubleshooting, or identifying a problem and then solving it, can be a challenge with WLANs because it is a new technology and there are so many different things that can go wrong. Troubleshooting is part science, based on a systematic approach, and part art, based on experience and "gut feelings."

❑ FAQs, or frequently asked questions, are a common user support tool. Some of the FAQs for the Cisco Aironet 340 and 3Com AirConnect are: What operating systems are supported? Should the laptop be on or off when I install the wireless NIC adapter? How do I assign an IP number and subnet mask to the wireless station? How do I know that my WLAN network is functioning correctly? What are some of the differences between the 3Com and Cisco WLANs?

KEY TERMS

bridge — A network hardware device that knows the segment on which the destination computer is located and that sends the frame to only that segment.

filtering — The ability to control the types of network traffic that pass from the wired Ethernet network to the WLAN stations.

forwarding — Passing through specific types of frames in the filtering process.

Internetwork Packet Exchange (IPX) — A protocol based on one developed by Xerox in the late 1970s and used in Novell NetWare LANs for many years.

User Datagram Protocol (UDP) — A network protocol sometimes used instead of TCP.

REVIEW QUESTIONS

1. All APs have a(n) _____ connection that allows them to connect to an Ethernet hub to provide wireless stations the same network resources as a wired client.

   a. RJ-11

   b. RJ-45

   c. X.500

   d. serial

2. The primary port of the AP is almost always the _____ port.

   a. serial

   b. input

   c. parallel

   d. Ethernet

3. A _____ is a network hardware device that knows the segment on which the destination computer is located and sends the frame to only that segment.

   a. router

   b. gateway

   c. bridge

   d. station

4. Changing a default address on the AP can cause it to _____ or force a reboot of the AP.

   a. lose its network connection

   b. crash the network

   c. reboot all of the WLAN stations

   d. change its firmware

10

5. Each of the following is an option for the type of connector and connection speed used by the Ethernet port on a Cisco AP except

   a. Auto

   b. 10Base-T

   c. 100Base-T

   d. 1000Base-T

6. Changes to the Cisco Ethernet Hardware page require Administrator privileges with Write capabilities. True or false?

7. The Ethernet Advanced page is used to change the operational status of an AP temporarily. True or false?

8. If the Packet Forwarding field is set to Disabled, the AP will no longer send frames to wireless stations. True or false?

9. A Domain Name System is a special file server that contains a database of Internet domain names and their corresponding IP numbers. True or false?

10. You can configure the Cisco Aironet 340 AP to work with the network's Domain Name Server. True or false?

11. The Domain Suffix of the URL http://www.soccer.com that would be entered on the Name Server page is _____.

12. The entry _____ for the Default Gateway indicates that no gateway exists.

13. The Ethernet setting _____ on the 3Com AirConnect disables any radio transmissions from the access point if it detects no activity on the Ethernet line.

14. _____ allows control over the types of network traffic that pass from the wired Ethernet network to the WLAN stations.

15. _____ is based on a protocol developed by Xerox in the late 1970s and was used in Novell NetWare LANs for several years.

16. Explain the different levels of filtering and how filtering works on a 3Com AirConnect AP.

17. List and describe the three different types of Ethernet frame formats.

18. What is Mobile IP?

19. Explain the Registration Timeout and Delay Time fields used with 3Com Mobile IP.

20. What are some of the major differences between the Cisco Aironet 340 and the 3Com AirConnect WLAN?

HANDS-ON PROJECTS

1. The Ethernet Identification page provides basic information regarding the configuration of the Ethernet port on the Cisco AP. If you are using the Cisco Aironet 340, follow these steps:

   a. Open a browser and enter the IP number of the access point to display the Summary Status screen.

   b. Click **Setup** from the Summary Status page, then click **Identification** on the Ethernet row under the Network Ports heading. This displays the Ethernet Identification page.

   c. Record the contents of the following fields:

      ❑ Default IP Address

      ❑ Default IP Subnet Mask

      ❑ Current IP Address

      ❑ Current IP Subnet Mask

   d. Explain why the contents of these fields are different or are the same.

2. The Ethernet Hardware page allows you to modify the connection to the Ethernet network. If you are using the Cisco Aironet 340, follow these steps:

   a. Open a browser and enter the IP number of the access point to display the Summary Status screen.

   b. Click **Setup** from the Summary Status page, then click **Hardware** on the Ethernet row under the Network Ports heading. This displays the Ethernet Hardware page.

   c. The drop-down Speed menu lists three options for the type of connector and connection speed used by the Ethernet port. Note the type of connection that is currently being used with the network. If it is set to Auto, ask the network administrator why he or she chose this setting.

3. The Ethernet Advanced page is used to change the operational status of a Cisco AirConnect AP temporarily. It can be a helpful tool when troubleshooting network problems. The Requested Status field allows you to change the operating condition of the Ethernet port. The Packet Forwarding field displays and allows you to change the forwarding capability of the Ethernet port on the access point. The Forwarding State field displays and allows the user to change how frames (packets) are being forwarded. Ask the WLAN administrator for the five most common types of network errors that are encountered. Which of the three fields could be helpful in diagnosing the causes of these errors? Why? Write a short paper on your findings and conclusions.

4. The Cisco Time Server Setup page synchronizes the AP's clock with the network's time server using the Simple Network Time Protocol (SNTP). Research time servers and SNTP. How can they be used? What are their advantages and disadvantages? If the network that you are using does not use SNTP, could its use benefit network users? Why? Write a one-page paper on your findings.

10

5. One of the Ethernet settings that can be adjusted on the 3Com AirConnect is the Ethernet Timeout setting, which disables any radio transmissions from the access point if the AP detects no activity on the Ethernet line. If you are using the 3Com AirConnect, follow these steps:

   a. Open a browser and enter the IP number of the access point to display the opening screen.

   b. On the tree in the left pane, click **Access Point**, then **Configuration**, then **System**. When prompted, enter the username **Administrator** and the password. This displays the System Setup page.

   c. Enable the Ethernet Timeout function by clicking the drop-down arrow and selecting **Enabled**.

   d. In the seconds field, enter a value between 30 and 255. You may want to ask your WLAN administrator for a recommended value. Reset the AP for the new values to take effect.

6. Filtering can take place at different levels. Some devices filter at a high level and can block an application from being requested, whereas other filtering can be done at an intermediate level, such as rejecting a request for a specific IP port. At the lowest level, filtering can block at a received frame based on the type of frame itself. Research frame filtering. Which level offers the most protection? Why? How difficult is it to implement this level of filtering on a typical firewall? What are some of the latest attempts to circumvent filtering? Write a one-page paper on your findings.

7. You can filter frames on a 3Com AP. If you are using the 3Com AirConnect, follow these steps:

   a. Open a browser and enter the IP number of the access point to display the opening screen.

   b. On the tree in the left pane, click **Access Point**, then **Configuration**, then **Filtering**. When prompted, enter the username **Administrator** and the password. This displays the Filtering Setup page.

   c. Configure the AP to pass through (forward) specific types of frames. Click **Forward** as the Type Filtering option. Ask your WLAN administrator for the protocol and frame type of the frames that should be filtered. Determine the corresponding protocol hexadecimal number and enter that number.

   d. Click **Add Filter**.

   e. Configure the AP to discard specific types of frames. Click **Discard** as the Type Filtering option. Ask your WLAN administrator for the protocol and frame type of the frames that should be discarded. Enter the four hexadecimal digits associated with the network protocol that is to be discarded, then click **Add Filter**.

   f. Click **Save Settings** to save any changes made on this page.

CASE PROJECT

Northridge Consulting Group

Northridge Consulting Group (NCG) again wants you to assist with a WLAN project. The accounting firm of Thompkins, Kirkpatrick, and Kid (TKK) is now providing laptop computers to its employees to use around the office. One of the offices is in a historical building known as Old Mulkey; the other is the firm's main office on Carter Street. The Old Mulkey office is using the Cisco Aironet 340, whereas the main office has installed the 3Com AirConnect. TKK has only one network specialist on staff for both sites, and her background in WLANs is limited. TKK needs a written WLAN manual for its staff, and has hired NCG. In turn, NCG has selected you for this project.

1. Select either the Cisco Aironet or 3Com AirConnect product. Create a manual for the local WLAN station. Divide the manual into three parts: installation, configuration, and use. Make this manual basic enough that someone with a limited networking background can use it.

2. Add an appendix on troubleshooting problems. Use your own experience and that of others to generate a list of problems and suggestions for how these problems should be solved.

10

OPTIONAL TEAM CASE PROJECT

NCG also wants you to create a manual for TKK on the access point as well an FAQ appendix. Create a team of three to four consultants. Each consultant should select one area of the AP manual (installation, configuration, troubleshooting, or FAQs). Research that area and work together to create an appropriate manual for the access point.

Glossary

4-pulse position modulation (4-PPM) — A modulation for diffused infrared 2 Mbps WLANs that translates two data bits into four light impulses.

16-pulse position modulation (16-PPM) — A modulation for diffused infrared 1 Mbps WLANs that translates four data bits into 16 light impulses.

Access Control List (ACL) — A list of approved MAC addresses contained in the access point.

access point (AP) — A device connected to the wired local area network that receives signals and transmits signals back to wireless NICs, and that acts as both the base station and bridge for a wireless network.

active scanning — The process of sending frames to gather information.

ad hoc — A mode in which wireless stations communicate directly among themselves without using an access point; also called *peer-to-peer mode* or *Independent Basic Service Set (IBSS)*.

Address Resolution Protocol (ARP) — Part of the TCP/IP protocol that associates a MAC address with an IP number.

Aironet Client Utility (ACU) — A Cisco utility program that is used to configure the WLAN network and perform user-level diagnostics on the wireless NIC.

American Standard Code for Information Interchange (ASCII) — An arbitrary coding scheme that uses the numbers from 0 to 255 to represent letters, numbers, and other characters.

amplitude modulation (AM) — Commonly used modulation for transmitting conventional radio station signals between 535 KHz and 1700 KHz.

antenna — A copper wire or similar device used to transmit radio signals that has one end exposed and the other end connected to the ground.

associate request frame — A frame sent by a station to an access point. The frame includes such information as the station's own capabilities and supported rates.

associate response frame — A frame returned to a station from the access point. The frame contains a status code and station ID number for that station.

association — The process of communicating with other wireless stations or the access point so that the station or access point can become accepted as part of the network.

authentication — The process that verifies that the user has permission to access the network.

authentication frame — A frame sent to an access point by a station when WEP encryption is used for authentication purposes.

backoff interval — A random amount of time that two computers wait before attempting to resend.

bandwidth — The transmission capacity of a network.

Barker code — A bit pattern used in a DSSS transmission; also called *chipping code*.

base 2 — The numeric system used by computers that represents any number by using just two digits, 0 and 1; also known as *binary code*.

Basic Service Set (BSS) — A WLAN mode that consists of wireless stations and one access point; also known as *infrastructure mode*.

beacon frame — A frame sent from the access point to all stations.

binary code — A code used by computers that can represent any number by using just two digits, 0 and 1. Binary code is the same as the *base 2* numeric system.

Bluetooth — A wireless standard for devices to transmit data at up to 1 Mbps over a distance of 33 feet (10 meters).

bridge — A network hardware device that knows the segment on which the destination computer is located and that sends the frame to only that segment.

buffering — The process that the access point uses to temporarily store frames for stations that are in sleep mode.

Card Information Structure (CIS) — A file that contains information about the PC Card installed, such as its speed, its size, and the system resources required.

care-of address — A temporary IP number assigned to a mobile station using Mobile IP.

Carrier Sense Multiple Access with Collision Avoidance (CSMA/CA) — The IEEE 802.11 standard procedure used by WLANs to avoid packet collisions.

Carrier Sense Multiple Access with Collision Detection (CSMA/CD) — The IEEE 802.3 Ethernet standard that specifies contention with a backoff interval if a collision results.

carrier sense — The process of listening before sending in order to detect other traffic.

carrier signal — A transmission over a single radio frequency that carries no useful information.

Cellular Digital Packet Data (CDPD) — An analog packet-switched transmission signal used by cell phones.

channel access methods — The different ways of sharing in a multipoint topology.

chipping code — A bit pattern used in a DSSS transmission; also known as *Barker code*.

circuit-switched — A technology that establishes a dedicated connection circuit between a sending and receiving device; that circuit remains open until the entire transmission is terminated.

Client Encryption Manager (CEM) — A Cisco utility program that is used for setting security features.

collision — A conflict between packets sent by two computers that transmit packets at the same time.

Common Management Interface Protocol (CMIP) — A protocol, based on the OSI model, that gathers network statistics.

Complementary Code Keying (CCK) — A code of 64 eight-bit code words used for transmitting DSSS at speeds above 2 Mbps.

configuration — Part of the 3Com MCM utility that is a collection of profiles.

contention — One type of channel access method in which computers compete with each other for the use of the network.

control frames — MAC frames that assist in delivering the frames that contain data.

data frames — MAC frames that carry the information to be transmitted to the destination station.

de facto standards — Common practices that an industry may follow.

de jure standards — Standards controlled by an organization or body that has been entrusted with that task; same as *official standards*.

detector — A device on light-based infrared WLAN systems that receives a signal.

differential binary phase shift key (DBPSK) — A modulation used for DSSS transmission that varies the phase of the waveform slightly to represent a 0 or a 1.

differential quadrature phase shift key (DQPSK) — A modulation used for DSSS transmission that varies the phase of the waveform slightly to represent the bits 00, 01, 10, and 11.

diffused — An infrared transmission that relies on reflected light to send and receive signals.

digital certificates — Electronic signatures that are issued by a trusted third party that validates the identity of a certificate holder.

direct sequence spread spectrum (DSSS) — A spread spectrum technique that uses an expanded redundant code to transmit each data bit.

directed — An infrared transmission that requires that the emitter and detector be aimed directly at one another.

disassociation frame — A frame sent by the new access point to the old access point to terminate the old access point's association with a station.

Distributed Coordination Function (DCF) — The default access method for WLANs.

Distributed Coordination Function IFS (DIFS) — The standard interval between the transmission of data frames.

DNS server — A file server that uses the Domain Name System (DNS) and contains a database of Internet domain names and their corresponding IP numbers.

Domain Name System (DNS) — Part of the TCP/IP protocol suite that associates an IP number with the name of a host.

Dynamic Host Configuration Protocol (DHCP) — Part of the TCP/IP protocol that temporarily distributes IP numbers to stations.

dynamic rate shifting — An 802.11b standard that adjusts data rates automatically to compensate for the changing nature of the radio signal.

electromagnetic waves — Waves through which light and heat travel.

emitter — A device on light-based infrared WLAN systems that transmits a signal.

encapsulate — In Mobile IP, to wrap a frame into a new frame and give it a different destination address; also called *tunnel*.

ether — A medium that early scientists theorized was the means through which light and heat traveled.

Extended Service Set (ESS) — A WLAN mode that consists of wireless stations and multiple access points.

Extended Service Set ID (ESSID) — A unique ID for the Extended Service Set WLAN.

Federal Communications Commission (FCC) — The U.S. governmental agency responsible for establishing how radio frequencies should be used in the United States.

filtering — The ability to control the types of network traffic that pass from the wired Ethernet network to the WLAN stations.

firmware — Semipermanent software that is embedded in a silicon chip; also called *flash memory*.

flash memory — Semipermanent software that is embedded in a silicon chip; also called *firmware*.

foreign agent — A forwarding mechanism that provides routing services to the mobile computer using Mobile IP.

foreign network — The remote network to which a computer relocates when using Mobile IP.

forwarding — Passing through specific types of frames in the filtering process.

fragmentation — The division of data to be transmitted from one large frame into several smaller ones.

frame — A packet of data.

frequency — A measurement of radio waves that is determined by how frequently the device that generates the waves moves or cycles.

frequency hopping spread spectrum (FHSS) — A spread spectrum technique that uses a range of frequencies and changes frequencies during the transmission.

frequency modulation (FM) — Commonly used modulation for transmitting conventional radio station signals between 88 MHz and 108 MHz.

gateway — A computer or router that forwards network communications from one network to another.

Gaussian frequency shift key (GFSK) — A modulation used for FHSS transmission that varies the frequency slightly within the channel to represent different bits.

gigahertz (GHz) — One billion hertz.

handoff — A change in association from one access point to another.

help desk — A central point of contact for users who need assistance.

hertz (Hz) — The number of cycles per second.

hexadecimal — The base 16 numbering system.

hidden node — A station in a WLAN that cannot be detected by all other stations.

home address — A static IP number given to a computer using Mobile IP.

home agent — A forwarding mechanism that keeps track of where the mobile computer currently is located.

Home Network — Cisco's term for an ad hoc network without an access point.

home network — The original network of a computer using Mobile IP.

HomeRF Working Group — A group of over 40 different companies from the personal computer, consumer electronics, communications, and software industries that established the SWAP standard.

hopping code — The sequence of frequencies used in an FHSS transmission.

host — A device on a TCP/IP network.

Hypertext Markup Language (HTML) — The standard language for displaying content on the Internet.

Independent Basic Service Set (IBSS) — A mode in which wireless stations communicate directly among themselves without using an access point; also called *ad hoc* or *peer-to-peer mode*.

Industrial, Scientific, and Medical (ISM) band — An unlicensed band of frequencies approved by the FCC in 1985 for use by wireless network products.

Infrared Data Association (IrDA) — A specification for a 115 Kbps directed transmission that is used for data transmissions between laptop computers and printers.

infrared light — Invisible light on the light spectrum that has many of the same characteristics as visible light.

infrastructure mode — A WLAN mode that consists of wireless stations and one access point; also called *Basic Service Set (BSS)*.

Institute of Electrical and Electronic Engineers (IEEE) — A standards body that created computer network standards to ensure interoperability among vendors.

Institute of Electrical and Electronic Engineers (IEEE) 802.11b — The networking standard for wireless local area networks.

interframe spaces (IFS) — Time gaps used for special types of transmissions.

International Standards Organization (ISO) — A standards body that developed specifications for computer networks.

Internetwork Packet Exchange (IPX) — A protocol based on one developed by Xerox in the late 1970s and used in Novell NetWare LANs for many years.

interoperability — The ability of a product manufactured by one vendor to work with a product made by another vendor.

kilohertz (KHz) — One thousand hertz.

light spectrum — All the different types of light that travel from the sun to the earth.

light-based WLAN — A wireless local area network that transmits data using light.

line of sight transmission — A transmission that requires that the sender and receiver be aimed directly at each other.

link manager — Special software in Bluetooth devices that helps identify other Bluetooth devices, creates the links between them, and sends and receives data.

Link Status Meter (LSM) — Cisco's site survey software that assists in the placement of access points.

Logical Link Control (LLC) — A sublayer of the IEEE Project 802 Data Link layer (Layer 2).

MAC address — A unique number that is burned into the network interface card when it is manufactured.

management frames — MAC frames that are used to set up the initial communications between a station and the access point.

management information base (MIB) — The repository where SNMP software agents store their data.

Media Access Control (MAC) — A sublayer of the IEEE Project 802 Data Link layer (Layer 2).

megahertz (MHz) — One million hertz.

micro browser — A tiny browser program that runs on a WAP cell phone.

milliwatt (mW) — One-millionth of a watt.

Mobile Connection Manager (MCM) — A 3Com AirConnect utility that stores the configuration information needed for each WLAN to which a mobile laptop may connect.

Mobile IP — An enhancement to the TCP/IP protocol that provides a mechanism to support mobile computing.

modulation — Adjustment of the carrier signal so it can also carry information.

multicast — A transmission mode that sends a frame from one sender to multiple receivers with a single transmit operation.

multipoint — A computer topology in which each computer has just one connection point and shares the medium.

narrowband — Transmissions that send all of their power in a very narrow portion of the radio frequency spectrum.

net allocation vector (NAV) — Temporary storage space used by a station in a WLAN.

network interface card (NIC) — A device, installed or built into a computer that is connected to the network, that plays a critical role in sending and receiving data between the computer and the network.

null data frame — The response that a station sends back to the access point to indicate that the station has nothing to send.

official standards — Standards controlled by an organization or body that has been entrusted with that task; same as *de jure standards*.

Open Systems Interconnection (OSI) model — A conceptual model of computer networking that is based on layers, in which each layer does specific functions and cooperates with the layers immediately above and below it.

orthogonal FHSS — A set of hopping codes that never use the same frequencies at the same time.

packet acknowledgment (ACK) — A procedure for reducing collisions by requiring that the receiving station send an explicit packet back to the sending station.

packet switching — A communications technology that breaks a message into small data packets and then seeks out the most efficient route to the destination as circuits become available.

packets — Small blocks of data.

passive scanning — The process of listening to each available channel for a set period of time.

PC Card — A peripheral the size of a credit card that is available for use as a modem, sound card, or hard drive.

peer-to-peer mode — A WLAN mode in which wireless stations communicate directly among themselves without using an access point; also called *ad hoc* mode or *Independent Basic Service Set (IBSS)*.

personal area network (PAN) — Two or more Bluetooth devices that send and receive data to and from each other.

Personal Communications Service (PCS) — A digital circuit-switched transmission signal used by cell phones.

Personal Digital Assistant (PDA) — A hand-held device used for taking notes and making records.

phase change — The variation of the phase of the waveform used in differential binary phase shift key (DBPSK) transmissions.

Physical Layer Convergence Procedure (PLCP) sublayer — A sublayer of the IEEE Project 802 PHY layer that reformats the data and determines when data can be sent.

Physical Medium Dependent (PMD) sublayer — A sublayer of the IEEE Project 802 PHY layer that defines the standards for the characteristics of the wireless medium and the method for transmitting and receiving data through that medium.

ping — A program that sends a series of packets to an IP number and then listens for a response.

Point Coordination Function IFS (PIFS) — A time gap interval that stations use when polling nodes that have a specific time requirement.

Point Coordination Function (PCF) — The 802.11 optional polling function.

point-to-point topology — A computer topology in which each device is directly connected to all other devices.

polling — A channel access in which each computer is asked in sequence whether it wants to transmit.

power management — An 802.11 standard that allows a mobile station to be turned off as much as possible to conserve battery life but still not miss data transmissions.

PowerBASE-T adapter — A hardware device that provides power to a 3Com AirConnect access point over an Ethernet cable.

privacy — Standards that assure that transmissions are not read by unauthorized users.

probe — A frame sent by a station point when performing active scanning.

probe response — A frame sent by an access point when responding to a station's active scanning probe.

profile — Part of the 3Com MCM utility that contains information about how the laptop must be configured to communicate on a WLAN.

Project 802 — The standards created by the IEEE for computer networking.

protocols — Rules for sending and receiving frames.

public key — Cryptography that uses matched public and private keys for encryption and decryption.

radio module — A small radio transceiver built onto a microprocessor chip embedded into Bluetooth devices that enable them to communicate.

radiotelephony (radio) wave — A wave created when an electric current passes through a wire and creates a magnetic field in the space around the wire.

reassociation — The process of a station dropping the connection with one access point and reestablishing the connection with another.

reassociation request frame — A frame sent from a station to a new access point asking whether it can associate with the access point.

reassociation response frame — A frame sent by an access point to a station indicating that it will accept its reassociation with that access point.

Remote Network Monitoring (RMON) — An SNMP-based tool used to monitor LANs that are connected through a wide area network.

remote wireless bridge — A device used to connect network segments using radio-based technology.

request for information (RFI) — A document sent to a vendor to gain general information about a vendor's products or solutions to a problem.

request for proposal (RFP) — A detailed planning document sent to vendors that provides precise specifications for the products and services that the organization intends to buy.

Request to Send/Request to Clear (RTS/CTS) — An 802.11 option that allows a station to reserve the network for transmissions.

Reverse Address Resolution Protocol (RARP) — Part of the TCP/IP protocol that associates an IP number with a MAC address.

roaming — Movement of a mobile wireless user through different access points and areas of coverage.

router — A device that examines the network and host number in a TCP/IP network and forwards it toward its destination.

RTS threshold — A size limit that specifies that only packets longer than this value are transmitted using RTS/CTS.

scanning — The process that a station uses to examine the airwaves for information that it needs in order to begin the association process.

Service Set Identifier (SSID) — A unique identifier assigned to an access point.

shared key — Cryptography that uses the same key to encrypt and decrypt a message.

Shared Wireless Access Protocol (SWAP) — A set of specifications for wireless data and voice communications around the home that can include computer equipment, cordless telephones, and home entertainment equipment.

short IFS (SIFS) — A time gap used for immediate response actions such as ACK.

signal-to-noise ratio (SNR) — A measurement that indicates how much of the radio signal is being affected by noise.

Simple Network Management Protocol (SNMP) — A protocol that is part of TCP/IP that allows computers and network equipment to gather data about network performance.

site survey — A software utility that assists in the placement of access points.

sleep mode — A power-conserving mode used by laptop computers.

slot — A time that a diffused infrared WLAN sends a pulse of infrared light; also called *time slot*.

slot time — The amount of time that a station must wait after the medium is clear.

SNMP management station — A computer on a network using SNMP that controls the management software.

SNMP trap — An alert message sent to an SNMP management station whenever a network exceeds a predefined limit.

SNMPv2 — The second version of SNMP that provides encryption, faster data transmission, and the ability to retrieve more information.

software agents — Special SNMP software that is loaded onto each network device that monitors network traffic.

spread spectrum — A technique that spreads a narrow signal over a broader portion of the radio frequency band.

synchronize — To set all stations and access points on the same time.

Telnet — An application protocol that is part of the TCP/IP suite that provides support for terminal emulation.

time slot — A time that a diffused infrared WLAN sends a pulse of infrared light; also called *slot*.

topology — The physical layout of the network.

traffic indication map (TIM) — A list of the stations that have buffered frames waiting at the access point.

Transmission Control Protocol/Internet Protocol (TCP/IP) — The standard protocol for local area computer networks.

Trivial File Transfer Protocol (TFTP) — A program used to transport data files that does not guarantee the connection between the devices and does not require a username or password.

tunnel — Used by Mobile IP, to wrap a frame into a new frame and give it a different destination address; also called *encapsulate*.

Type I — A category of PC Card that is a maximum of 3.3 millimeters thick and is used primarily for adding additional RAM to a laptop.

Type II — A category of PC Card that can be up to 5.5 millimeters thick and is often used by modem cards and wireless NICs.

Type III — A category of PC Card that can be up to 10.5 millimeters thick and is often used to accommodate a portable disk drive.

unicast — A transmission mode that sends a frame from one sender to a single receiver.

User Datagram Protocol (UDP) — A network protocol sometimes used instead of TCP.

virtual carrier sensing — An 802.11 option that allows a station to reserve the network for transmissions.

voltage — Electrical pressure.

WAP gateway — A device that translates HTML to WML so that it can be displayed on a WAP cell phone; also called a *WAP proxy*.

WAP proxy — A device that translates HTML to WML so that it can be displayed on a WAP cell phone; also called a *WAP gateway*.

Web browser — Software that runs on a local PC and makes a request from the World Wide Web file server for a Web page.

Wi-Fi certification — The seal granted by the WECA that guarantees that a wireless LAN product will work with products from other vendors.

Wired Equivalent Privacy (WEP) — An 802.11 standard that provides an optional specification for data encryption between wireless devices to prevent eavesdropping.

Wireless Application Protocol (WAP) — A standard for transmitting, formatting, and displaying Internet data for devices such as cell phones.

Wireless Ethernet Compatibility Alliance (WECA) — A standards group that certifies wireless LAN vendors whose products meet the IEEE 802.11b standard.

wireless home networking adapter — A device that connects to a home computer to transmit and receive data over radio waves.

wireless local area network (WLAN) — A local area network that is not connected by wires but instead uses wireless technology.

Wireless Markup Language (WML) — The language for displaying Internet content on WAP cell phones.

wireless network interface card — A card installed in a computer that performs the same functions as a standard network interface card, except that it does not have a cable that connects it to the network.

Index